AAR
AMERICAN ACADEMY OF RELIGION

ACADEMY SERIES

Series Editor

Aaron W. Hughes, University at Buffalo

A Publication Series of The American Academy of Religion and Oxford University Press

Of Borders and Margins
Hispanic Disciples in Texas, 1888–1945
Daisy L. Machado

Yves Congar's Theology of the Holy Spirit
Elizabeth Teresa Groppe

Hsieh Liang-tso and the Analects of Confucius
Humane Learning as a Religious Quest
Thomas W. Selover

Gregory of Nyssa and the Concept of divine Persons
Lucian Turcescu

Graham Greene's Catholic Imagination
Mark Bosco, S.J.

Coming to the Edge of the Circle
A Wiccan Initiation Ritual
Nikki Bado-Fralick

The Ethics of Animal Experimentation
A Critical Analysis and Constructive Christian Proposal
Donna Yarri

Paul in Israel's Story
Self and Community at the Cross
John L. Meech

Crossing the Ethnic Divide
The Multiethnic Church on a Mission
Kathleen Garces-Foley

God and the Victim
Traumatic Intrusions on Grace and Freedom
Jennifer Erin Beste

The Creative Suffering of the Triune god
An Evolutionary Theology
Gloria L. Schaab

A Theology of Criticism
Balthasar, Postmodernism, and the Catholic Imagination
Michael P. Murphy

Incarnation Anyway
Arguments for Supralapsarian Christology
Edwin Chr. Van Driel

Disability and Christian Theology
Embodied Limits and Constructive Possibilities
Deborah Beth Creamer

Meeting God on the Cross
Christ, the Cross, and the Feminist Critique
Arnfríður Guðmundsdóttir

Muslims, Scholars, Soldiers
The Origin and Elaboration of the Ibāḍī Imāmate Traditions
Adam R. Gaiser

Race and Religion in American Buddhism
White Supremacy and Immigrant Adaptation
Joseph Cheah

Journey Back to God
Origen on the Problem of Evil
Mark S. M. Scott

Beyond the Walls
Abraham Joshua Heschel and Edith Stein on the Significance of Empathy for Jewish-Christian Dialogue
Joseph Redfield Palmisano, SJ

Types of Pentecostal Theology
Method, System, Spirit
Christopher A. Stephenson

Other Dreams of Freedom
Religion, Sex, and Human Trafficking
Yvonne C. Zimmerman

Liberalism Versus Postliberalism
The Great Divide in Twentieth-Century Theology
John Allan Knight

Image, Identity, and The Forming of The Augustinian Soul
Matthew Drever

Righteous Rhetoric
Sex, Speech, and the Politics of Concerned Women for America
Leslie Dorrough Smith

AAR

AMERICAN ACADEMY OF RELIGION

Righteous Rhetoric

Sex, Speech, and the Politics of Concerned Women for America

LESLIE DORROUGH SMITH

OXFORD
UNIVERSITY PRESS

OXFORD
UNIVERSITY PRESS

Oxford University Press is a department of the University of Oxford.
It furthers the University's objective of excellence in research, scholarship,
and education by publishing worldwide.

Oxford New York
Auckland Cape Town Dar es Salaam Hong Kong Karachi
Kuala Lumpur Madrid Melbourne Mexico City Nairobi
New Delhi Shanghai Taipei Toronto

With offices in
Argentina Austria Brazil Chile Czech Republic France Greece
Guatemala Hungary Italy Japan Poland Portugal Singapore
South Korea Switzerland Thailand Turkey Ukraine Vietnam

Published in the United States of America by
Oxford University Press
198 Madison Avenue, New York, NY 10016

Library of Congress Cataloging-in-Publication Data
Smith, Leslie Dorrough, 1975–
Righteous rhetoric : sex, speech, and the politics of concerned women
for America / Leslie Dorrough Smith.
p. cm.
Includes bibliographical references.
ISBN 978–0–19–933750–7 (cloth : alk. paper) 1. Concerned Women for America.
2. Christian women—Political activity—United States—History.
3. Women in Christianity—United States—History—20th century.
4. Conservatism—Religious aspects—Christianity. 5. Conservatism—United States.
6. Rhetoric—Religious aspects—Christianity.
7. United States—Church history—20th century. I. Title.
BR517.S455 2014
267'.43—dc23
2013031771

1 3 5 7 9 8 6 4 2

Printed in the United States of America on acid-free paper

To Annemarie, Cole, and Micah

Contents

Acknowledgments

WHILE IT IS customary to acknowledge that no work is created in solitude, this particular one was created in the midst of a crowd. I am convinced that it is a good thing that we do not know what lies in our futures, for had I known some ten years ago (then childless) that I would be researching and writing the lion's share of this book with three young children in tow, I might not ever have attempted it.

Yet the extraordinary help, advice, and training that I received from many different individuals created the conditions of this project's possibility. In particular, I am indebted to Wade Clark Roof, Catherine Albanese, and Eileen Boris for their incredibly helpful feedback on a much earlier incarnation of this project, which was then a dissertation, and for being a supportive doctoral committee and all-around excellent professors. I am also indebted to Brett Miller, who, quite a long time ago, taught me how to critically think, and to do it with a sense of humor. I also want to thank Russell McCutcheon for his tremendous influence in my study of discourse, rhetoric, and religion when I was a Master's student at Southwest Missouri State University (now Missouri State University). I am deeply grateful for his friendship, guidance, and support. My thanks also goes out to my dear friend Becky Brown, whose assistance preparing the manuscript was invaluable. In addition, I remain indebted to two anonymous readers of an earlier draft of this book, whose comments were immeasurably helpful.

My family has stood behind me throughout this project. To my mother, Barbara Brown-Johnson, and my parents-in-law, Dick and Mitzi Smith, I offer my sincerest thanks for doing what terrific parents do: love, support, cheer, help, listen . . . and babysit. In particular, I offer thanks to my mother for teaching me through example what things are worth the struggle.

I am most grateful, though, to my immediate family. My husband Brian's enthusiasm for my academic career has always been steadfast. Brian has also been a much needed voice of reason across the several years that this project consumed, calling me to balance and rest at times when both were needed but I was resistant to take them.

I became a mother at the same time that this project came to life. That I would have two more children in a relatively short span is, perhaps, not the trajectory of events that most would imagine when a budding scholarly career comes to mind. In all honesty it was not my initial vision, either, but it has been the most tremendously rewarding experience of my life, and the timing could not have been more perfect. This book is dedicated to Annemarie, Cole, and Micah.

Righteous Rhetoric

Introduction: Chaos Rhetoric and the Public Construction of American Morality

"Language is the site of history's enactment."[1]

—JOAN WALLACH SCOTT

"Americans have survived their own unprecedented wickedness. Many times."[2]

—JAMES MORONE

IN AUTUMN OF 2003, I became a mother. Like most new parents, I was poorly prepared for the relentless demands that a child poses, and I quickly found myself drowning in a never-ending cycle of laundry, sleepless nights, and feedings that all blurred into one another. While these daily logistics were overwhelming in themselves, I was equally as consumed with figuring out how I would maintain my professional identity while also caring for my infant daughter.

I had just started my Ph.D. program at the time I became pregnant and was (appropriately) worried about whether I could complete my degree in a timely fashion. Although I took the sound advice of a professor by putting my scholarship on hold and taking an official leave of absence, I did so begrudgingly, not yet understanding how the care of another human could consume so much time that an official break was warranted. Once my daughter was born, however, that maternity leave slipped away as soon as it started, and I found myself feeling conflicted and guilty for surrendering her to daycare while I returned to my research. I felt endlessly pulled a million different ways, wondering if I was doing any aspect of my life particularly well.

My newly reinvigorated research only made matters worse, it seemed. Once back to work, my first project was an analysis of the rhetoric used by prominent evangelical figures to discuss gender and family life; judgments on the wisdom of working motherhood were a central part of this discourse. In particular, I was intrigued by the popularity and longevity of the work of Beverly LaHaye. LaHaye is founder of Concerned Women for America (CWA), one of the nation's largest politically-engaged conservative Christian organizations for women, as well as wife to Tim LaHaye (pastor, co-author of the *Left Behind* series of apocalyptic novels, and conservative political activist). She has spent a considerable portion of her public career writing for women facing the many contradictions involved in juggling their professional and family commitments.

In the 1970s, LaHaye's work made her something of a modern-day conservative prophetess, sounding the call to scores of American women about the dangers posed to American culture by what she considered the godless doctrine of secular humanism (and its twin offspring, Communism and feminism). In the vision offered by LaHaye, God created an ordered and exacting world where men are men and women are women, and to threaten such order with feminist liberation, abortion, gay rights, or governmental aid programs is to ultimately undermine the authority of the godly family, male-headed and female-nurtured.

LaHaye specifically targeted career-aged women pondering the choices that feminism had just recently made possible, and true to form, her pronouncements were rarely neutral. In one of her books, she warns career-aged women that children whose mothers are absent for any extended period of time are, in a sense, orphans; to forfeit one's identity over to the feminist drive toward career, liberation, and independence guarantees children whose souls are dry and empty from emotional abandonment even if their backs are clothed.[3] In the same breath, she blames parental neglect and abuse (here including working mothers as "neglectful") for causing children to become radical feminists and mass murderers (equating the two without explanation).[4] In an equally pointed passage, she recalls a conversation she overheard in a restaurant wherein a husband verbally abused his wife because he felt that she looked haggard. While LaHaye expresses concern about the harshness of his attack (even remarking that it "ruined her dinner"), she ultimately defends his message, saying "Who knows how many years he had been looking at that tired mess? With all the helps available today, there is no need for a woman to let herself get into this situation."[5] She explains:

> I feel very strongly that when a woman fully accepts herself as a creation God has made, she will do her very best to prune, trim, manicure, and even paint the object of God's love and care. What a pity to see a Christian woman who has developed her inner beauty but has done nothing to the frame she must house it in.[6]

For those unfamiliar with this sort of rhetoric, it may seem easy to presume that LaHaye is a has-been whose brand of moral hype renders her now decades-old advice books obsolete. After all, she wrote these words during the time when liberal feminism was growing in social visibility, representing a threat to many conservative ideas about gender.[7] Her response to this "danger," as she put it, was to found CWA, an organization that she has described as an avenue for conservative women (and "like-minded men") to have a voice in political issues that directly affect women and family.[8] In fact, much of the "concern" behind the name "Concerned Women for America" is tied directly to worries that liberal feminism will drive America to ruin, and these sentiments still run strong within the organization today. The group's website provides frequent updates and emails to remind members that liberals are actively attempting to undermine conservative Christian values, all working under the infiltrating presence of feminism, gay rights, "big" government, abortion, and secularism in the public schools, to name just a few.[9]

These ideas are not at all isolated to LaHaye or CWA, but reflect the larger philosophy behind the Christian Right, the name that scholars have given to a strong coalition of politically engaged American conservative Christian groups (many of which are Protestant). This activist network has been in existence in one form or another for well over fifty years.[10] As a prominent member group of the Christian Right, CWA's half million members and active sympathizers look very much like the rest of the movement: they emphasize Jesus as a personal savior, claim to take the Bible's injunctions seriously (if not literally), advocate the importance of evangelizing others, and understand America as a fundamentally Christian enterprise that, having been mired in secularism and sin, must be returned to its noble religious beginnings.[11] LaHaye, now in her eighties, has become more the symbolic figurehead of the organization than its day-to-day leader (officially stepping down in 2006), but CWA's organizational structure is still closely aligned with her past activism.[12] True to her intentions, CWA is not a church or other religious organization; rather, political activity is CWA's raison d'être. This open political involvement has been the key distinctive of the Christian Right's member groups, setting them apart from other religious conservatives not so comfortable—or interested—in the political spotlight.

For CWA, this spotlight has been focused on sexual and reproductive issues. This is also nothing new, for American religious campaigns linking social demise with sexed or gendered morality have existed since at least the colonial period and have almost always garnered more social support than campaigns focusing on other "vices."[13] A century ago, the early fundamentalists saw flappers, female preachers, and suffragists as a sign of the death of the very relationships that knit society together. Still today, CWA argues that sexual ethics, heterosexual marriage, and traditional gender roles are in constant threat of attack from liberal forces even as they remain iron-clad institutions that comprise the very fibers of the social fabric.

As an example of CWA's political activism on such issues, consider the following 2007 article written by one of the organization's current leaders, Janice Shaw Crouse. Crouse claims that Planned Parenthood and other "leftist and pro-abortion" organizations wrongly depict the demographic profile of women who consider abortion.[14] Instead of presuming that most women who choose abortion do so because they are sexually naïve teens who find themselves unexpectedly pregnant, Crouse cites statistical evidence indicating that most out-of-wedlock births are to women over age twenty who clearly understand that sex can lead to conception (and thus, to Crouse, truly "unintended" pregnancies do not exist). She concludes:

> When more than three-fourths of the 1.5 million unwed births are to women age 20 and older, these results cannot be blamed on youthful immaturity. These post-teen behaviors can only be characterized as reckless and irresponsible, given what is well known about (a) the skyrocketing incidence of sexually transmitted diseases among sexually active unmarried women, as well as (b) the abysmally high rates of poverty of children living in female-headed families and (c) the well-documented risks of negative outcomes attributed to children living in father absent households. These toxic fruits are a cocktail made up of sexual revolutionaries pushing promiscuity, secular liberalism's unrelenting attacks on the boundaries of religion and morality, and radical feminism's raging hostility toward marriage.[15]

In the logic employed within this piece, to be a sexually active, unmarried female is to be complicit in a problem framed as one of the most significant of our time. Abstinence is but one answer to this problem, but marriage is the real solution, for marriage provides the stability and support necessary to create a family. The nuclear family is thus posed as an entity through which major social problems are resolved: if "fatherless" households create poverty, social dysfunction, and the spread of disease (as the logic goes), then the heterosexual, nuclear family halts that downward spiral. Yet, to Crouse, feminism's "raging hostilities" have made marriage an unattractive option to many women. Following the logic still further, feminism does not simply advocate for abortion rights; insomuch as it makes families impossible and praises frequent sexual activity, feminism *causes* abortion, the spread of disease, poverty, child abuse, and ultimately, destroys the nuclear family.[16]

This book explores this sort of emotionally laden rhetoric about America's impending demise—as interpreted through things like the dangers of feminism or the "death" of the family through the legalization of gay marriage—considering how it may actually be the secret to conservative Christian political vitality. More specifically, I use a rhetorical analysis to address how a type of speech that I call *chaos rhetoric* is used by CWA to transform public religious talk about sex, gender, and reproductive issues into a powerful political engine that portrays conservative Christian norms as mainstream American values. This book concentrates on how and why rhetoric regarding sex, gender, and reproduction is among the most useful and emotionally charged means through which groups like CWA authorize their attempts to transform American culture and politics.

What is chaos rhetoric? Chaos rhetoric is a type of declension speech that attempts to persuade an audience by stressing an imminent threat to a beloved entity (which could include everything from children, to liberty, to the nation itself). In claiming the deterioration of this entity, chaos rhetoric portrays a world where threat, disorder, fear, and chaos reign. Groups who create such rhetoric usually offer their own politically expedient solution to the very threat they rhetorically crafted, a solution that positions the group as the embodiment of goodness, stability, and order. Rather than simply calling these fear tactics, I use the term *chaos rhetoric* not only to highlight the hyperbolic nature of the speech, but also to reveal its shifting character: what is chaotic in one cultural circumstance or time is a nonevent in another. Thus, speaking about the emotional efficacy of chaos rhetoric involves understanding how the threats that a group manufactures are useful only under particular socio-historical circumstances. What this means is that such threats must be constantly re-fabricated to maintain emotional (and thus persuasive) appeal.

This book will examine how CWA's public rhetoric depends almost entirely on threats to a particular sexed or gendered order rather than arguing more positively for that order itself, all to push the public to resolve the fear or threat in a manner commensurate with the group's political ideals. Whether urging its membership to oppose an amendment on gay marriage on the grounds that such marriages will lead to gay adoption (and thus child molestation), or speaking out against sexual education in schools using the reasoning that children will be taught *how* to have sex, chaos rhetoric does not persuade by advertising the superiority of the group's understanding of sex and gender (although this is its eventual byproduct), but by positing the dangers that will arise if that order is ignored.

My focus on disorder as an analytical framework is inspired, in part, by the theoretical work of Judith Butler, whose observations on identity construction are featured in the coming chapters. Much of Butler's work describes identity as a process whereby a culture normalizes and thereby approves certain traits through a process of contradistinction: those who do not bear such "normal" qualities become the point of contrast through which others who do can assert their own dominance, and in so doing, re-valorize the status quo as a natural (and, by extension, superior) social phenomenon. Butler thus highlights the persuasive capital that social groups invest in the creation of a pathological subject against which they define their own identity.[17] As this book will show, CWA is constantly involved in such a process, negotiating its own identity by casting (and re-casting) its portrayal of its opponents in light of the present political circumstances, thereby maintaining its cultural relevance at any given moment. As a result, who and what CWA is, in the most general sense, is not defined by a self-evident standard, but is the product of whether the public has first adopted its negative representation of its rivals. From that foundation, CWA can begin to shape its own persona.

This represents a somewhat different approach to the one taken by many scholars of conservative Protestantism, who tend to focus their attention on what are perceived to be the absolute, ordered, unshifting elements of the movement. For instance, consider this rendering of evangelicals (an umbrella term used to describe many conservative Protestants) by scholar Jason Bivins:

> . . . however potent and disordering is worldly evil, God's moral order is without ambiguity and thereby more resilient. This situates moral agency in a context where behavioral and doxological norms are irrevocable and absolute; they cannot be altered via interpretation, nuance or partial convictions.[18]

Bivins concludes that evangelicals "privilege certitude, fixity, and commitment over ambiguity, fluidity, and multiplicity."[19] This description reinforces Christian Smith's now mainstream "embattled but thriving" thesis, which suggests that rather than deteriorating in the modern world, the rigid order of evangelicals (which translates into strong ideals and firm social boundaries) places them at tremendous advantage in pluralistic environments because people are drawn to strong and stable identities so long as those identities do not grow too countercultural. Like any movement that stands the test of time, evangelicalism must change if it is to survive, he notes, although in the midst of more superficial changes, certain core elements of the religion usually remain untouched, preserving the movement's ordered distinction.[20]

My assertion in this book is that while these remain relatively accurate assessments of how most conservative Protestants see *themselves*, such portrayals overlook the more nuanced, complex social dynamics that actually create the public support upon which such movements depend. Although most scholars will acknowledge that all groups must change to survive, most are not accustomed to thinking about how certain conservative groups famous for their dichotomous worldviews constantly renegotiate almost all of their concepts or practices, particularly those previously marketed as eternal and absolute. Rather than treat terms like "eternal" and "absolute" as accurate depictions of the world, my interest lies more with considering how these adjectives are conscious, strategic descriptors chosen by evangelical and other conservative elites to create persuasive value in their public speech, and not simple descriptors of a strict worldview. Such change is critical to appeal to a public that is, itself, always in flux. If groups like CWA were limited to certain arguments that remained relatively static in content and cultural meaning over time, then they would lose the capacity to create an always-relevant, constant menace lurking on the fringes of society, which is one of the most persuasive platforms from which such groups can speak.

In this sense, emotion is key to the efficacy of chaos rhetoric. In his study of the formation of moral protest movements, James Jasper shows that emotions are central, if perhaps even prior, to the logic behind activism. Jasper describes logic and emotion as mutually reinforcing entities; activists must, he says, "weave together a moral, cognitive, and emotional package of attitudes" in order to embark on a protest.[21] Yet because the urge to protest often begins with a "moral shock," or a highly emotional event that incites outrage, the activist impulse is often first rooted in strong feelings before anything else.[22] The primacy of emotion describes how most of us make the bulk of our decisions: we act on some inchoate feeling, from whether to trust a new person we meet to what clothes to wear. While logic may temper or even change what an impulse tells us, the power of "gut feelings" often remains strong.

This is not meant to imply, however, that emotions are some sort of essential, interior guide, providing a roadmap toward truth and away from evil (a common claim made by many evangelicals, among others). Rather, here I treat emotions in line with Émile Durkheim's model, approaching them as learned responses to the power dynamics of a social group, all of which typically supports the status quo.[23] The concept of sentiment is central to Durkheim's famous definition of religion as "collective effervescence," a concept predicated on the notion that religion, or "the sacred," is nothing other than a social group worshiping itself, having objectified its norms and values through the emotional vehicle of shared sentiment.[24] This sentiment is critical to the creation of social solidarity, or the feeling of being tied to others in a common cause.

As a progressive feminist, I did not enter into my research on CWA expecting to find many moments of personal agreement or any such common cause. Yet the more that I read the CWA website, the more I was intrigued by how easily I could allow the logic behind its arguments to work on the guilt so ubiquitous to parenting and family life in general. To be clear, I did not personally find their claims particularly logical or desirable. Despite this, I was struck by how high the stakes were drawn so that responding the "wrong way" in a situation concerned with gender and family was portrayed as one of ultimate consequence. It is one thing to be concerned about whether my daughter's time in daycare might have fostered some sleeping problems at home, or perhaps tantrums; it is an entirely different thing to consider that this choice of childcare has unintentionally created a future mass murderer, as LaHaye's earlier comments suggest.

Even if the scenarios used by CWA may seem, to some, far-fetched, one need not fully ascribe to the complete theology or rationale of a speaker to find the core elements of her or his message persuasive.[25] Thus, while I do not share CWA's conviction that sexual education programs in public schools will cause teens to have rampant sex, contract HIV, or contribute to skyrocketing teen pregnancy rates, I can relate to the concerns over how my children's future sexual habits will affect their lives. In this way, even if readers do not fully agree with CWA's argumentation, the uneasy feelings left by its rhetoric linger as an emotional investment made by the group that can be cashed in when needed.[26] For CWA and other politically involved Christian groups, personal, theological conversion often takes a backseat to sympathy at the voting booth.

In this way, the emotional is the political; it is the internalization and perceived individualization of an otherwise social norm reflecting society's contours at a specific moment, which can be used to constitute an equally specific threat. Consider an episode of the hit TV series *Mad Men*, set in the 1960s, where young Sally Draper's mother, Betty (who is taking long drags from a cigarette while noticeably pregnant), catches Sally playing in a plastic dry-cleaning bag. Instead of fearing her suffocation, as many today might, Sally's mother expresses irritation that the clothes once contained in the bag are on the floor.[27] Audiences who watch the award-winning show often remark on the many behaviors deemed "normal" during much of 1960s America (smoking during pregnancy, constant alcohol consumption, driving while intoxicated, etc.), which today are generally considered unacceptable. Of all of the possible ways that Sally could have been portrayed, the fact that the show's writers sought to include this scene is likely connected to its modern shock value. Context, then, is critical to our emotional lives, and by extension, to our conceptions of normalcy, order, and threat. While Durkheim describes emotions as an ingrained biological trait, much like a reflex, he also argues that the context in which emotions are evoked, and to what service they are employed, is determined by the group's drive to preserve not only its norms, but also its very existence.[28]

What this means, practically speaking, is that we are all, to some degree, trained how to feel. Society's earliest lessons involve learning the "proper" emotional response to certain stimuli, from what is scary (snakes and spiders) or dangerous (strangers) to what is loving and safe (our parents, or a security blanket). Julia Kristeva has shown that things that repulse social groups do so not because of any inherent quality within those things, but because they disturb the overarching order that the group presupposes, thus threatening to undo the epistemological basis on which rests the culture's defining power structures.[29]

Transgendered persons, for instance, experience significant discrimination in American culture today. Yet in those few cultures that openly accept the existence of a "third gender," or a gender often regarded as somewhere in between male and female (such as the "Two-Spirit" people that have held some degree of historical prominence in certain Native American groups), to be transgender is often nothing more than one of several, acceptable gendered options.[30] A culture that does not depend solely on heteronormativity to define its power structures does not need to cast transgendered individuals as "freaks" or "perverts," labels that many transgendered people often hear. In this sense, social categorization works to provide cognitive cohesion and control precisely by designating certain things dangerous or abnormal—while others remain safe and pure—in a way that feeds the social power exchange at that moment. Emotions thus assist in the process of this categorization: they are the teaching tools used by a culture to make claims on who to trust, who is dangerous, or who is an ally, creating a much cleaner, more direct version of events not muddied by nuance, details, or even sometimes, evidence.[31]

For those who oppose the activist work of groups like CWA, it will be tempting to see its production of chaos rhetoric as a damaging cultural force driven by fear-mongering and political interests. Reinforcing that conclusion is not, however, part of the goal of this project. To categorically demonize chaos rhetoric as an illegitimate form of communication overlooks how it is a very normal part of the persuasive process for almost all groups, not just CWA, the Christian Right, or other conservative Christians. This conclusion also undercuts how important the emotions of fear and anxiety can be in the maintenance of society. If one did not fear the possible outcome of touching a hot stove, or running in front of a moving car, then injury (or death) would be a constant, legitimate threat.

Groups have great interest, then, in deciding what should be regarded as fearful and spreading those ideas widely so as to guarantee the group's own physical and ideological survival. Thus, my interest in how chaos rhetoric operates (and specifically, how CWA deploys it) lies in examining how the group has managed to link together certain emotive symbols in such a way as to render certain things fearful or dangerous (such as gay marriage, abortion, and feminism) that are not otherwise fearful to people with different political interests, for like many other things, fear is in the eye of the beholder. Understanding the multi-layered symbolic creation of chaos rhetoric thus not only lays bare many of the group's agendas, but it also explains how groups can garner widespread social sympathy for platforms that may defy modern standards of logic or that may be otherwise devoid of concrete scientific proof. Managing fear production to meet its own political aims is thus an important part of any group's chaos rhetoric, no matter what the political interests of that group may be.

Why Chaos Rhetoric?

When many scholars discuss the Christian Right's frequent use of fear-based speech, they are not uncommonly reviving an older perspective on the movement that claims that conservative Christians cling to the stability of moral absolutism because they are psychologically fragile individuals who do not cope well with cultural change. That is not the approach I take here, for not only do I presume that plenty of non-conservatives are change-averse, but also that conservative Christians of many stripes are a very heterogeneous group of people with often divergent views.[32] However, the job of the elite leaders who comprise the public face of the Christian Right is to persuade an otherwise diverse public of a rather uniform set of political planks, and it is upon these spokespersons that this book will focus. Chaos rhetoric is critical to achieving this persuasive task because it is specifically crafted for public consumption, and is thus intended not only to maintain the allegiance of conservative Christians, but also convince the public at large. As I will show, the chaos rhetoric of such elite figures has been critical to the formation of many of America's most enduring jeremiads.

Jeremiads, or large-scale cultural critiques that emphasize moral failure and call for moral redemption, have been an "essential American literary form."[33] James Morone notes that the jeremiad's persuasive efficacy depends first on its hearers adopting a certain utopian vision of the nation. From "pulling yourself up by the bootstraps" to "liberty and justice for all," such utterances and ideals have been fundamental to the symbolic creation of an imaginary America where everyone who works hard will prosper, where all are truly free and empowered to determine their own destinies, and where moral behavior is not only self-evident and uniform, but is also always rewarded. In addition to these nationalistic ideals, the social ideals specific to many groups have also been popularized culture-wide through jeremiads, including the superiority of the heterosexual nuclear family, the inherent goodness of childbearing by the proper individuals, and the centrality of religion to any healthy and functioning society.

When such visions inevitably don't materialize, however, the jeremiad makes possible blame and scapegoating by locating responsibility for social problems (whether real or perceived) on the poor morals of certain members of the population. This is where chaos rhetoric steps in: it is frequently featured within nationalist jeremiads not only because it reminds the reader of the superiority of the dominant group's values or norms, but it also focuses on what is at risk in their compromise. This is a very convenient built-in mechanism, for it allows the more privileged authors of the jeremiad to deflect their own culpability in the creation of social problems, or at the very least, to maintain a utopian vision without conflict.[34] Outsiders, minorities, and the poor are often the jeremiad's targets for blame.

Take, for instance, the following piece of CWA chaos rhetoric attacking the Employment Non-Discrimination Act (ENDA), a bill that would outlaw employers from making employment decisions based on a person's sexual orientation or gendered identity. The email featuring this rhetoric, sent to CWA members, is entitled, "Could your employer be forced to hire a cross-dresser—and punish Christians for disapproving?":

> Dear Pro-Family American,
>
> I need your help right now. As I write, the House is preparing for a . . . hearing on the Employment Non-Discrimination Act (ENDA) . . . . . . Imagine a country where it's illegal to teach your children what the Bible says about right and wrong . . . where loving God's Word and living out Christian morality could cost you thousands of dollars in fines or even send you to jail. . . .
>
> (The) ENDA . . . would force all employers with 15 or more employees to add "sexual orientation" to their workplace rules, forcing devout Christians to give homosexuals special rights that other employees don't have . . . That's why I'm writing you today . . . I need your help to stop this terrible assault on our children, families, and the biblical principles we love.[35]

Embedded within this textual jeremiad are the declension tones that characterize chaos rhetoric. Links in the text take the reader to articles claiming that the ENDA will force school systems to hire pedophiles as schoolteachers. The rhetoric connects employment legislation with pedophile schoolteachers via the emotionally powerful symbol of innocent, helpless children; it simultaneously asserts that the reason why the ENDA is a topic of discussion at all is because Christianity holds second-class status in America. The rhetorical threat presented to the audience depends not only on the image of the persecuted Christian—portrayed as an ethical figure silenced by a law blind to morality—but also on the character of the blameless child victimized by the sex acts of immoral adults. Whether such things are really the actual outcome of the ENDA is not nearly as important as is the creation of public sympathy.

It may seem a matter of mere semantics to emphasize chaos over order in considering the rhetoric of the Christian Right, but this distinction is actually of great significance in tackling the dynamics of rhetorical persuasion. CWA *does* emphasize moral absolutes, of course, but like any other group that claims eternal and unchanging platforms, it must deflect attention from the ways that it is forced to alter those "absolutes" in order to maintain its political relevance, thus preserving the appearance of an eternal vision. The ordered position for which it attracts attention and loyalty is thus a shifting one: it is useful at that political moment, but prone to change under the weight of cultural fluctuations. So whereas dancing and rock-and-roll might have been an abomination to some Christian groups in decades past, many today might find those particular disputes irrelevant, concerning themselves instead with other issues (such as gay marriage) that have more direct impact over the present contours of society.

In this way, chaos rhetoric is multi-functional: not only can it manufacture the emotions that help create social sentiment, polarize audiences, and incite activist behavior, but it also verbally deflects attention away from the seams of its own social construction, shifting the threat to a new specter while letting the old one quietly die. Under this reading of conservative power, one mistakes the purpose of CWA (and, for that matter, all groups espousing "eternal" values) by presuming that its goal is to endorse truly timeless positions, for those must almost always, by necessity, change.

Take the Bible, for instance. Most who espouse a literal reading of the Bible are selective in what "literals" they choose to adopt and how they choose to adopt them (Snake-handling? Speaking in tongues? Killing the unrighteous? A ban on jewelry wearing?), and thus a "literal reading" is heavily dependent on the way that the word "literal" is construed at any given moment. Similarly, in light of the blossoming of academic biblical scholarship over the past few decades, many evangelicals today regard the term "Bible" as a document filled with nuance, language, metaphor, and historical context in a way that earlier conservative Christians did not, who instead tended to see the Bible more as a scientific document, filled only with cold, hard facts. Moreover, this sort of distinction does not begin to grapple with the physical variations in Bibles themselves, from translation differences to debates over the degree to which certain biblical commentaries should be included alongside the biblical text. Even changing perceptions about the great unchanging being itself—"God"—have caused the entire conservative Christian enterprise to be performed far differently depending on whether God has been seen more as cosmic judge, friend, or father.

Consequently, it seems difficult to assert that even the most enduring notions have survived the years unchanged. Rather, it seems more appropriate to consider "Bible," "God," and other such presumably stable conservative Christian entities not as hegemonic, unwavering theological positions, but as *labels* that are used flexibly over time to unify otherwise disparate political aims and viewpoints. The goal of groups like CWA thus becomes manipulating the meaning and symbolic value of those labels in such a way as to generate a continual stream of ideological loyalty.

Such "flexible absolutism," to borrow Susan Harding's term, has been a significant ingredient in the Christian Right's longevity, propelling it to great cultural highs and sustaining it through various cultural lows.[36] If this aspect of chaos rhetoric has been used by CWA to demonize its opponents, it has also been used to craft itself into a righteous, mainstream, and progressive organization. True to Janet Jakobsen's sense that "elasticity and elusiveness in meaning is often the case with powerful symbols,"[37] this book will show how CWA has used chaos rhetoric to render terms such as "feminist," "elitist," "liberal," "conservative," "child," and "family," among others, in a specific, often shifting, manner so as to locate the group's opponents as fringe or radicalized entities, simultaneously painting its own image in a multiplicity of flattering and powerful ways. CWA's "absolute" platforms are thus hardly eternal, for rhetorical flexibility is one of the skills needed to negotiate the variable political winds.

What this means, practically speaking, is that the persuasive impact of CWA's chaos rhetoric is not limited to the already influential bloc of conservative Protestant culture, but has been crafted so as to have widespread public appeal. As I will show, this is achieved anytime the public sympathizes with its chaos-laden claims about the imminent ruin of families, children, nation, and faith through the volatile imagery of sex and gender. The power of chaos rhetoric does not require, or even request, full-blown theological adherence, for whether the public calls itself "Christian" is a relatively moot point in CWA's campaigns so long as that public lends support to the larger conservative political movement that it claims to represent.

Why Sex (and Religion)?

Various American groups have been raising the alarm over the nation's declining sexual morality since the country's genesis, and still today, this theme stands at the center of many controversial political and cultural debates. Studies of voting habits indicate that ballot issues involving sex and its related realms of gender and reproduction often evoke fierce voter loyalty, and recent Gallup polls show that abortion, homosexuality, and sexual education in schools, among other concerns, are topics around which there is little national consensus.[38] When one considers the number and scope of laws that have regulated sexual behavior over time (including bans on homosexuality, polygamy, statutory rape, interracial relationships, and sodomy, to name just a few), it becomes clear that American culture tends to treat sex as an inherently moral issue, or at the very least, a matter fundamental to the preservation of social order.

Not only are "our choices about sexuality so vital to our life projects," as Kathleen Sands remarks, but they are also the primary way that society determines whether we are seen as moral—and thus valuable—citizens.[39] Sexual, gendered, and reproductive norms have provided some of the most expedient ways of denigrating one social group while elevating another.[40] This is why, over time, recurring moral campaigns about sex have frequently warned of the overabundant reproduction of African Americans, or the perverse sexual acts of the poor: sexual panics have historically been raced and classed as a way to demarcate the boundaries of power, privilege, and status.[41] "In this sense," Nancy Fischer notes:

> . . . drawing lines between who is considered sexually pure and who is impure is not a simple matter of a culture going through some 'natural' process of determining its own particular norms and sorting out who follows rules and who breaks them, but is one more way that dominant groups demonstrate their power against minorities.[42]

This is but one reason why sex and religion talk often go together. As this book will discuss, one of the primary ways that sex is elevated from mere biology to ultimate morality is through the authority granted to religious rhetoric, like the kind produced by CWA. Religious speech is a bit of a chameleon, however: when it is not used in instances of overt "God-talk," it can masquerade as "tradition," "common sense," or secular "morality," all in the service of creating the image of a mainstream and neutral moral code that is nevertheless built on the ideals and agendas of specific religious claims. It can be difficult to find news stories about sex, gender, or reproduction that do not consult a religious official as an expert on the matter (even when, ironically, that person is celibate); similarly, most religions carefully proscribe rules about acceptable sexual acts.

Religious language is distinct in the special, elevated authority that it grants to human behaviors, so that arguments that employ religion are often perceived by the public to be superior to others when contests arise.[43] As a result, those who reject the dominant religious worldview – or even the moral standards stemming from it – are not represented as people who are simply exercising their personal preferences, but as individuals who are immoral, evil, or simply illogical.[44]

A Note About Terms

Scholars have devoted significant time to differentiating the various types of conservative Protestants who, in their politically active form, inspire this book. In most cases, they have attempted to describe them theologically. Thus, most American Conservative Protestant (ACP) groups are defined by their beliefs, which remain close to the original list that distinguished the early twentieth-century fundamentalists from other Christians: belief in the verbal and original inspiration and inerrancy of the Bible; the deity of Jesus; Jesus's virgin birth, substitutionary death, resurrection, and return (or "second coming"); and the existence of the Holy Spirit.[45] In more popular parlance, the umbrella term "Born Again Christian" implies adoption of these concepts, and usually carries with it the moral burden to convert others, as well.

In most scholarship, the terms *fundamentalist* and *evangelical* are used in place of "ACP," and theologically speaking, the two are relatively similar in their espousal of the aforementioned list. The difference, as it is often told, lies in the degree of social engagement with which each group is comfortable, with fundamentalists arguing for more social separatism and evangelicals advocating for more cultural involvement. But many scholars are carefully questioning the terms that they use to describe these conservative Christian groups; among other issues, *fundamentalist* has had widespread pejorative use and *evangelical* has been deployed so generically that it describes virtually anyone who is a conservative Christian (and an assortment of not-so-conservative Christians, as well). While these terms have specific historical meanings (some of which will be detailed in Chapter 1), for this book, parsing out such details is not usually a critical matter. Since the 1970s, many conservative Christian groups that went on to political activity (the early Christian Right) agreed to disagree on the particulars of their identity politics and, instead, work together for their common cultural causes. In addition, because the internet provides groups that wish to advertise their positions widespread public access, the sheer variety of religious and political organizations to which the public is exposed means that denominational labels and church loyalty simply do not bear as much weight as they did in the past.

In this book, I will use the term ACP to refer to the American conservative Protestant public in general (no matter their degree of political involvement), differentiating them from the Christian Right, a term used to describe the elite leaders of mostly ACP-based movements who claim that American culture is in dire moral trouble and is in significant need of a godly, Bible-based renovation that can and should be achieved through political activity. While the politics of the Christian Right are not limited to ACPs alone, conservative Protestants comprise the majority of the activists who make up its networks. At various points, I will also refer to "conservatives" and to "Christian conservatism" to speak more broadly about those who generally support conservative social politics without necessarily identifying as Protestants or even as religious people.

With this said, I am hesitant to mark these groups using only theological labels, since even a brief examination of the Christian Right's activism will show that many of its public campaigns are not primarily interested in the goal of "winning souls for Christ" if this does not explicitly translate into support for certain political issues. To this end, my own definitional rubric does not entirely discount the theological components behind such political action, but does not essentialize them, either. In other words, I do not treat beliefs as stand-alone phenomena disconnected from cultural contexts, nor do I sanitize them as something immune from politics. Rather, I approach doctrines and theological statements as pieces of rhetoric designed to forward religious groups' aspirations of social power, a spacious category that could include everything from having the cultural privilege to normalize one's religious views to the ability to pass a legal ban on gay marriage. Similar to the previous discussion on emotion, belief *in* something is not simply an inward cognitive act, but the process of adopting certain social views of reality that are historically contingent and humanly constructed (and thus political). In much the same way that Joan Wallach Scott describes the category of "experience," my assumption is that talking about belief as a self-evident (and thus automatically authoritative) category is not sufficient to describe the fullness of human behavior, for while scholars have often used the category of belief to differentiate between groups (just as they have used "experiences" to accomplish the same task, Scott notes), this category is often used as "uncontestable evidence" and an "originary point of explanation."[46] This practice is analytically problematic because it fails to ask about the nature of belief, why certain beliefs emerge in the first place, the socio-historical conditions of a certain belief's popularity, and perhaps most importantly, how beliefs function to "constitute subjects who see and act in the world."[47]

In light of this, I often refer to the outcome of such beliefs as "social power" or "political power," two terms used to describe the motivations that CWA and other Christian Right groups have in pursuing their activism. In describing these motivations, I am sensitive to John Shields's critique that scholars often employ psychological or sociological models to explain conservative Christian activism when the rationales provided by such groups seem distasteful or even irrational to the scholars who study them.[48] Yet presuming that a more unbiased view means taking conservative Christian claims at face value falls prey to the very sort of *sui generis* treatment of belief refuted above. For my part, I do not see a conflict between viewing *all* groups as entities that devise tangible goals to accompany beliefs for which they have crafted supporting logics, while also understanding the social function of such beliefs to simultaneously provide non-tangible rewards such as psychological security, social status, and the like. Thus I approach CWA as a group that achieves social or political power not only when it successfully changes laws, but also when its members experience things such as cultural normalcy and a sense of moral superiority.

With this dissection of "belief" in mind, the term "religion" also deserves attention. Instead of approaching religion as an essence or thing, in this book I treat religion as a *tactic*, exploring how religious rhetoric often uses allusions, symbols, and explanations that are distinct in the power continuum of language precisely because they appeal to an external, transcendent authority (God, or more generally, morality), which then presumably renders the speech impervious to criticism, hiding its human creation and granting it extraordinary status.[49] Because I am concerned with how religious speech operates in the public sphere, I will not spend time here considering whether the claims of religion are categorically true or false—my interest is simply whether the public sympathizes with the rhetoric that features those claims. On a more theoretical level, though, I see considerable risk in talking about religion as something distinct from politics, as is common in the academy. Any religious claim is automatically a power claim (and is thus political in the widest sense of the term) because it asserts that its legitimacy comes from an ultimate and unquestionable source. Consequently, in this book I treat religious speech as political speech, and presume that separating the two creates a false dichotomy.

CWA: A Rhetorical Engine

The primary purpose of this study is to offer a model for how chaos rhetoric works, and with this understanding, to question how large social movements like the Christian Right also operate. But because achieving this goal requires placing CWA's chaos rhetoric under the microscope, so to speak, the book also provides a thorough topical analysis of CWA's platforms. As one of the most politically and culturally potent members of the Christian Right, many of the conclusions drawn about CWA's use of chaos rhetoric can be applied to the larger Christian Right movement, or, as I will show, to any social movement that attempts to persuade the public.

CWA is an organization of particular interest because it has been a loud and long voice in political debates on morality and proper sexual identities, claiming not only to represent ACPs at large, but also mainstream America. From the time of her first public political engagements in the 1960s, Beverly LaHaye has stood apart from most other Christian Right figures in the sheer endurance and longevity of her activism. Together with her husband, Tim, the pair has built an extensive media empire. By most recent estimates, CWA has a budget of approximately $8 million dollars and claims to be the largest women's organization in the United States.[50]

Yet the ability to communicate effectively and expansively is not simply a matter of technological mastery. What continues to differentiate CWA from other conservative groups is its ability to reach outside of the evangelical world to shape the larger cultural currents in a way that makes the "personal the political," to borrow the feminist motto. CWA's goal to "[help] our members across the country bring Biblical principles into all levels of public policy" has translated into political and legislative action groups, frequent media appearances by CWA staff on mainstream (and other) media outlets, an extensive legal team, and a widespread, national grassroots campaign.[51] This grassroots base is CWA's human engine, which, when notified by the organization to act, has been known to flood legislators and public officials with letters, phone calls, and emails. As one CWA observer has noted:

> The effects of such efficient organizing can be devastating as thousands of letters and phone calls bombard Capitol Hill in a matter of days. Legislators in both houses and in both parties, particularly those who depend on conservative support, know that a "wrong" vote on one of these hot issues will come back to haunt them at the next election. Even centrist legislators are affected by the deluge, regardless of their own opinions on an issue: the safest political position is often with the majority of the activists, as opposed to the majority of citizens or voters. They may not expect the support of the CWA crowd, but they definitely don't want to be targeted by them as a special enemy in the next election.[52]

While CWA has capitalized heavily on its success as an example of kitchen-table politics, its deep political ties in Washington cannot be overstated. Most of its spokespersons and senior staff have been or continue to be lobbyists, aides, presidential speech writers, media pundits, United Nations delegates, and others whose political ties run deep.[53] It is true that many other well-connected Christian Right groups have built this same political infrastructure, but what most of them lack is the identity as a women's organization. In something akin to niche marketing, CWA borrows heavily from the longstanding historical argument that women bear a special religious or moral essence, and thus it frequently claims that it occupies a unique cultural position that enables it to speak authoritatively on moral issues regarding sex, gender, and reproduction in a way others cannot. Distinguishing "true" women from "false" or misguided ones is an important part of this self-portrayal, however, for feminists, lesbians, and other sorts of "liberal" women represent not the grand spectrum of female diversity, but are signs of its perversion. At certain points in its rhetoric, CWA even discounts their female identity altogether, claiming that "real" women must be bold enough to take charge of the course of the nation, rescuing it from the "counterfeits" who threaten its destruction.

With the continuing vitality of Christian Right groups like CWA, it may seem ironic that a 2009 edition of *Newsweek* magazine featured an article touting the "End of Christian America."[54] In the article, author Jon Meacham observed that while religion is still a powerful force in America, overtly religious arguments in the public sphere no longer hold the same power as they once did. Based on statistics indicating that fewer Americans than ever label themselves "Christian," Meacham concluded that religion, as a whole, is on the decline.

As much as Meacham may have tapped into a shift in the power dynamics of religion in America today, it seems a critical error to equate the diminishment of personal religious affiliation with the public decline of religion, for this presumption depends on thinking that religion's social power is found mostly in private, individual conversion or blatant religious talk. Instead, a more accurate picture of American religious power might be found in the tremendous time, energy, and money that groups like CWA spend in avoiding the constant invocation of overtly religious speech, but in still persuading both politicians and the public on what it portrays as self-evidently moral grounds. As this book will repeatedly show, because it is a fundamentally political engine, CWA is not primarily interested in making believers out of Americans, but in making them voters whose votes it can control.

Methods

Beverly LaHaye's cultural import places her in the footsteps of many other famous, politically active Christians who have sought mass-media dominance as a mechanism to transform the nation's political scene. One need only consider the early twentieth-century evangelistic radio shows of Charles Fuller; the mid-century international dynamism of Billy Graham's open air "Crusades"; the extensive televangelist broadcast networks of the 1980s (featuring names such as Jim Bakker, Jerry Falwell, Pat Robertson, and Jimmy Swaggart); and the present-day barrage of books and websites attributable to figures like the LaHayes, as well as a new generation of evangelicals like Rick Warren, Joel Osteen, and Bill Hybels, among others. While television, radio, internet, and print media have all been critically important to CWA's growth, the organization has joined most other contemporary social movements by conducting a large portion of its public business in the virtual world. My engagement with CWA's rhetoric occurred through careful readings of the articles that comprise its most expansive and accessible resource: its website.

The reasons for limiting my research to CWA's website (versus the other available media produced by the organization) were motivated primarily by matters of scope and consistency. The CWA website offers the fullest picture of the group's rhetoric if very simply because it is used as a storage receptacle for the majority of its other media engagements (including podcasts, transcripts, print, and occasional video), which are then re-marketed as web content and featured alongside the many legal-style briefs that comprise the bulk of its online presence. Knowing the many voices and styles that together constitute the website, it might seem natural to assume that the vantage points expressed by its contributors range widely in tone or content. This, however, is not the case, and across the better part of a decade that I regularly read the site, I rarely (if ever) found an errant article or contradictory statement. This merits some attention, for those unfamiliar with the speech of Christian Right groups may easily find the excerpts contained here shrill and extreme. They are, however, representative. This heightened tenor is how chaos rhetoric is designed, for unless negative emotion is a part of the reader's experience, political action is unlikely.

One noteworthy difference between online and other media venues is the dynamic and often interactive nature of the internet. While the internet is now so ubiquitous that it may seem that the medium itself needs no critical introduction, research into online religion has evoked questions regarding how this particular form of communication is different from its more physical, face-to-face counterpart. Many have claimed that democracy, access, and anonymity are the new terms of possibility that the internet offers the world of religion, a point of heightened contrast to the many instances of hierarchically entrenched religion (what has been called "organized religion") of the physical world.[55] The internet's ability to compress time, create a sense of authority, and enable easy networking and activism has undoubtedly changed the face of religion forever.[56]

Yet despite the temptation to see "virtual religion" and "physical religion" as two separate realms, more recent theoretical models have portrayed cyberspace as a mere extension of the physical world, one that is intrinsically conservative insomuch as it reinforces existing power structures.[57] When one considers the internet as a reflection of cultural politics, the most elementary issues surrounding how religion is defined re-emerge. Foremost among these is whether religion is an inherently political phenomenon. Assuming that it is (as I have earlier argued), the distinction that some scholars have made between "online religion" and "religion online" becomes a questionable one. The former is often described as the purely informative broadcast of data about a religion through the medium of the internet (such as one might find through a Wikipedia search for "Catholics" or "Mormons"), while the latter describes one's actual participation in religious practices online, such as prayer, sermon-watching, or tithing.[58]

The problem with the labels "online religion" and "religion online" involves the way that the very terms themselves create an artificial dichotomy, for how religion is portrayed ("online religion") can go very far in determining whether it appears attractive or reasonable enough to identify with or practice ("religion online"). Moreover, this distinction limits what counts as "religion" to predictable, often Christo-centric acts (prayer, tithing, sermon-watching) that represent only a small sliver of the larger realm of behaviors, attitudes, and positions influenced by religion's claims. In the case of CWA, for instance, readers are urged to take political action by contacting their legislators or signing petitions just as much (if not more) than they are to pray and tithe—that is, to practice "typical" Christian acts. Because the CWA website portrays itself as a database supporting the many causes of conservatism, it becomes difficult to distinguish between traditionally religious behaviors and other encounters that inform the reader's position on a political topic through a secular-sounding, yet religiously wrought, lens. Instead, CWA presents most of this information in more neutral form, claiming that what it offers is purely informational, common-sense knowledge.

With this in mind, the distinction between "online religion" and "religion online" may obscure more than it clarifies, yet the internet has nevertheless opened up a world of possibilities for political groups seeking public attention and response, making an easier task of large-scale persuasion. Besides for the ability to quickly and easily access mountains of information, the "point and click" nature of online culture has made activism in the name of religious or moral principles no more than a finger-stroke away. While it still bears all of the residues of the physical, social world, the CWA website has created the conditions through which certain types of rhetoric are more easily facilitated and thus more easily take hold.

Because I understood the CWA website as an inherently political engine, I was interested in approaching it in such a way that might mimic the average user who turns to it for information. During most of my visits there, I interacted more passively, clicking only on the prompts provided by the website (such as "Religious Issues" or "Family Issues") to see where and how the organization sought to lead the reader. On other occasions, I conducted my own searches using terms such as "abortion," "gay marriage," or "homosexuality," among others. At still other junctures, I searched using the names of political figures (such as "Obama," "Pelosi," or "Sotomayor") when articles headlined by the organization related public policy issues specifically to those individuals. Search terms were kept purposely short to mimic what the average user might enter, and links were freely followed from there so long as they remained on the site. When appropriate, I included visual images in the analysis that contributed to and thus affected the presentation of the rhetoric.

I considered all articles featured on the website, even when written by people with no direct organizational ties to CWA. Because the Christian Right is a vast network of often interrelated groups that rely on one another for both rhetorical and physical support, it would be impossible to limit discussion of a particular group to its paid staff. As a result, I was not as concerned with the identity of the writer as much as I was interested in the fact that CWA found the article as an important piece of rhetoric and sought its inclusion on its website. For instance, I did not hesitate to include an article by Christian Right founder Paul Weyrich, for while not an employee of CWA, Weyrich's presence on the site makes an important statement not only about CWA's politics, but also about how it envisions its own political lineage.

After examining the articles using the criteria mentioned above, I selected those for inclusion in this book with several other measures in mind. First, with a few exceptions, I focused on pieces published since the year 2000. The result is that this book provides a snapshot of the events that concerned CWA for roughly the first decade of the twenty-first century. Second, I was interested in identifying articles that drew upon sexualized, gendered, or reproductive imagery to elicit reader persuasion. Because these topics are invoked so frequently to craft an argument about a multitude of issues, finding such articles was not difficult. Finally, I sought to preserve a sense of how CWA portrayed itself to the public, and thus gave special attention to the placement of certain articles on the website. Some of the articles were selected for inclusion because they were prominently featured on the website's homepage, were linked as "additional reading" from one of those highly visible articles, or had been emailed directly to members. These were chosen to highlight what sort of rhetoric CWA deliberately emphasized as it built its public persona.

As mentioned, CWA portrays itself as an informational tool to equip readers with the necessary knowledge needed to take political action. I regarded the factual claims within each article neither as necessarily true nor false, but as instances of chaos rhetoric containing intentionally manipulated symbols designed to persuade the public in a particular way. As I will discuss throughout the book, chaos rhetoric's signature is not necessarily its connection with reality, but its persuasive value. One group may create a chaos rhetoric that is logically and scientifically sound but rather weak in its emotional appeal, while another may defy reason altogether but craft a very convincing story that successfully evokes public outrage. In each case chaos rhetoric has been crafted, but only to the degree that social perceptions are changed can one call the latter truly effective, despite its lack of factual data.

If there was any claim made by CWA that I rejected outright, then, it was the notion that what it offers the public is neutral information, or "just the facts." This is not because CWA has a particularly unique problem with impartiality, for all groups that take on a political position and desire to persuade the public have something at stake in portraying reality in one way over another. Because the processes of categorization and definition—distinguishing immoral from moral, sinner from saint, patriot from traitor, and so on—remain among the most fundamental political practices, there is no time when describing a situation or recalling an event is self-evidently true to all those who witness it. In short, there are many ways to tell a story.

With this in mind, I analyzed the selected articles by focusing on how the structure and language of CWA's arguments were shaped to persuade the public, and how the themes or symbols that formed the content of this structure were both selected and used. Within each article I identified various recurring symbols, how they were employed in the rhetoric, what logic was used to persuade the reader of the naturalness of that particular symbolic portrayal, and what identifiable linguistic patterns (such as word choice, argument order, or logical progressions) were present. Even more specifically, I identified the natures and types of chaos rhetoric that appeared, cataloguing in each instance what sort of order was constructed against which proposed threat.

Apart from how it depicted its enemies, I also noted how CWA crafted its own self-depiction. Here I found a multitude of shifting rhetorical tactics. At certain points, CWA described itself as the last remnant of American righteousness, while at others it proposed that its positions were so widespread that they represented the vast majority of Americans. CWA takes advantage of a tremendous amount of rhetorical flexibility to represent itself in whatever way is most advantageous at the moment. This is typical of groups that successfully dominate a media form, portraying themselves as *the* public rather than members within *a* public, even as they describe themselves at other times in a countercultural or subaltern way.[59]

Overview of the Book

While many works addressing the rhetoric of Christian Right groups have been published, this book represents a reversal of several common methods or assumptions that typically ground such research. When the Christian Right was experiencing a particularly vital moment during the 1980s and 1990s, many scholars understood its focus on sexuality issues as a distinctive element of late twentieth-century Christianity.[60] Yet in Chapter 1, I will show that the rhetoric linking a failure in sexual ethics with national decline is actually a longstanding historical trope that has been revived by conservative religio-political representatives during times of social upheaval, and that its presence has been a quintessential part of American culture. The intent and outcome of most of these campaigns has been to restore white, patriarchal, heterosexual power. Starting with the endorsement of the "separate spheres" ideal by many nineteenth-century Christian organizations, this model of gender dichotomization and traditional sexual roles has been revived and reclothed across the nation's history. From concern over white women's use of birth control in the early twentieth century, to the present debate regarding the legality of same-sex marriage, morally charged language about sex has been strategically interjected into American social debates as a mechanism to control the reins of political power. By the time CWA emerged in the 1970s, it had become yet another rhetorical engine that reproduced a more modern, yet consistently historical, version of earlier chaos rhetoric regarding sex, gender, and reproduction, and it built heavily on the notion that women's natural moral tendencies legitimized its claim to speak for all Americans.

The next three chapters question the common presumption that the social allure of Christian Right groups lies with their rigid morals and absolutist statements. Building on the historical lessons of the first chapter, Chapter 2 demonstrates how CWA garners social support by threatening a specially constructed sense of order that is both built and maintained by relegating its opponents to categories of abjection. This chapter considers the role of religious symbols in creating a chaos rhetoric that manages to elevate sex to a particularly sensitive moral realm. But rather than rely solely, or even mostly, on overt theological arguments, CWA more frequently invokes logic, science, and populist claims to defend its positions, thereby presenting itself as a mainstream social group that is not only logical and reasonable, but objective. This is a critical claim to consider, for chaos rhetoric does not typically conceal reality outright, but presents only a very limited version of events that can be tweaked to the group's political favor.

Chapter 3 reverses the popular notion that the Christian Right stands for eternal and timeless platforms. This chapter deals with the flexibility of chaos rhetoric, particularly concerning the term *feminism*. Here CWA presents itself as a traditional institution that rejects liberal feminism and, simultaneously, a progressive institution embodying "true" feminism's historical legacy. It does this in large part by pathologizing its opponents, a move of delegitimization as well as contrast whereby it can shape its enemies' symbolic value in more negative terms and then dynamically produce its own identity in a positive light. In all of its self-portrayals, the organization claims to be the representation, protection, and embodiment of the best (and thus most righteous) segments of American culture.

Continuing with the assumption that religion is a tactic and not an essence, Chapter 4 considers CWA's central political platforms and the manner in which it must project a certain understanding of nationalism in order to gain the greatest political impact, along the way reversing the idea that what CWA does is, in some central way, religious but not political. CWA has named these platforms "The Six Core Issues," which include "Family," "Sanctity of Life," "Education," "Pornography," "Religious Liberty," and "National Sovereignty." Under the auspices of these topics, CWA's entire symbolic repertoire is on display in its portrayal of the nation as a powerful entity that is nevertheless rendered vulnerable by sexual norm violations. Here CWA continuously draws upon the emotionally laden symbol of the innocent child who is preyed upon by sexual deviants or moral relativists. By equating the protection of children with a specific reading of sexual morality – and with this with national strength – groups like CWA can more easily justify their voice in national affairs by depicting themselves as the guardians of true morality, and thus true patriotism, fighting against a despotic government. Tellingly, CWA does not raise the specter of the death of Christianity as a problem in itself, but warns more often of the death of *America* as the result of Christianity's demise.

The final chapter of the book makes a claim that may seem entirely counterintuitive: there is very little that is rhetorically unique about CWA and similar Christian Right groups, if only because the tactics that chaos rhetoric enables are so extraordinarily widespread. Why, then, do scholars spend so much time considering the influence of a movement that is otherwise rather mundane? Here I consider whether and how portrayals of the Christian Right as a unique phenomenon are the claims of an academic community that, in itself, is politically uncomfortable with acknowledging the normalcy of CWA's tactics, specifically, and conservative politics, more generally. To admit the rather commonplace nature of CWA's rhetorical work robs the academic community of the ability to generate much of its own chaos rhetoric, which frequently holds that groups like CWA represent some sort of cultural or theological deviation. Nevertheless, certain points of distinction do exist, but these have far more to do with the ability of Christian Right groups to fuse their own identities with the nation-state itself than with theological or tactical distinction.

If, as Morone observes, sex, gender, and the family are realms that have been at the crux of defining American concepts of fear and danger – and thus sin and salvation – then these issues cannot be understood as "mere" politics, for in their manipulation and deployment lies the ability to categorize and thus control the most basic structures of society.[61] Exploring the historical, theoretical, and rhetorical dimensions of CWA's symbolic universe is key to understanding the process by which chaos rhetoric transforms the ordinary realm of human political contestation into something that appears much more extraordinary.

1

Second Verse, Same as the First: A History of American Conservative Sex, Gender, and Reproduction Rhetoric

> *In Chicago, a couple attending the University of Chicago's graduate school made it very clear that I was "Neanderthal" in my approach to family planning because I reaffirmed God's first commandment to humans, "Be fruitful and increase in number; fill the earth and subdue it" (Gen. 1:28). They had been so brainwashed by the humanistic family planners of our educational system that they considered avoidance of a family a patriotic service. However, I was suspicious (as I told them personally) that the real reason largely reflected selfishness. At that point the wife's anger erupted, and she revealed the extent of her humanistic brainwashing by parroting the women's libber's line, "What do you think I am? A baby factory? I want to pursue a career!". . . . In a practical way, when a Christian couple decide [sic] not to have children, they exclude a potential child from the potential blessing of eternal life as God planned for him or her.*[1]
>
> —TIM AND BEVERLY LAHAYE, The Act of Marriage (1998)

IN LATE 2011, more than a decade after the LaHayes published the above statement on the damage wrought by those who choose not to bear children, the world population reached an estimated seven billion people. While a flurry of commentators spoke about the population crisis that the planet was already experiencing, CWA's Janice Shaw Crouse responded with an entirely different message:

> While these warnings are espoused by seemingly reputable organizations and claim to be steeped in research, in reality, they are mere

> scare tactics designed to elevate environmentalism over human expansion. The phrases "giv[ing] women access to family planning" and "motivat[ing] women to reduce their fertility" are simply codes for easier access to contraception and elective abortion.[2]

Crouse asserts that while the world population is higher than it has ever been, birth rates are actually dropping, something that she attributes, in part, to individuals choosing cohabitation and career development over marriage and childbearing: "A loss of faith has played a key role in diminishing birth rates," she argues, which has subsequently created these "sub-par living arrangements" that "foster an ethic of selfishness and disdain for large families. . . ."[3] In its simplest terms, Crouse confirms that there is a crisis, but it is the exact opposite of what those who warn of a population explosion suggest. The real crisis is a liberal lie, fueled by selfish agendas, which condones the inherently unethical acts of abortion and chosen childlessness.

Statements deriding individuals who do not follow the traditionally gendered path towards the nuclear family and heterosexual reproduction have had a long tenure in American public rhetoric. From the turn of the twentieth century to the turn of the twenty-first, the many conservative voices that have engaged in such speech show how central sex, gender, and reproduction have been to American culture's self-description. This chapter explores several historical moments across the twentieth and twenty-first centuries wherein chaos rhetoric has been used to symbolically fuse together sex, morality, religion, and the nation, ending with its contemporary incarnation in the work of CWA. From one century to the next, a predictable theme ties the period together: When social power structures are threatened by new players, new mores, or other cultural challenges, religious or moralistic rhetoric about the demise of sexual ethics has often quickly emerged as a way of stabilizing these shifting sands back into the hands of the status quo, using chaos rhetoric to create and support the jeremiad of national, moral decline.

Lest one too quickly conclude that this is the work of religious authorities alone, the speakers who have employed this rhetoric have not necessarily represented religious institutions. Regardless of their affiliations, they all found religious and moralistic speech readily available for their use in inciting public persuasion. Secular voices can bolster the legitimacy of an otherwise religiously inspired chaos rhetoric in times where religion's outward authority may seem to be on the wane. Yet these sources remain critically important even in periods of great public religiosity if only because they lend another layer of plausibility to the argument: Perhaps the church teaches that God hates homosexuality, but if a well-known doctor now indicates that homosexuals spread disease, then there is yet another layer of logic to influence how one thinks or votes about the issue.

This chapter starts by examining the sex, gender, and reproduction rhetoric employed within the context of early twentieth-century fundamentalism, which became a template for later Christian Right platforms. In the decades after the public rise (and then fall) of early fundamentalism with the Scopes "Monkey Trial," a new form of ACP emerged, embodied in the person of Billy Graham. Graham capitalized on the social events of the mid-twentieth century to create a mainstream religious rhetoric. His speech strongly fused politics, religion, and issues of popular culture into a new sort of American Christian empire. In the midst of McCarthyism's concern over the preponderance of un-American behavior and the Kinsey Reports' shocking findings on the sexual habits of the average American, many conservative Christians found enemies all around—and their Communist, anti-Christian ways were evidenced, in part, through their sexual habits.

This conservative empire kindled by Graham proliferated under the weight of the gender, sex, and reproductive changes that characterized the next two decades. During the 1960s and 1970s, the Christian Right not only specifically defined Christian morality and American patriotism through the lens of sex (via campaigns against the Equal Rights Amendment, abortion, homosexuality, and feminism, among others), but also amplified the degree and scope of its political involvement. In light of the clear departure from the traditional nuclear family idealized during the 1950s, the Christian Right fought back over the next several decades to preserve the normalcy of such relationships, drawing consistently on secular humanism and big government as the new cultural specters causing the family's decline.

Despite the fact that the 1980s and 1990s were a time of conservative cultural dominance, the rhetoric of forced Christian isolationism at the hands of the government persisted and was influential in the proliferation of a multitude of new Christian Right interest groups. CWA is one such example of a mobilized response against the gendered shifts of the 1960s and 1970s that gained both institutional and political power in the 1980s. Like its historical predecessors, CWA has continued the trend of couching the health of American culture in terms of sex, gender, and reproduction.

To tell the story of how and why groups like CWA exist is to trace a moralistic path back as far as America's beginning, one that has linked sexual morality (understood in conservative Protestant terms) with a robust nationalism. This vision of nationalism has long described a certain type of moral fortitude as a prerequisite to full citizenship and human rights. From the patriotic appropriation of Puritan John Winthrop's famous sermon to the early colonists describing their "City on a Hill," to the series of widespread religious revivals since the country's inception, American religious rhetoricians have long promoted the country's sense of divine chosenness and moral mandate.[4]

Yet, at the same time, the call to moral purity has been specifically and narrowly defined so as to constitute an act of cultural exclusion. If "morality" is the name given to the proscription and evaluation of not only behaviors, but also identities, rights, privileges, and resources, then crafting a moralistic ideal inseparable from nationalistic fervor makes possible the creation of legal or other sanctioned civic avenues through which to oust or silence dissenters. Filled with the various threats that accompany moral demise, the conservative Christian voices throughout American history have been clear: the very survival of the country hinges on the triumph of the righteous and the expulsion of the unrighteous. Issues of sex, gender, and reproduction have often been portrayed as the marker dividing the two.

Chaos Rhetoric and the Early Twentieth Century

Recalling the history of twenty-first century chaos rhetoric involves a continual return to shifts in class, race, and sex, those ever-important categories through which most cultures distinguish between people and the relative cultural worth that they are granted. In the American conservative Christian story, some of the most important expressions of such social power were established near the end of the nineteenth century. The Victorian era is often remembered for its valorization of the "separate spheres," the model for ideal families that gained religious justification during this period and that has continued to enjoy healthy resurgences ever since. Certain segments of Victorian culture elevated this ideal to something of a cultural art form: to balance out the domain of men—the ruthless, dog-eat-dog environment of an increasingly changing, corporate, industrialized world—women were cast as the god-ordained keepers of the home. The home was described as an oasis of kindness, gentleness, and moral purity, the site for fostering what were believed to be women's "true" religious inclinations.

As Betty DeBerg describes it, however, this idea was popularized because of a shift from an agrarian to an industrialized economy that destabilized both labor systems and gender roles, a shift that rather suddenly interjected women into work that had been seen as traditionally masculine.[5] Seeking to right the cultural unrest, many Christians lent this gendered separation an explicitly religious reading. As the chaos rhetoric was framed, God created men's and women's natures such that they should occupy these different spheres, and for one to cross over into the other represented an unnatural, and ultimately ungodly, arrangement. The institution of marriage thus became one of domestication and virtue; if infiltrated by lust, recreation, or self-indulgence, the marriage relationship promised only to undermine Protestant ideals of "moral earnestness, austerity, and self-control."[6] From these concepts emerged the gendered ideals that historians have labeled the "separate spheres," as reflected in the preaching of Henry Ward Beecher:

> Man is strong—woman is beautiful. Man is daring and confident—woman is diffident and unassuming. Man is great in action—woman i[n] suffering. Man shines abroad—woman at home. Man talks to convince—woman to persuade and please. Man has a rugged heart—woman a soft and tender one. Man prevents misery—woman relieves it. Man has science—woman taste. Man has judgement—woman sensibility. Man is a being of justice—woman of mercy.[7]

Through much of the rhetoric of the period, preachers described the Christian message as an inherently feminine philosophy; Christian morality was read synonymously with female virtue insomuch as Christianity was "essentially nurturing, altruistic, loving, affective, and passive."[8] This gendered reading applied to the Christian scriptures as well; in 1869, popular preacher Harold Bushnell depicted the Old Testament as the masculine law, while the New Testament represented God's feminine grace.[9]

If the white Victorian woman was ideally moral, gentle, kind, and nurturing, however, she was also asexual. This idea endured into the first few decades of the twentieth century when, in popular literature and social rhetoric, it was simply presumed that a "bad" boy was criminal, but a "bad" girl was sexual. This view helped reinforce popular racist notions held by the public about the errant sexuality of racial minorities, which at least partly explains why many social workers during the early twentieth century took it for granted that African American girls were sexually active.[10] These ideas remained very popular for decades thanks in part to the fame of G. Stanley Hall, a late nineteenth- and early twentieth-century psychologist who, in his research, openly approached sexuality as one of the most reliable gauges by which one could measure moral capacity (and, by extension, social worth).

Hall described adolescent sexual desire as a slippery moral slope, warning that, if left unchecked, rampant sexuality would open the floodgates to all sorts of criminal behavior. He discussed sexuality in ways typical of his time: marital sex was a social good; adultery was morally bad, yet frequent; and homosexuality was rare yet so heinous that it caused the complete moral devaluation of those engaged in such acts. Hall's solution to the social ill of overly and wrongly sexualized youth (masturbation was of particular concern) was religion. He argued that Christianity's capacity to provide Jesus's love and acceptance to confused and experimenting teens would short-circuit the transformation of desire into perversion, in all of its forms.[11]

But like many others of his day, Hall was sensitive to the social critique that many men were rejecting the church on the grounds that it had turned too "soft" and feminine with the presence of women at its helm.[12] Daniel Scott Smith has called this emergence of female religious and domestic power "domestic feminism," a term that describes not only the institutional and organizational clout that many middle- and upper middle-class women achieved within church structures, but also the degree to which they began to exercise greater agency in matters within the family and home, like childrearing and birth control.[13] This newfound outlet of power was also expressed in service organizations that sought to rid the public of immorality, such as the women's campaigns against alcohol before and during the Prohibition era. The Women's Christian Temperance Union (WCTU), organized in 1873, was perhaps one of the most visible faces of female religious dominance. Headed in the early twentieth century by women's rights advocate Frances Willard, the organization not only sought to eliminate vice, but located gender segregation, war, child labor, and women's inability to vote as a sign of cultural sin.[14] In many ways, Willard played an integral role in fusing female religious power with social change.

As Hall's concerns demonstrated, though, not everyone celebrated this gendered shift in power. At the same time that women grew more powerful within church organizations that fostered their supposedly natural religious inclinations, many male church administrators, ministers, and observers became nervous about this arrangement. In his own chaos rhetoric, Bushnell argued that women's innate passivity and delicacy did not equip them well for the political struggles of the world.[15] Fueled by such sentiments, the early part of the twentieth century saw female religious power replaced with the rise of theological arguments for women's subservience and submission; men, not women, were cast as the new guardians of orthodoxy as women lost their Victorian claim to moral superiority.[16]

How could this happen, if women were still collectively regarded as bearers of an inward moral compass? Opponents of women's rights argued that while women might have naturally ethical inclinations, they did not have an emotional temperament strong and stoic enough to suit them for public leadership. Even certain women advocated against their own political empowerment. The largely female National Association Opposed to Women's Suffrage (NAOWS), started in 1911, claimed that granting women the right to vote would erode traditional gender roles, public morality, and the dignity of femininity, the latter of which belonged more in service to others than in the public world of politics.[17] In an irony that would recur over the decades, the NAOWS featured politically engaged, vocal women who spoke out against politically engaged, vocal women.[18]

In shifting the pendulum of power back to men, conservative Christianity repeatedly turned to masculine imagery in an attempt to attract the men it previously saw as naturally unreligious. Male social service movements (not unlike WCTU) formed that were devoted to public service and the "calm, sane, and logical" evangelization of the un-churched; these adjectives could not, presumably, describe their female counterparts.[19] Strength and virility characterized the fundamentalist Christian gospel, as in baseball player-turned-fundamentalist preacher Billy Sunday's prayer: "Lord, save us from off-handed, flabby-cheeked, brittle-boned, weak-kneed, thin-skinned, pliable, plastic, spineless, effeminate, ossified three karat Christianity."[20]

These contests over gendered authority, both in the churches and society at large, were one force that signified the tipping point leading to a new breed of Christian conservatives who not only were quite visible, but who also positioned themselves as an alternative to the dangers and disorders of female religious power.[21] If "fundamentalism" was the name given to the early ACP movement, known for its adherence to certain key Christian principles, then fundamentalists were extant long before the early twentieth century.[22] It was during that time, however, that the movement's more public face materialized.[23] The flapper and the emergence of early feminism, alongside a continually growing immigrant population, encouraged chaos rhetoric linking moral depravity with job loss, crime, and the threat to the white, native-born, Protestant family. These were all signs of the palpable tensions that existed over the place of the white male worker and the supremacy of white ACP culture through which fundamentalism operated.

What did white, upper-class Americans have to fear? Immigrants topped the list. Not only did they seemingly threaten to steal the jobs of white men, but their moral capacities were consistently questioned, often through the language of sex. Early twentieth-century American immigration policies consistently relied on a sexual degeneration model to classify certain potential citizens (namely, the non-white and poorer classes) as bad candidates for citizenship because it was presumed that they bore compromised moral and physical abilities. This model was based on the notion that sexual abnormalities (understood to mean everything from homosexuality to arrested genital development) were the precursor to moral perversion, which was itself a precursor to economic dependency on the state. Thus immigration policy was constructed around the popular perception that admitting sexually "suspicious" immigrants to the United States would bog down the country with the social ills and poverty that their sexuality all but guaranteed.[24] As testament to the power of this argument, immigrants suspected of homosexuality were deported for this reason alone through the 1960s, and still as late as the 1980s, an overt admission of homosexuality could launch an investigation into a potential citizen's immigration status.[25]

Hence, early fundamentalist chaos rhetoric consistently warned of the moral degradation coming from infiltrating outsiders as well as corrupt insiders who violated traditional sexual norms. Theologically speaking, fundamentalism's pre-millennialism supported this reading of moral "others." This doctrine, which claimed that society would grow more evil in advance of Jesus's second coming, allowed fundamentalist preachers to construe changing gender roles and other "abnormalities" within sexual and family life as a sign of a comparably eroding society and thus the imminence of the apocalypse.[26] While this dichotomous gender model served as a culture-wide gauge for acceptable family life, it demanded a level of economic stability that made it realistically accessible only to wealthier whites.[27] Thus, the rhetoric worked on many levels: Not only did it establish white (and gendered) normativity, but the racial and economic tensions lingering in the American South, in particular, helped to construct the enduring bourgeois connection between poverty and moral (often read as sexual) depravity.

This was nowhere clearer than in the issue of interracial marriage, one particularly contentious site used to work out gendered, sexualized, and racialized norms through the language of morality. Anti-miscegenation laws from the late nineteenth through the early twentieth centuries delegitimized marriages between whites and other racial groups (including blacks, Asians, Filipinos, and American Indians, among others) on several grounds. The most consistent argument offered by the courts was that "mixing" races not only compromised the purity of whites, but was also a sign of the triumph of unnatural lust.[28] Indeed, a growing nativist impulse explained the poverty experienced by racial minorities and the working classes as the result of their aggressive displays of sexual desire, thus accounting for the subsequent "vice and promiscuity" that abounded among them.[29] While cultural stereotypes perpetuated the notion that both black and white men's sexual appetites were robust, white men were often cast as the victims of black women's animalistic libidos. In fact, black women's attempts to seduce weaker-willed white men into sexual impropriety was used as the dominant explanation for why white men epidemically raped them.[30] As black women's moral opposites, the purity, civility, and asexuality of white women could civilize and redeem white males whose indiscretions were reduced to momentary weakness rather than inherent moral depravity. Thus, the dignity of marriage was gauged, in part, via race.

By the close of the first three decades of the twentieth century, fundamentalism and other conservative social movements had targeted most underprivileged groups as the instigators of sexual deviancy and thus moral corruption. A declining white birth rate (in part the result of this "domestic feminism"), combined with rising numbers of non-whites and immigrants, made it appear that the morally depraved were gaining the upper hand.

These fears were both created and exacerbated by the open, public discussion on reproductive control started by women's rights advocate Margaret Sanger, whose name, Ellen Chesler notes, "was virtually synonymous with the birth control cause."[31] Sanger was one of the first to publicly recognize that the ability to control the terms under which reproduction took place was the simultaneous ability to provide women greater agency in almost every aspect of their lives. Controversially, Sanger also forthrightly described women as sexual beings.[32] However, as much as this agency enabled women's further cultural empowerment, it was also incredibly provocative (if not outright scandalous), as it portended the unraveling of the gender ideals that gripped so much of privileged culture.

In an attempt to halt the activism of Sanger and others who radically re-imagined reproduction and gender, popular religious publications forged a robust alliance between (white) motherhood and religion. In these publications and the growing religious rhetoric spawned from them, responsibility for the moral fortitude of children—and thus the course of the nation—was placed directly in women's hands. Popular religious chaos rhetoric decried white women's use of birth control techniques as sinful and unnatural methods of hiding and proliferating vice that threatened white moral dominance, while also creating the possibility of consequence-free lust, marital infidelity, and fornication.[33]

No matter the argument, the white woman's desire to have fewer children was read by religious conservatives and many others as self-indulgent evidence of a decline of the Protestant values of hard work and self-sacrifice.[34] In a statement that pre-dates by a century the Crouse and LaHaye quotes that begin this chapter (yet mimics their very content), Theodore Roosevelt warned of the same issues in 1911:

> The American stock is being cursed with the curse of sterility, and it is earning the curse, because the sterility is wilful [*sic*]. It is due to moral, and not physiological, shortcomings. It is due to coldness, to selfishness, to love of ease, to shrinking from risk, to an utter and pitiful failure in sense of perspective. . . . Exactly as the measure of our regard for the soldier who does his full duty in battle is the measure of our scorn for the coward who flees, so the measure of our respect for the true wife and mother is the measure of our scorn and contemptuous abhorrence for the wife who refuses to be a mother. . . .[35]

If ideas like Sanger's represented a completely new way of approaching sex, gender, and reproduction, so, too, other changing intellectual currents drew into question religion itself. Issues of biblical inerrancy, human uniqueness, and the power of Enlightenment rationalism were all confronted during the 1925 Scopes trial. The trial became a public stage on which the many tensions characterizing the struggle between early twentieth-century traditionalists and progressives came to the fore. In the proceedings, Tennessee schoolteacher John Scopes was convicted of teaching evolution in his high school biology classroom, and although he was subsequently found guilty, his defense team symbolically won the case.[36] Cast as the backward, uneducated, biblical literalists standing ignorantly in resistance to the intellectual, progressive, scientific truth, fundamentalists experienced an intense public shaming.

Yet, in the jury box of society, some of the loudest supporters of anti-evolutionary campaigns were white women. Anti-evolutionary thinking complemented the popular maternalist sentiment of the time by capitalizing on the moral dangers posed to children by Darwin's controversial theories, which removed God from the picture as the creator and designer of earthly life. Since women were seen as responsible for both the educational and moral development of children, to interject evolution into the classroom was akin to de-feminizing women insomuch as they were unable to fulfill their most basic role of raising religious children with a strong moral sense.[37] African Americans were generally divided over Scopes. While those affiliated with Christianity tended to support the prosecution, a vocal minority of both Christian and secular black leaders expressed concern that creationism was being used, in part, to fight the evolutionary notion that all humans had a common origin, and thus shared a common equality.[38]

While today the Scopes trial is often remembered as the first public, legal debate on the teaching of evolution in schools, it also involved the wholesale ridicule of traditional Protestant religion mixed with the emerging roots of a later, politically charged Christianity. Fueled by tensions surrounding World War I, many fundamentalists felt that the fundamentalist/modernist debate was not about theology but the actual moral course of Western civilization.[39] In kind, many fundamentalist groups connected anti-evolutionism and anti-modernism with anti-Communism, providing the first inklings of what George Marsden has called a "fundamentalist super-patriotism."[40]

But however strong such patriotism was often portrayed, it was simultaneously cast as vulnerable to assault, and predictably, sex was believed to be its most potent threat. As World War I began, rhetoric from many sides capitalized on sex as the foundation breaking under the weight of the conflict. As in many wartime situations, women who supported their country's war effort disturbed traditionally gendered work roles out of necessity, taking on the jobs that absent soldiers had once held. In response to this shake-up, conservative media publications in both the United States and Britain crafted chaos rhetoric warning that women freed from their soldier boyfriends and husbands would threaten the nation's integrity. Not only would they would be prone to infidelity, thereby weakening their country's moral backbone in its time of vulnerability, but such rhetoric also warned that male absence would create career-oriented women and lesbians.[41] While homosexuality had yet to become the central issue that it would be later in the century, even then its presence was seen as a sign of corruption, as the Allied forces often described the German ranks as being filled with homosexuals.[42]

Many of these same ideas infused the Ku Klux Klan, which experienced a resurgence during the 1920s. It is likely difficult for many Americans today to think of the KKK as "mainstream," yet the sentiments expressed by the group during its periods of greatest strength were championed by many middle- and upper-class white Protestants and were a part of the ideological basis for a large number of the platforms espoused by the later Christian Right.[43] While various manifestations of the KKK have been brutally violent, Kelly J. Baker notes that the 1920s version of the movement sought mainstream status by downplaying this aspect of Klan activity while also very publicly touting itself as a beacon of true Protestantism. In many ways, the Klan was a pivotal part of the national religious culture of early twentieth-century America.[44]

The Klan's central position was that the "low morals" of minority groups (particularly Catholics and Jews) compromised the moral fortitude of white native-born Protestants.[45] To reinforce this, the KKK and the related Women's Ku Klux Klan (WKKK) movement described their members using terms of nationalist and gendered purity. Calling themselves "100% American Men" and "100% American Women," respectively, these terms worked as both descriptors and recruiting tools for those who sought to prove both their patriotism and their gendered conformity.[46] Hence the KKK's public call was to "[summon] white men to protect threatened white womanhood and white female purity."[47] The importance of chaste, moral, white women was a frequent theme in Klan literature, integral to a plotline wherein such women were consistently threatened by the flapper's corrupting influence or the black rapists' potential brutality.[48]

If the popularity of the KKK's message is any indication, it seems that fundamentalism's public image was wounded at a time when many of its impulses were already mainstream. Add to this the growing prominence of Catholic politicians, the greater acceptance of liberal Protestantism, and the eventual repeal of Prohibition, and many ACPs began to feel their cultural influence wane.[49] The period after the Scopes Trial was not a time of fundamentalist demise, as older historical models suggest, but was instead a period of intense reorganization. This distinction is key. From 1925 to the 1950s, the movement took advantage of new sociocultural outlets (such as parachurch organizations and the media) through which it could express itself and its ongoing revivalist themes, many of which fused the integrity of the nation with the health of conservative religion.[50] Attaining such a hold on culture was in no small way crucial to the movement's later social force. With a distinct sense of hurt and embarrassment over the public shaming of the 1920s, fundamentalists revisited the same themes but were ready to face their detractors in a much different way.

The Mid-Twentieth Century

There would be no decisive, visible upswing in a politically organized ACP for years still to come, although many of its supporting sentiments continued to infuse American culture. Throughout the 1930s and 1940s, fundamentalism's pre-millennialistic sense of the inevitability of cultural decline provided a framework through which events like the Great Depression, World Wars I and II, and the Holocaust could be retrospectively (if not presently) read.[51] Many fundamentalists used these events to contextualize themselves as God's faithful remnant awaiting the end times, maintaining their own moral purity through their characteristic separatism.

This separatism came under intense critique with the public emergence and social engagement of evangelist Billy Graham. Graham, the "unquestioned leader and exemplar of evangelical Christianity" during the 1950s and 1960s, has preached the Christian message to more people than anyone else in history.[52] Beginning his famous public revivals (called "Crusades") during the late 1940s, Graham was at the helm of a vast call to foreign and domestic Christian mission work that, in effect, became a revival of revivalism itself.[53] He drew upon and synthesized concerns over race, gender, and politics, casting these issues as specifically Christian matters.[54] Like the fundamentalists before him, he was vocally patriotic and anti-Communist, merging social and fiscal conservatism with religion in the sermons he preached to the literally hundreds of millions of people who attended his events over the years. Graham's proposal that Christianity was the solution to the problem of "godless Communism" was perhaps stronger than any other American religious message for decades.[55]

If Graham was the epitome of the Christian preacher during the middle of the twentieth-century, his rhetorical fusion of sex, nation, and religion is representative of how deeply many Christians understood the indivisibility of these three. A dramatic change in social rhetoric about sexuality emerged with the 1948 and 1953 publications of the controversial Kinsey Reports, two studies of American sexual activity authored by psychologist Alfred Kinsey. Kinsey's research suggested, among other things, that homoerotic experiences were actually rather common among American males (Kinsey noted that about 60–75% of Americans exhibited sexual behavior deemed "abnormal" by experts), and that humans' natural tendency was towards frequent sexual exchanges that were both heterosexual and homosexual in nature.[56] In stark contrast to other psychologists of his day, he did not find that homosexual activity was a gateway to social degeneracy.[57] In effect, Kinsey's conclusions rendered the heterosexual, monogamous family more the result of certain social pressures inspired by Christian morality rather than a divine institution imprinted upon human nature.

Many Christian voices responded in a tide of anger against Kinsey, who was strenuously attacked. Graham, among others, maintained that Kinsey's findings were of the same ilk as the rhetoric propagated by atheists such as Nietzsche and Freud insomuch as Kinsey promoted a worldview antithetical to the Bible.[58] While Graham insisted that there were clear theological grounds supporting the heterosexual model of sex and marriage (publically remarking that "there is 'no unisex in the Bible'"), his most effective technique against Kinsey was couched in nationalist terms.[59] True to the spirit of the Communist scare upon which Graham so effectively capitalized, the preacher used chaos rhetoric that referred to Kinsey's researchers as "secret agents" who collected the lurid stories of radicalized men and women whose sexual behaviors were far from mainstream.[60] Like many Christian voices responding at the time, Graham saw Kinsey as not only factually wrong, but as a menace poisoning the prospects of a strongly Christian America. Graham and many others were convinced that stemming the sexual vice that plagued America (and that, he felt, Kinsey promoted) would invoke God's favor. Experimenting with this hypothesis, the federal government attempted to ban the distribution of *Playboy* magazine through the US mail in the fall of 1958.[61]

As Graham demonstrated, McCarthyism had bred a general and versatile language through which conservatives could address almost every issue of concern; teaching cultural pluralism in schools, for example, became an instance of the infiltration of Communism.[62] In a context where virtually anything could be construed as un-American, many social conservatives also saw feminists and gays as groups co-responsible for what they perceived to be the fragile condition of the country. Interjecting the threat of homosexuality more directly, the image of the physically and morally weak gay man was juxtaposed in public rhetoric with the strong American (straight) male defending the country's honor.

This danger was construed as a sexual, and thus moral, assault on the government. Stories openly circulated about how government-employed homosexuals held such compromised personal moralities that they were vulnerable to enemy infiltration. This threat seemed so palpable that in April 1953 gay men and lesbians were barred from federal jobs.[63] Similarly, in 1956, *Life* magazine questioned whether Americans should fear that overly authoritative modern mothers had created a breed of weak men incapable of standing up to the Communist challenge.[64] While the state was generally more focused on exposing and ridding its ranks of homosexual military men, during the period of the early Cold War, a more comprehensive inquiry into rumors of lesbianism was initiated. Lesbianism was considered harder to root out because it was presumed that women's naturally affectionate natures would make romantic relationships between them more difficult to detect. Margot Canaday notes that the specter of lesbianism was constituted by military authorities not only to weed out homosexuality, but also to "help maintain gender hierarchy after women's integration eliminated a historical barrier between male and female service."[65] Provisions within the GI Bill were also modified to deny benefits to any soldier receiving a dishonorable discharge because of engaging in homosexual acts.[66]

If most Christians agreed that Communists, liberals, and homosexuals were a problem, many had also reached a similar consensus on the emerging civil rights movement. As early as the 1950s, Graham stood relatively alone among ACPs in asking for an end to racial intolerance, modeling this by insisting on integrated seating at his Crusades.[67] Despite Graham's overtures, racism was still a way of life in America and for many Christians, in particular, as a young Jerry Falwell's 1958 delivery of a pro-segregation sermon suggests. Falwell later denounced the sermon as inconsistent with his beliefs, citing it as an artifact reflective of ubiquitous cultural sentiment rather than a theological absolute.[68]

Although important legal strides in racial integration marked the 1950s (*Brown v. Board of Education*, for one, outlawed school segregation in 1954), such legislation was not uniformly enforced if in part because so much of Christian America opposed it. This and other rulings sparked the formation of thousands of Citizens' Councils, organizations that rekindled many of the values seen in the KKK just decades before. These included an emphasis on the moral failure of non-whites and the poor, "responsibilities over rights"/anti-welfare rhetoric, and the location of social problems in a totalizing approach towards personal morality.[69] While their intentions for segregated public policy were ultimately unsuccessful, the group's emphasis on morality as the precondition to civil and human rights was a crucial step in the growth of later social conservatism.

Rhetoric denouncing the moral failure of non-whites continued to be endemic in Christian speech during this time, but focused particularly on the dangers to white schoolchildren. *Brown*, which was tremendously unpopular among Southerners, was followed within a decade by *Engel v. Vitale* (1962), which ruled the practice of institutionalized school prayer unconstitutional. The social shifts started with *Brown* and continued with *Engel* effectively fused segregation with Christianity insomuch as they together portended America's progression down a slippery slope of secularism and national demise.[70] The image of endangered white children had always been present in conservative speech, but as women's rights advanced and the Supreme Court struck down both school segregation and school prayer, the expediency of the schoolchild symbol held even greater social purchase. As with the Scopes trial, the schoolroom was rhetorically cast as the place where Communists, libertine women, and other secularists were ready to prey on America's innocents.

Many conservatives who spoke out against desegregation and the civil rights movement, in general, claimed not to harbor personal animosity towards blacks or to support racism, but framed their opposition against a federal government that was curbing basic rights such as free association and private property. This, they argued, made America a Communist enterprise in the making.[71] But even as such legislation passed (leaving many African Americans and other racial minorities legally more free but still poverty-bound), many white Christians were quick to recuperate the decade's old sense that civil rights were due only to those who could assert their moral worth, and there was heightened suspicion among the privileged classes over the benefits of social welfare spending.[72] Concern over the sexual habits of African Americans as well as their criminal lives continued to persist in ACP speech, and remained a particularly powerful way to explain their widespread disenfranchisement. In popular conservative Christian rhetoric, "Christian" became a stand-in term for the whites opposed to desegregation, while "Secularists" described those who supported racial civil rights.[73] Racial integration was thus read as both a symbolic and literal compromise of Christian authority.

The 1960s and 1970s

The gender ideals of the 1950s are often canonized in American storytelling as the pinnacle of the nuclear family. In reality, the decade preceding the sexually dynamic 1960s was far more gender-conflicted than pristine, in part because women who had been encouraged to work for the war effort found their jobs dried up at the war's end. While a great majority voiced a desire to continue paid work, more often they were encouraged to retreat to the "haven" of the home.[74] A growing cultural discontent with this expectation was reflected in Betty Friedan's *The Feminine Mystique* (1963), in which she famously identified "the problem that has no name":

> The problem lay buried, unspoken for many years in the minds of American women. It was a strange stirring, a sense of dissatisfaction, a yearning that women suffered in the middle of the twentieth century in the United States. Each suburban housewife struggled with it alone. As she made the beds, shopped for groceries, matched slipcover material, ate peanut butter sandwiches with her children, chauffeured Cub Scouts and Brownies, lay beside her husband at night, she was afraid to ask even of herself the silent question: "Is this all?"[75]

Helping to inaugurate liberal feminism's public resurgence, Friedan gave voice to the sense of entrapment that many middle- and upper-class white women experienced from traditional sexed and gendered norms. Friedan was just one part of a building countercultural sentiment that questioned the logic of gendered conformity and tradition, which is perhaps one dominant reason why evangelical declension narratives often fixate on the 1960s as the moment when "America's exalted and sacred status [was] compromised."[76]

This sense of moral erosion was launched early in the decade, when, in 1960, the Food and Drug Administration (FDA) approved oral contraceptives ("The Pill"), reliably freeing sex from conception and giving women control over their reproductive capacities. This accompanied a growing shift in perceptions that framed premarital sex not only as unproblematic, but desirable; marriage and childbearing increasingly became options instead of destinies. At the same time, public awareness of homosexuality was growing, and pornography and explicit sexual guide books became more mainstream.[77] By the mid-1960s, a time then defined in part by youth culture and anti-authoritarian sentiment, sexual education programs were becoming an increasingly common feature within schools.

In response, a great number of legal cases that received attention in the 1960s involved conservative Christians looking for ways to fight sexual education curricula, and many conservative organizations whose anti-Communist platforms now sounded less relevant (such as the John Birch Society) began to garner support by deploying chaos rhetoric that framed sexual education as a well-honed Communist plot.[78] While most activists were concerned that education about sex would cause sex, the most common legal reason provided for the opposition was that sexual education was an imminently moral domain that belonged in the home.

Evangelicals frequently pointed their fingers at feminists as the cause of the erosion of these sexual moral standards. As LaHaye would later describe it, "Feminism and the sexual revolution are tentacles of the octopus Humanism, which is seeking to destroy Christianity and Christian principles in America."[79] When Friedan and others founded the National Organization of Women (NOW) in 1966, their goals included ending gendered employment discrimination and providing access to contraception and abortion, among others. Within five years, NOW added lesbian rights to its agenda, a move that came shortly after the public emergence of the gay rights movement in 1969. It made sense, then, that feminists saw the ratification of the Equal Rights Amendment (ERA), a constitutional amendment that would have banned discrimination based on sex, as a natural extension of their work.

Thanks in part to many conservative activists like LaHaye, however, the ERA was never ratified. Throughout the 1970s, a Catholic lawyer named Phyllis Schlafly was the main organizer against the ERA, successfully persuading many Americans that the ERA would dissolve a husband's obligation to provide financial support for his wife, create federal funding for abortions, force women into military combat situations, mandate sex-integrated bathrooms, and enable gay marriage.[80] An astounding army of grassroots conservative women organized behind Schlafly's cause, understanding the ERA as an assault on their identities as conservative women. Beverly LaHaye was one of them, and she later reflected that the ERA was a "cleverly designed tool to invite governmental control over our lives," that, had it succeeded, would have resulted in a court system "glutted with lawsuits filed by rabid feminists."[81]

Before her entry onto the national scene in the 1970s, LaHaye's activist work was focused more at the grassroots and state levels on issues such as the ERA and public school curricula. She has always been closely involved in political matters with her husband, Tim. Tim LaHaye has had a long and successful career as a conservative political and cultural activist. Starting out as the pastor of a Baptist church in Southern California in the 1960s, his first major political involvement targeted secular humanism in public education. This particular topic led him and others to start a private Christian school network, lobby for and provide instrumental support to conservative political candidates (especially in the cases of Jack Kemp and Ronald Reagan), and help develop numerous organizations (CWA among them) committed to lobbying in support of conservative politics.[82] The LaHayes were like many other conservatives who vocally argued that the government violated *their* civil rights when it passed laws enacting racial integration and gender equality, a rhetorical theme used repeatedly in the years to come.[83]

Racial issues had not subsided for many ACPs, for still they were seen as a compromise of the white nuclear Christian family. The Supreme Court's passage of *Loving v. Virginia* (1967) threw out anti-miscegenation laws, thus legally permitting interracial marriage. Although the Supreme Court proclaimed that marriage was a fundamental component of human happiness for all citizens, the case was criticized heavily by white Christians who once again claimed that the "separate but equal" argument was God's design for the relationship between racial groups. A significant portion of the ACP community continued to locate interracial marriage as a sign of a declining moral order.[84]

In all of these shifts, what had ultimately transpired was a "critical reappraisal of the nuclear family."[85] Abortion was a particularly important part of this reappraisal, and it turned into a consensus issue driving and enabling Christian Right unity. Ironically, before the passage of *Roe v. Wade* (the 1973 decision legalizing abortion), many ACP denominations and conservative politicians endorsed some sort of legal abortion, particularly in cases of rape, incest, or to preserve the health of the mother. In 1971, for instance, the Southern Baptist Convention—the nation's largest ACP denomination—even passed a resolution endorsing the liberalization of state abortion laws for the benefit of women.[86] Daniel Williams notes that it was only after *Roe v. Wade* was endorsed by feminists, was portrayed as one possible outcome of the sexual revolution, and had legally codified a right to privacy as something that could be read as explicitly female, that many conservative groups rethought their previously moderate views towards abortion policy and turned sharply to the right.[87] By the later 1970s, chaos rhetoric portraying abortion as murder had grown more mainstream among many ACP leaders. LaHaye, for one, drew on the symbolism of Nazi Germany to liken abortion to a second Holocaust, the horror of which liberal government officials and feminists preferred to keep quiet so as to implement their humanist agendas.[88] But alongside the rhetoric of murder emerged an underlying—yet extremely powerful—sense that abortion's real offense was its ability to cover up sexual misconduct. Jerry Falwell argued that women who pursued abortions were "pregnant because of sin. . . . I cannot understand a mother wanting to abort a child who was conceived with her husband."[89]

Gay rights were an equally critical matter in building the infrastructure of what would become the early Christian Right. While most conservative Christians opposed gay rights on principle alone, it was Anita Bryant's 1977 campaign against homosexuality that propelled the issue onto the national scene. A former beauty pageant contestant and commercial actress, Bryant drew heavily upon child and nationalist imagery to create a well-used genre of chaos rhetoric that charged "militant" homosexuals with the predation of American children (and thus her famous anti-homosexual pamphlet entitled "Save the Children!"). She invoked what Mark Jordan describes as "a rhetoric of compassion and cursing" as she sounded the call to protect children and attack homosexuals in the same breath.[90] In her use of militaristic language and her symbolic attachment of homosexuality with Communism (the "Battle Hymn of the Republic" was one of her campaign jingles), she translated McCarthyism's threat into homosexuality, thus positioning homosexuals as the opposite of true American patriots.[91] Above all else, she relied heavily on her identity as both a woman and a mother to market her campaigns as inherently moral and common sense.[92] Bryant's activism sparked a series of books and other new media from early Christian Right activists, including Tim LaHaye's 1978 book *The Unhappy Gays*, which provided a litany of reasons why homosexuality is harmful. Through an apocalyptic reading of the Bible, LaHaye argued that the antichrist would likely be a gay man (something he extrapolated from the growing influence of gay rights in American society). LaHaye openly advocated political action against homosexuals as a literal fight against the incarnation of evil.[93]

Thus, the 1960s and 1970s represented a period of intense reorientation for ACPs as the proposal and passage of various pieces of civil rights legislation challenged the white heterosexual hegemony upon which the movement had long depended for its power. In the main, conservatives responded by insulating themselves and their children from such cultural shifts through the development of private schools free from racial integration, sexual education, and multiculturalism.[94] But as this attempt at separatism became more difficult to preserve, many conservatives began to consider new ways for them to change the wider culture to fit their own values. From this, the Christian Right was born.

Many date the actual genesis of the Christian Right to the 1979 founding of the Moral Majority, one of the first visible groups explicitly devoted to aligning the political system with its conservative Christian agenda. While the celebrity of founder Jerry Falwell helped the movement's popularity, much of its social force nevertheless came from like-minded grassroots activists whose work preceded the Moral Majority by several years, many of whom were women.[95] Reviving aspects of traditional, dichotomous gender ideals once again, many Christian Right groups portrayed these women as authorities on matters of family values whose inherent sense of moral direction had prompted their activism. Much of this took place in the form of anti-ERA campaigns early on, but their work against abortion, gay rights, and feminism were an equally significant part of their advocacy. The high degree of public female involvement in the Christian Right enabled by feminist activism is one of the great ironies of the movement, as most of these women spoke against feminist ideals.[96]

As testimony to the centrality of women's voices in the burgeoning Christian Right, Beverly LaHaye founded CWA in the same year that the Moral Majority came to life. LaHaye pointed to the formation of NOW, political support for the ERA, and what she perceived to be the anti-family bias of President Jimmy Carter as powerful catalysts in her decision to mobilize ACP women into a large-scale political engine.[97] Focusing more intensely on direct political involvement, CWA moved its offices to Washington, DC, within five years of its inception.[98] In a retrospective book discussing the history of the organization, LaHaye openly thanked feminists such as Betty Friedan, Gloria Steinem, and Bella Abzug for "open[ing] my eyes" to the "blatantly pro-lesbian tactics of radical feminists" that she witnessed at a series of conferences on women and family sponsored by the Carter administration.[99] The conferences convinced her that immediate action was necessary:

> . . . five friends and I talked nonstop about the . . . convention and the feminist movement. We had been trying to live as good Christian women, being decent mothers and citizens, but we had been completely ignorant of the social forces that threatened to destroy our families and our nation. It was time to get busy and do something to oppose the feminist movement—or any movement that purposed to destroy the sanctity of our homes.[100]

How, exactly, could a self-proclaimed evangelical president offend so many Christian Right activists? When born-again Christian Jimmy Carter was elected to the presidency in 1976, religious conservatives experienced renewed optimism that their platforms could infuse American culture. *Newsweek* magazine declared it "The Year of the Evangelical."[101] To many, Carter held a sort of homespun, populist appeal that was sorely needed in a country drained from the Vietnam War and still reeling with political mistrust from the Watergate scandal and President Richard Nixon's impeachment.

But the love affair was certainly short-lived. While Carter's campaign emphasis on family issues initially held great allure to many conservatives, what Carter meant by "family" proved disappointing. To the Christian Right, in particular, his offenses were legion. The aforementioned conferences were part of Carter's initiative to address the quality of life of women and children in America and inform federal programming devoted to those same populations. What LaHaye and many other conservative women did not realize was that pro-ERA, pro-lesbian, and pro-abortion rights activists had also been invited to participate.[102] Representatives of many conservative groups boycotted several of these conferences to protest Carter's refusal to remove more progressive voices from the table, and their frustration eventually led them to a dramatic walkout. In the late 1970s, Carter also attempted to enforce a previously enacted IRS regulation that, had it succeeded, would have revoked the tax-exempt status of any private school not visibly committed to racial integration. This caused an uproar among ACPs who had heavily invested in the formation of predominantly white private Christian school networks, and this catalyst, perhaps before many others, was pivotal to inciting the early activism of the Christian Right.[103] For many conservative Christians, their "born-again" president stood for platforms that were a far cry from how they envisioned their country's moral destiny.

The 1980s and 1990s

CWA was one of many Christian Right organizations riding high on the wave of conservative sentiment that helped to create Ronald Reagan's victory over Carter in the 1980 election. Undoubtedly, Reagan's conservative social views were instrumental in acquiring the Christian Right support that proved critical to his election, but many other groups with differing agendas also influenced Reagan's victory. Natasha Zaretsky observes that Reagan's rhetoric about the nation depended heavily on the image of an endangered family.[104] Beyond his literal discussion of nuclear families, Reagan described many facets of both domestic and foreign policy in terms of how they affected "the family" that was the nation. Zaretsky notes,

> Perception that the family was under siege from destructive outside forces had played a crucial role during the perceived decline of the 1970s. A politician who evoked that image . . . could bridge traditional divisions of class, culture, religion, and geography, thus linking the political universe of the secular conservative businessman opposed to government to the evangelical mother incensed by the content of her child's school curriculum to the patriotic black single mother concerned about her son in the army.[105]

With Reagan's entrance into the White House came a resurgence of the chaos rhetoric that had initially united conservatives in the 1950s: moral decline, Communism, and secularism were all construed as entities that threatened to assault the family, both narrowly and widely understood. Reagan's distaste for affirmative action and civil rights in general was a reassuring move to many white conservatives who saw in both a threat to their worldviews. The administration drew heavily on racialized portraits of sexual immorality to advance its platforms; Reagan often juxtaposed "welfare queens" and "ghetto hoodlums" with "decent, hard-working Americans."[106] These statements and a host of others like them centered on the figure of the poor black unmarried woman and her offspring as the source of American moral decline. Reagan's ability to draw on the symbol of the family (here narrowly understood) as a parallel for national unity is indicative of the sort of elasticity that the term "family values" developed, becoming a way of clothing religious speech in secular garments.[107]

Drawing heavily from the family metaphor, CWA's early campaigns focused on helping conservative women re-envision themselves as assertive Christian activists instead of the insipid housewife stereotype. This is evidenced in LaHaye's 1984 publication of a book entitled *Who But A Woman?*, which contextualized CWA's work as something undertaken by ordinary women.[108] The organization's 1980s activism centered largely on educational matters, mirroring Reagan's own commitment to the re-institutionalization of school prayer. CWA focused on demarcating "parent's rights" as a legitimate legal entity that could fight against the perceived humanist forces in the public schools, the textbook industry, and the National Education Association (NEA). As early as 1982, CWA was very visibly involved in legal cases addressing secularism in public education, and its commitment to such cases (wherein it often provided legal representation and funding to the Christians involved in litigation) became its hallmark for several years. In one particularly noteworthy case (*Mozert vs. Hawkins City Schools*, 1984), CWA provided legal representation to a mother who unlawfully removed her children from school because she found their textbooks religiously offensive. Arrested on Thanksgiving eve, CWA describes how it was responsible for returning her from jail "in time for Thanksgiving dinner with her family."[109]

CWA's early identity was also tied up heavily with anti-abortion activism. As LaHaye tells it, CWA was one of the first organizations to fight against the practice of late-term abortion.[110] While conservatives approved of Reagan's use of strongly Christian rhetoric about the humanity of the fetus, leaders of the Christian Right had grown savvy to the fact that presidents' promises were fickle; it was Reagan, after all, who appointed Sandra Day O'Connor, a pro-choice woman, to the Supreme Court in 1981. Also, abortion rates did not decline under Reagan's watch. While he had verbally agreed with the content of the Helms-Hyde Bill, which legally granted personhood to the fetus, the administration did little to see the bill through to passage.[111]

Conservatives hoped that Reagan's attorney general, well-known physician and abortion opponent C. Everett Koop, would help in policy implementation by using his office as a political platform to preach an anti-abortion stance. Koop refused, and further disappointed conservatives when, after the emergence of AIDS, he strongly and unwaveringly called for massive public sexual education campaigns that emphasized condom use. This position offended the abstinence-only platforms of both the Reagan administration and the Christian conservatives who supported him. CWA's focus on issues of sexuality coincided roughly with the public emergence of the AIDS crisis. At about the same time that Koop's AIDS public education campaign promoting condom use began, CWA flooded the major TV networks in a postcard campaign to ban condom advertising.[112]

The AIDS epidemic pushed gay rights into a new public spotlight. As it became evident that gay men were among the primary transmitters of AIDS, the AIDS crisis, wrote Koop, "pitted the politics of the gay revolution of the seventies against the politics of the Reagan revolution of the eighties."[113] The public hostility over gay rights compromised the formation of a quick and unified public prevention campaign, something further complicated by incendiary comments about gays coming from representatives of the Christian Right.[114] Many Christian Right leaders openly connected AIDS as a punishment from God for homosexual behavior, as in conservative political leader Pat Buchanan's remark, "The poor homosexuals. They have declared war on nature and nature is exacting an awful retribution."[115] In kind, Jerry Falwell described AIDS as "the wrath of God upon homosexuals."[116]

Koop wrote that the issue of AIDS was so politically volatile that he was almost completely cut off from publicly speaking about it for five years.[117] Jennifer Brier notes that the administration's slow move towards action should not be read as a sign of Reagan's personal refusal to deal with AIDS, but was, rather, a signal of how deeply the administration was fragmented over a politically favorable plan of attack.[118] Crafting a strategy that would please social conservatives—themselves a sorely divided constituency on the matter—was a delicate and protracted process.[119] Through its policies, the Reagan administration confirmed that it considered AIDS a political liability more than an urgent public health epidemic.

By the late 1980s, many of the core organizations within the Christian Right began to lose steam. This decline was due, in part, to the gaffes committed by many elite figures that alienated them from the public at large.[120] Tim LaHaye, for one, was forced to resign as co-chair of Jack Kemp's presidential campaign after word was leaked of his anti-Catholic statements, while Jerry Falwell's defense of South African apartheid won him little public acclaim.[121] Scholars began to document the fall of the Christian Right, presuming the movement was in steep decline. This perception generated a new rhetorical angle used by Christian Right leaders to defend themselves against charges that their efficacy was waning. Falwell publicly described media claims of conservative decline as the same sort of discrimination faced by racial minorities. The problem was not the

Christian Right, he claimed, but the media and other liberal forces seeking to defeat conservatives through prejudicial and defaming speech.[122]

But as usual, decline was not in the cards. One of the most predictable aspects of the Christian Right has been its ability to stage its own regeneration after what appears to have been its cultural death. Such revitalization culminated in perhaps the most important development of late 1980s politics, which was the formation of the Christian Coalition. The Christian Coalition was an organization that effectively sealed the tight relationship between evangelical Christianity and the Republican party.[123] Founded by media-mogul-turned-presidential candidate Pat Robertson and directed by young graduate student and conservative strategist Ralph Reed, the organization's most central function was to get conservatives out to vote, a feat achieved in part by bringing together politically-minded conservative organizations under the banner of traditional morals. One of the organization's most notable activities was the publication of voting guides that provided those loyal to the Christian Right options on how (and, only thinly veiled, for whom) to vote. The consequence of these guides was not only several important political triumphs, but a series of politicians eager to court the movement. Reed's face appeared on the May 1995 cover of *Time* magazine, testament to what he had managed to accomplish in the previous five years. Accompanying a black- and-white headshot of Reed surrounded by shadows, the headline read: "The Right Hand of God." The subtitle continued, "Meet Ralph Reed, 33. His Christian Coalition is on a crusade to take over U.S. Politics—and it's working."[124]

After the 1992 presidential election of Democrat Bill Clinton, the Christian Coalition was largely responsible for the sweeping Republican victories in the 1994 congressional elections. Rumors of Clinton's alleged sexual indiscretions (which gained great visibility in the Monica Lewinsky scandal), his pro-choice stance on abortion, his controversial "Don't Ask, Don't Tell" policy regarding gays in the military, and his so-called "socialist" federal healthcare plan fueled the conservative fire.

The result was policy that called for more comprehensive government intervention at the same time that it eschewed government altogether. Reed was able to formulate policy recommendations in the form of a plan entitled the "Contract with the American Family," which called for greater governmental control over individuals on issues of sexual and private morality. This contract took its name from a parallel plan devised by members of the Republican Congress called the "Contract with America," which, ironically, espoused the dangers of big government. A central piece of legislation that emerged from the Contract With America was the Personal Responsibility and Work Opportunity Reconciliation Act of 1996 (popularly known at the time simply as "welfare reform"), wherein children with unwed parents were legally encoded as "illegitimates" and heterosexual marriage was posed as the solution to the poverty experienced by welfare recipients. In no uncertain terms, the act made clear that the government had the right to name unmarried sex as a transgressive act.[125] The ability to use such rhetoric to both fight big government and, simultaneously, to expand its territory through moralistic speech, is but one sign of the historical fluidity of the "family" symbol.[126]

The 1990s represented a period of tremendous organizational growth for CWA, as well. On the media front, CWA created a successful radio program and monthly magazine (called *Beverly LaHaye Live* and *Family Voice*, respectively), both of which culminated in the 1996 launch of the official CWA website.[127] At CWA's 1998 annual convention, LaHaye announced the formation of the Beverly LaHaye Center for Traditional Women's Studies as a counterpoint to the more liberal university-based academic field.[128] This organization was later subsumed into the Beverly LaHaye Institute (BLI), one of CWA's official think tanks. BLI represents a virtual library of research-style briefs and essays that cover everything from feminism and abortion to homosexuality and religious liberty. Today, these works are often prominently featured on the organization's website.

The New Century: Resurrecting the Old?

CWA's activism through the early twenty-first century closely followed the larger Christian Right's political concerns. By the first decade of the 2000s, a ban on gay marriage was at the top of the Christian Right's platform, and just as the issue of sexual education had revitalized conservative organizations in the 1960s, gay marriage boosted the perceived public relevancy of organizations within the Christian Right that had otherwise been flagging. In 2001, CWA founded the Culture and Family Institute (CFI), a think tank devoted exclusively to anti-gay rights activism. The CFI's positions were well-aligned with other Christian Right leaders, including James Dobson (founder of the Focus on the Family media empire and its political arm, the Family Research Council), who in his own chaos rhetoric, publicly claimed that the legalization of gay marriage would mean the literal disintegration of lifelong, heterosexual marriage, and with its passing "a chaos such as the world has never seen."[129]

While CWA's focus on abortion, gay rights, and feminism have remained steady, these themes took on new incarnations with the attacks of September 11, 2001. For many Americans, 9/11 signaled a different understanding of the world and America's place in it, as well as the solidification (and often, simplification) of moral rhetoric surrounding that event. Consistent with the Christian Right's pattern of fusing nationalism with Christianity, CWA engaged in a vocal campaign in support of President Bush's "War on Terror," and for continued military involvement in Iraq and Afghanistan. For several years an eye-catching message on the CWA website's homepage read "Support Our Troops/ Let Them Win!" When the reader clicked on the image, she was led to an essay on how CWA members had an "obligation to lend our moral support" to the troops protecting America's national sovereignty.[130]

As with a diverse array of other organizations, national sovereignty and a robust patriotism have been prominent themes on the CWA website since the 9/11 attacks. Yet in the days immediately following 9/11, CWA strongly resuscitated the rhetoric linking sex and immorality with national decline. This occurred in its response to other Christian Right leaders' remarks, as well as in the structure of its own rhetoric.

In a televised interview on September 13, 2001, featured on Pat Robertson's *700 Club* program, Robertson prefaced his live conversation with Jerry Falwell with the remark that because of American sexual, reproductive, and gendered sin, "God Almighty is lifting his protection from us." In his now-famous chaos rhetoric about who was responsible for causing 9/11, Falwell noted,

> The abortionists have got to bear some burden for this because God will not be mocked. And when we destroy 40 million little innocent babies, we make God mad. I really believe that the pagans, and the abortionists, and the feminists, and the gays and the lesbians who are actively trying to make that an alternative lifestyle, and the ACLU, People for the American Way, all of them who have tried to secularize America. I point the finger in their face and say: 'You helped this happen.'[131]

Despite the fact that Falwell later recanted his remarks, CWA was quick to attack those who criticized him, claiming that his comments were not inconsistent with orthodox Christian faith.[132]

Perhaps more than any other cultural event, 9/11 revealed how effectively CWA has symbolically intertwined sexual morality with patriotism. CWA capitalized heavily on hijacking and terror symbolism in the months after 9/11, equating liberals with terrorists who were hijacking the sexual morals of America for their own bidding.[133] But even literal references to sex and 9/11 monopolized the organization's attention for several weeks. In one particularly heated series of articles that were featured on the website, CWA attempted to redress allegations made by a gay rights activist that the first recorded casualty of 9/11, Catholic priest Father Mychal Judge, was gay. Judge's heroism was the topic of many early reports about the tragedy since he was one of the first on the scene attempting to rescue those trapped inside the World Trade Center. By the time the news of Judge's sexual orientation had broken, CWA had already heavily capitalized on Judge's story as an example of the noble sacrifice of a religious man. When, eight months later, another CWA article conceded that there was sufficient evidence to prove that Judge was gay, CWA headlined the article by explicitly separating itself from Judge: "Fr. Mychal Judge's Sexual Conduct Does Not Alter Moral Code."[134]

In a culture that is growing ever more open to issues that once were taboo (such as gay marriage), the twenty-first century challenges that CWA has faced have often involved convincing its members that the terms "liberal" and "moral" are mutually exclusive, no matter what appearances may be.[135] When Democrat Barack Obama was elected to the presidency in 2008, CWA amplified rhetoric that his danger lay primarily in his duplicity. Metaphorically juxtaposing Obama with the Emperor in the fabled "Emperor's New Clothes," Crouse, speaking for the organization, remarked:

> His voting record is as far left as is possible. He spelled out on his official website his plan of action in all its leftist glory. Those who cared to look could find all the relevant details. The problem is that most did not want to look; they didn't want to have the "emperor" exposed. Now, though, we have to face reality — the emperor is fully clothed, in liberal garb from head to toe. So the nation has a president-elect who will drastically alter society, weaken family structure, and undermine religious freedom.[136]

The sense that Obama and other liberals have engaged in overt political deception has been at the forefront of CWA rhetoric since Obama's presidential campaign began. This was likely due, in part, to Obama's ability to capture the vote of part of the "Joshua Generation," the name observers gave to a demographic of young voters who identified as evangelicals but who were nevertheless more politically progressive.[137] The growing numerical and political prominence of this population is likely a strong reason why CWA continues to deploy chaos rhetoric that reminds members that support for liberal ideas or platforms amounts to delegitimizing Christianity itself, for a wide moral lens is tantamount to blindness.[138] In response to those evangelicals who found Obama's message alluring, CWA has repeatedly explained this appeal as nothing other than a fantastic ruse wherein Obama "learned the language of evangelicalism and he spoke it fluently when it served his purposes."[139]

If one believes, in fact, that appearances are deceiving, then what will sustain CWA across the shifting political tides in the future will be its ability to effectively recuperate the movement's most enduring chaos rhetoric that has historically worked to revitalize conservative sentiment. As this chapter has shown, this rhetoric has invoked the naturalness of dichotomous gender roles; the literal and figurative dangers faced by innocent children and moral women; the significance of sex as both a gauge of moral worth and the source of catastrophic social breakdown; and the danger lurking with the morality of social "others," a category with the elasticity to subsume race, class, gender, and sexual orientation.

While many of the Christian Right groups that proliferated during the 1980s and 90s have since disbanded or faded into relative obscurity, CWA's presence remains vibrant, despite the fact that it does not articulate a particularly unique political platform when compared to the larger movement. Yet CWA holds certain points of distinction that have mattered significantly to both its influence and survival. Central to its vitality is its identity as the largest conservative women's group in America. By capitalizing on both the identity "woman" and "America," CWA is able to lay claim to these issues of sex, gender, and reproduction as platforms on which it holds special expertise while also linking them specifically to national decline, another realm that it claims under its purview. As the next chapter will discuss, CWA does not attack its opponents primarily with Bible verses and "God-talk." Rather, it employs a calculated rhetoric that dodges overtly religious language, depending, instead, on heavily scientific and rationalistic speech that reflects the carefully crafted use of certain symbols and images that effectively mainstream its message. In a recuperation of the long lineage of conservative chaos rhetoric about sex, the result is that CWA's vision of moral fortitude is designed to subsume and become *America's* vision, rather than the perspective of just a "religious" few.

2

The Architecture of Chaos Rhetoric: Emotion, Myth, Persuasion

Sex is . . . a social activist, a maker: it makes babies, friends, and enemies, and is a conduit for disease. It is, in a word, a thoroughly public reality. . . . Sex is power. Religion is power. Historically, both have proved that they can move mountains. So when sex and religion get together, we are dealing with power squared.[1]

—DANIEL MAGUIRE

ONE WOULD BE hard pressed to find many Americans today who could not deliver a small speech on why it is important to protect the environment, whether they personally believe it to be of much concern. Despite the fact that the concept of an ongoing ecological crisis has gained mainstream attention, most Americans would generally hesitate to link personal virtue with whether one recycles in the same way that they might critique theft or adultery; it seems inappropriate to insist that composting is a moral matter. The issue is not the gravity of the problem, for if the worldwide ability to continue sustainable food production is compromised, then few will doubt that this is one of the most significant troubles in history. Rather, the more pressing question is how the category of ethics has been constructed in such a way that certain acts and events are labeled by the public as uniquely immoral issues, while others are simply called personal preferences or fine individual ideals.

Arguably, it seems that the distinguishing line is that those things labeled "moral issues" have the capacity to directly impact a culture's dominant power structures. But even in those circumstances that are generally construed as ethical, what is immoral to one person may be perfectly acceptable to another. Since the category "moral decline" is itself a perception (for those who are unconcerned with environmental issues do not, presumably, call themselves "immoral" on those grounds), speaking about the erosion of a society's or group's morals is itself something of a persuasive political act, for those who hear this rhetoric must be convinced not only that the issue should be regarded as an ethical one, but that it is also of such magnitude that a diversity of different opinions about the topic should not be tolerated.

This chapter dissects the architecture of such moralistic talk as it appears in chaos rhetoric, exposing how it works, how it is structured, and in what contexts it operates. As earlier mentioned, chaos rhetoric is a type of speech used by a group to naturalize its own political agendas. It persuades by using fear, threat, and anxiety imagery to generate social sympathy for a position that aligns with the group's own political platforms, which the group offers as the resolution to the very threat it rhetorically created.

To understand its architecture, it is important to first address some of the theoretical concepts behind chaos rhetoric, investigating how abjection, emotion, and religion are deployed as techniques used to elevate sex to a matter of seemingly ultimate, ethical importance. Along the way, I will consider how CWA uses chaos rhetoric to capitalize on both its religious and secular self-portrayals to craft a sense of its own cultural authority. Finally, I will show how CWA has used four specific tactics common to chaos rhetoric, examining how oversimplification, a defensive focus, issue deflection, and urgency stand at the center of its persuasive clout. Taken together, an examination of these tactics reveals how the social shifts most often described through chaos rhetoric are usually those that strike at the interstices of a group's cultural dominance.

Producing Reality

While the term *rhetoric* has been defined in a multitude of ways, I use the term here simply to describe the process by which language creates (a particular) reality. The larger cultural context in which rhetoric is crafted is often described by social theorists as *discourse*, a term popularized by Michel Foucault to indicate the entire realm of knowledge, power, and agency structures that exists within a culture. These structures enable not only physical control over the population, but more fundamentally, ideological control over the terms of its existence.

This happens most simply through what might be discourse's most basic act: categorization. The ability to label something in a particular way is an almost unequaled power; advertisers know well that how they portray an item directly determines its public demand. If a product can be construed as the latest and greatest, or as a "special exclusive offer," its social and economic values climb. In this sense, rhetoric is a form of social advertising that employs the culture's discursive channels to achieve certain political ends. Rhetorical theorist Kenneth Burke refers to this process as the construction of a "terministic screen."[2] Viewing language as a series of screens, or filters, that direct the attention of an audience towards one interpretation of events (rather than another), language becomes the mechanism through which otherwise meaningless data is crafted, manipulated, and shaped into a seemingly inevitable reality.[3]

The work of the terministic screen is evident in William Saletan's study of a political consultant who, in the late 1980s, achieved a seemingly unlikely feat: he successfully persuaded socially conservative Arkansans to vote for a bill that supported government funding for abortions. At the time, many Arkansans held a negative view of women's issues, which often evoked images of a welfare mother whose sexual irresponsibility made the public morally and financially responsible for her "abortions of convenience." Yet by recasting legal bans on abortion not only as undue government intervention but also as the further victimization of female rape victims (those who could "legitimately" have abortions), conservative voters were able to enter into a new ideological space where they did not have to compromise their sense of moral responsibility wrought through the image of the sexually permissive woman. The shift in language, Saletan notes, "changed abortion from a welfare issue to a crime issue."[4]

Saletan's research reveals the workings of what Foucault calls "the power-knowledge nexus," a term that describes the inseparability (and to some degree, indistinguishability) of knowledge from power. The ability to create the terms of reality (or, put another way, to determine and manage the categories that define a culture) is the key to almost any expression of social order, authority, and control.[5] Like the ability of countless raindrops to create rivers, and thus canyons, across millions of years, the diffused nature of power means that individuals within a culture are shaped by the constant, inundating messages that they receive about the culture's norms and constraints, which they, in turn, adopt, embody, and thus reinforce. In this way, power is effective because, Foucault notes, it is "exercised from innumerable points," leading the individual members of society to regulate their own behaviors without ever asking where such norms come from.[6] While many have read Foucault's diffused model of power as an indication that no single group's particular interests are fed through the power-knowledge nexus, this is actually contrary to his own account. At certain points, Foucault clearly describes the norms created through discourse as those consistent with the perspectives and interests of the privileged, which others have naturalized and adopted as their own.[7]

Rather than focus on who has created the social standards that are perpetuated or resisted, however, Foucault is interested in how such concepts are passed on. Beyond the simple force of inundation on which the diffused power model is based, Foucault suggests that individuals adopt others' interests as their own through the joint vehicles of secrecy and anonymity. Power functions at its greatest efficiency when it is at least partially concealed—that is, when it is understood by the members of a culture as simple common sense, or the "natural" shape of things, rather than an externally imposed constraint.[8] This naturalizing aspect of power also depends in part on anonymity, for some of the most enduring ideas that cultures embrace are not easily traceable to a particular person or entity.[9]

For instance, in many Western cultures, it is completely permissible for women to bare certain parts of their bodies in public (such as the face, neck, arms, legs, and feet), while in other cultures, exposing some or all of these body parts for public viewing is deemed largely unacceptable. The women of these respective cultures know how to publicly clothe their bodies not because there is an extensive dress manual that they are handed upon reaching adulthood, but because their own perceptions about proper dress are rooted in a vast cultural knowledge into which they were effectively socialized from the time they were small children, one wherein certain female body parts remain morally neutral in one culture and circumstance, even as they connote indecency and immorality in another culture.

In either case, the way that a "proper" woman dresses is directly connected to cultural perceptions about her (whether as a sexual object, as a person whose modesty must be carefully protected, and/or as a person whose worth lies in her appearance or sexuality, etc.), and yet despite this, only a relatively small number of women likely spend considerable time consciously thinking about the connection between their cultural agency and their clothing. The way that things like dress codes are naturalized and made to appear self-evident indicates the degree to which historically constructed power dynamics can be transformed into practices perceived as simple inevitabilities.

Fear and Abjection

If discourse involves crafting and adopting certain social presumptions on which a culture builds and naturalizes its view of reality, it is critical to consider how some ideas become more popular (and are thus adopted) over others. In the case of chaos rhetoric, the emotions that drive it cannot be effectively evoked without the reader or listener first adopting a series of largely unquestioned cultural attitudes and social norms that make the fear or threat contained within the rhetoric seem a viable reality.

Put simply, something needs to be culturally identified as *frightening* before most individuals will be *frightened* of it. Most of us do not have to be persuaded to be fearful of a literal threat to our lives (say, through a car accident or disease), but we do have to be persuaded that sexual education programs can be just as lethal, as CWA has before suggested. This process of persuasion transpires by making sexual education (which, the logic goes, leads to sexual permissiveness, which leads to disease acquisition, which leads to death) appear *naturally* lethal—a matter of common sense—instead of the historically contingent argument made by a particular group attempting to change legal approaches to both sex and education.

Much of what a culture finds fearful or repulsive is not, however, tied to an essential feature of these cultural "boogeymen," but is carefully constructed by the culture itself in its chaos rhetoric. In her work on the logic behind the social construction of fear, Julia Kristeva demonstrates how groups relegate certain persons, behaviors, and things to realms of abjection. Abjected things, Kristeva notes, repel, disgust, and frighten. [10] Jasper amplifies the concept in his observation that abjection occurs when something compromises the sense that the world is a stable place, that one knows what to expect from it, and that one's routines and actions predictably impact it.[11] This is why abjected things must be portrayed not simply as peripherally or occasionally dangerous, but as wholly and essentially so. More than merely things we do not like, abjected things cannot logically be assimilated into a culture's epistemological structures. Kristeva elaborates:

> It is thus not lack of cleanliness or health that causes abjection but what disturbs identity, system, order. What does not respect borders, positions, rules. The in-between, the ambiguous, the composite. The traitor, the liar, the criminal with a good conscience, the shameless rapist, the killer who claims he is a savior . . .[12]

CWA uses abjection imagery consistently in its depiction of feminists, who are never portrayed in the group's rhetoric as happily married, heterosexual, or childbearing. Rhetorically speaking, none of those adjectives (happy, married, heterosexual, childbearing) can be placed together with "feminist" because CWA has portrayed feminists as existing outside of the group's order that these adjectives define. The only way that such a person ("feminist") can be made intelligible through CWA rhetoric is through her misery and foreclosure of family life. Similarly, CWA never holds out the possibility of a "healthy" gay marriage since the phrase "gay marriage" is itself abjected and thus fundamentally signifies dysfunction; nor can gay people be productive citizens, since being gay, by definition, represents a state of moral defilement inconsistent with good citizenship. This is but one reason why the term almost always appears in quotation marks ("gay marriage") in CWA speech: to CWA, it isn't truly marriage, but the co-opting of an accepted institution ("marriage") illegitimately used to describe an abjected state ("gay").

Theorists who study fear rhetoric cite a multitude of reasons why groups employ fear and abjection imagery, but most agree that fear is critical to gaining an audience. As earlier mentioned, social movements will often use a narrative shock, or some sort of highly elevated threat, to draw in the prospective member: the rhetoric poses such a grave danger that the listener cannot help but pay attention.[13] From there, the task of the movement is to continue to generate sufficient anxiety and fear so that the groups' members exist in a state of ongoing anger and righteous indignation. Injustice is a particularly important emotion to generate because it justifies expressions of both public outrage and activism.[14]

The ability to label fearful or abjected things in such a way not only helps social groups know who or what to oppose, but is integral to crafting the groups' own identities. When a culture relegates something to an abjected realm, that act of relegation can never wholly exist outside of the group's own self-construction since the abjected state or thing helps to define the borders of that culture in opposition. The identity of each is known in part because it is not the other.[15] For instance, even if many of CWA's members find some aspects of comprehensive sexual education curricula (which includes information on contraceptive use) important or informative for teens to know, the fact that liberals have endorsed such programs means that CWA is very unlikely to waver on its support for abstinence-only educational programming (which does not provide such information). Similarly, CWA's self-definition as a women's rights organization must be crafted very carefully so as not to sound too much like the liberal feminist organizations that it opposes (a topic addressed in the next chapter).

Practically speaking, this means that how a culture crafts an abjected realm says much about its own identity formation. In *The Psychic Life of Power*, Judith Butler argues that in order to become a known, recognizable part of our culture, we must reject or foreclose on a multitude of identities that our culture says we cannot be in order to become one of a series of acceptable options.[16] Applying this same concept to gender in her other works, Butler asserts that existence itself is a state of melancholy, a state of self-*rejection* that is self-*abjection*. Consider how we are all born with the ability to speak any human language if properly socialized, yet our capacity for language is narrowed and sharpened as time goes on to include only those languages that we are taught to speak and hear. Similarly, our identities are honed as we are shown who we can and cannot be, and "we" are thus born from a necessary degree of self-foreclosure.[17] Those who adopt an unacceptable or abjected outlet of identity will pay the social price by humiliation, exclusion, invisibility, or physical harm; one needs only to consider the treatment that many homosexuals endure in heteronormative cultures in order to see abjection at work. While Butler openly rejects certain features of Kristeva's model (most pointedly, Kristeva's presumption of a cross-cultural, psycho-symbolic realm from which most humans construct culture), both theorists locate the building of one identity in the very closely related sacrifice of another: individuals become acceptable by rejecting those acts or identities that mainstream society will not permit them to have.[18]

This identity-crafting function of abjection means that groups like CWA benefit from fixating on the subjects of their abjection as dangerous entities that are everywhere, always ready to infiltrate.[19] If the threat is lurid and ever present, fear becomes a self-replicating mechanism to maintain a group's own boundaries of identity, which need frequent reinforcement to remain stable in an always changing, information-heavy world. Fixation on the abjected subject ensures that individuals are constantly reminded what to fear and why, and from this reminder of what *not* to be, they grow more secure in the adoption of their identities.

Mythmaking: The Engine of Chaos Rhetoric

If fear and abjection are the rhetorical creations of a culture making statements about those things that threaten its epistemological structures, how do cultures convincingly create abjected realms in their chaos rhetoric? Practically speaking, how are the logics used to justify this fear created, represented, and adopted such that sexual education courses can be portrayed as something as deadly as gun violence? The process by which such naturalization transpires is a phenomenon that Roland Barthes calls *mythmaking*.

In Barthes's use of the term, mythmaking does not designate falsehood or deceit, but involves the ongoing and ubiquitous techniques that groups use to naturalize a relationship between things that may otherwise have no inherent connection. From a rhetorical standpoint, mythmaking occurs when a group or culture superimposes a politically advantageous "layer" of meaning on top of an already emotionally familiar (and often beloved) subject in its rhetoric, enmeshing the unfamiliar with the familiar.[20] In the case of chaos rhetoric, this secondary, less-familiar layer is introduced in an oppositional or abjected manner such that it threatens the aforementioned familiar and loved social symbol, infusing the relationship between the two with a robust dose of judgment-altering negative emotion. This negativity pushes the reader to be more likely to adopt the terms of this relationship automatically. The threat that is interjected between the familiar and the unfamiliar seals them together in such a way that history is transformed into nature, to borrow Barthes terminology; the rhetoric makes the constructed and contingent appear natural and timeless.[21]

When singer and conservative activist Anita Bryant launched her 1970s campaign against gay rights (mentioned in the last chapter), she effectively employed such mythmaking in the chaos-rhetoric she produced, which was comprised of just three simple words. Bryant named her campaign "Save Our Children," explicitly linking homosexuality with child abuse and exploitation.[22] By juxtaposing a highly emotional, familiar symbol (the innocent child) with an "other" (homosexuals), interjecting the relationship between the two as one of danger or threat (children need to be saved from homosexuals), "children," "homosexuality," and "danger" became symbolically enmeshed. Images of children, invocations of reason, and nationalist themes (including freedom, rights, and individualism) are featured so prominently in CWA's chaos rhetoric because they are emotionally evocative, and thus are likely to induce persuasion.

Indeed, the rhetorical fusion of children, endangerment, and homosexuality is a frequent trope used by CWA. Consider CWA's response to a 2002 statement by the American Academy of Pediatrics that held that children raised in households with gay or lesbian parents showed no harmful outcome. CWA countered with the following statement:

> The AAP report will be used to advance the "reckless liberal experiment of placing young children and even babies in homosexual-led households."[23]

In the style of rhetoric-building that Barthes suggests, CWA's speech overlays familiar symbols of innocence ("even babies") with the adjectives "reckless," "liberal," and "experiment," which are then fused with "homosexual-led households." Here, a good parent's presumed focus on safety, responsibility, and love is symbolically stripped from gay and lesbian individuals, disabling them from functioning under any positive connotations. Significantly, the author does not use the terms "parent" or "family"–undeniably, two words with great emotional weight—but further delegitimizes gays and lesbians by labeling them as "leaders" of "households." Under the terms of this chaos rhetoric, the union of "homosexual" with "good parent" becomes an illogical proposition.

Reiterating a similar theme, another article by CWA addresses a growing student-led trend in many schools to hold a "Day of Silence," a time where participating students choose not to speak in order to recognize the silencing and bullying endured by many lesbian, gay, bisexual, and transgendered students nationwide. CWA's response follows:

> Can you imagine officials at a middle school, junior high or high school setting aside a day to promote "tolerance" for heavy smoking and drinking among children? How about a day where teachers encourage kids to "embrace who they are," pick up that crack pipe and give it a stiff toke? Neither can I. The public would go ballistic, and for good reason.
>
> But that hasn't stopped officials in thousands of schools across the country from promoting other politically correct and socially "in-vogue" behaviors that—both statistically and manifestly—are every bit as dangerous as the aforementioned "frowned-upon"

> behaviors. That's exactly what the homosexual activist "Day of Silence" is all about —advancing, through clever, feel-good propaganda, full acceptance of the homosexual lifestyle among children.[24]

While the more overt chaos rhetoric featured here parallels the dangers of homosexuality with the dangers of drug use, this is not the only operant metaphor at play. The terms "tolerance," "propaganda," and "homosexuality" are all linked, equated, and then collapsed with danger. If tolerance is propaganda, and propaganda is danger, then "homosexual activists" can be described as "clever" insomuch as what they have to offer is nothing more than self-serving (and harmful) political talk that preys on innocence and goodness (i.e., children). This rhetoric also reinforces homosexuality as a behavioral choice, an important move in the latent claim that homosexuals are responsible for their own marginalization.[25] When promoted in the political realm ("tolerance," "propaganda"), homosexuality becomes a form of chosen aberrance that has no other function than to prey upon and ultimately harm innocent children.

In this way, chaos rhetoric is not only persuasive because it is emotionally alluring, but because it conveniently provides a built-in resolution designed for adoption by those in this emotionally suggestive state. Critically, insomuch as it rhetorically creates its own moral panic, Bivins notes that fear rhetoric "aim[s] simultaneously to raise and symbolically to resolve terrors, establishing normative and behavioral guidelines which fold safety, certainty, and sanctity together."[26] To resolve the dangers of homosexuals, one must deny them legal recognition, prohibit their employment options, and forbid them from adopting children. To solve the problem of children who fall sway to situational ethics and a dangerously flexible understanding of tolerance, one must remove evidence of controversial cultural differences from schools. As will be repeatedly evident, CWA rarely poses a threat that it does not follow with its own politically advantageous solution.

As testament to the efficacy of this tactic, consider the following email received by CWA members one August, at the beginning of the school year for many American colleges and universities. The subject line reads: "They put my daughter in a homosexual studies class!" The email opens with the story of a college freshman urgently texting her father to inform him that her advisor had placed her in a "homosexual studies" course—quite against her will. The email continues:

> It literally took just hours before liberals had confronted this young Christian conservative student – overwhelming her with their radically-charged agenda. Don't think for a moment that this was a coincidence. In fact, it's quite likely that Christian conservative women are being aggressively targeted this time every year in hopes of indoctrinating them into embracing an anti-family, big government, feminist agenda that runs counter to everything they've been taught at home. As this shocking story reveals, on college and university campuses across America right now it is OPEN SEASON on Christian conservative women, and I am more determined than ever to reach these young Christian women through our Young Women for America (YWA) chapters. Through YWA chapters, conservative women are already being empowered to make a profound impact, communicating and influencing legislators and policymakers on today's pressing social and cultural issues![27]

In what ends up being a fundraising email to start more YWA chapters nationwide, CWA provides the solution to the threat: money. Such funds are critical to stop an omnipresent, infiltrating force—liberalism—which, akin to how a hunter seeks his prey, "confronts," "overwhelm[s]," and "aggressively targets" innocent conservative young women in an "OPEN SEASON" that is the philosophical hallmark of American colleges and universities. From a structural perspective, the chaos rhetoric operates by linking liberalism with conservative college freshman, fusing the two together in a relationship that draws on the hunter/prey metaphor. Because of this looming threat, the only way that the CWA reader can protect such innocents is to fund the start of an organization that guarantees their ideological safety.

But the name of the organization operates as an important part of the rhetoric as well. In an acronym that closely resembles its own (YWA), CWA portrays its more youthful arm as an extension of itself—that is, an entity that is morally righteous. Although such righteousness is religiously wrought, it is not portrayed in explicitly Christian terms but in nationalist language. CWA and YWA's very names indicate that they are *for America*, not for Christianity or Christian morality (despite the fact that they frequently invoke both). In an intriguing move that substitutes nationalism for religion, collapsing the two together as a unified whole, CWA further uses the structures of chaos rhetoric to make an implicit statement about how America is, at its core, a Christian enterprise. The resolution to liberalism is thus a form of nationalism, implying along the way that the two oppose one another.

"Secular" Authority: Religion in Disguise?

Even though the degree of overt religious language publicly deployed by CWA vacillates, the languages of religion and morality are nevertheless vital ingredients in its chaos rhetoric, assisting in the naturalization process critical to persuasion. If, as earlier mentioned, we can think of religion as an institution that claims to draw power from a transcendent source that is impervious to human criticism, then it might seem that groups would use religion's presumably iron-clad arguments constantly, evoking "God-talk" wherever possible.[28] This is not, however, the trend among many religious groups today. In CWA's case, it favors a much more careful rhetorical balancing act that permits moments of overtly religious rhetoric that are tempered by appeals to educational credentials, science, reason, and populist appeals to a "common sense" morality. This multifaceted tactic of casting the net widely, so to speak, is critical to its success because it must convince even the non-religious of the solidity of its platforms; voting against gay marriage on the grounds that God hates homosexuality is, quite obviously, the position of an already-religious person.

Yet even among America's self-described religious population there exists a tension between what is appropriately religious and what is fanatical. Religious conservatives who have attempted to summon social power through overt religious rhetoric have at times endured ridicule, something antithetical to securing the mainstream appeal needed for widespread political influence. When, in 1987, televangelist Oral Roberts told his television audience that God would strike him dead if he was unable to raise eight million dollars, many believed his claim and answered with ample funds (Roberts ended up with over nine million dollars in donations from his supporters).[29] Despite his success, however, Roberts became the butt of an endless variety of media jokes, his theological legitimacy was hotly contested by other Christian groups, and he was generally portrayed as both a charlatan and a backwoods preacher.

It is this kind of paradoxical relationship with religion that makes certain religious statements taboo if mainstream persuasion is the goal. Yet one could reasonably argue that, in the American context, religious groups can still benefit from the moral authority that religion holds while avoiding overtly religious speech. If Janet Jakobsen and Ann Pellegrini are correct that American morality rhetoric is so closely conflated with religion that there is little ideological room for the concept of a value system outside of the dominant Protestant model, then talking about morality is almost automatically a cultural exercise in religion.[30] It is a rather reliable, one, too, for its religious roots are so mainstream as to appear non-existent. When, for instance, the Supreme Court has rendered decisions against the legality of gay rights on the basis of conformity to the "traditional values" of American culture, the court has long relied on a definition of "tradition" that is explicitly Christian.[31] Rather than see this as a violation of the separation of church and state, most Americans have construed these judicial decisions as a self-evident moral base because they, too, have adopted and naturalized those otherwise religious ideals as simple common sense.

This perception of a collective cultural reservoir called "morality" or "common sense" is closely linked to the phenomenon of rhetorical resonance. Building from the work of philosopher Gilles Deleuze, Linda Kintz describes *resonance*—an otherwise acoustical term that describes how sound is intensified through a number of sympathetic vibrations—as the phenomenon wherein large groups of people with otherwise disparate agendas can be drawn together and their political power synthesized through emotional appeals that they all find similarly attractive.[32] A person does not have to believe that God hates abortion or that the Bible teaches against it in order to vote against abortion rights; he merely has to empathize with images of aborted fetuses or tales of women injured by the procedure. Perhaps he does not even know why he feels compelled to vote against abortion; it just seems like "the right thing to do." As Kintz notes, people do not have to be lockstep adherents of conservative Christianity to amplify the social power of the Christian Right, for if they are even mildly sympathetic to some of its positions (for whatever reason), then they are more likely to endorse its platforms.[33]

In effect, Christian Right groups like CWA have sought to mainstream their messages through images that are attractive to everyone from their most devoted followers to the public at large. Such widespread appeal depends on symbols that are both ambiguous and emotionally evocative. In the same vein as Barthes and Foucault, Kintz describes how conservative groups often draw on familiar, safe images (such as "family values") that, while relatively devoid of concrete meaning, generate tremendous emotional capital.[34] This is why CWA can hold up the "family values" banner in attacks on feminists, gays, the United Nations, the ACLU, and many other, varied organizations. So long as it can construe the phrase as something consistent with its own platforms, "family values" operates as an emotive symbol that can be flexibly interpreted in whatever way is politically expedient. Under this reading of groups like CWA, their goal is hardly individual theological conversion, but the acquisition of political sympathy.

Yet if the ambiguous terms often endemic to morality talk (including "family values," "moral decline," "protecting our freedoms," etc.) permit religion's roots to hide within a secular-sounding argument, there are still moments when even overt religious speech has made otherwise religious pronouncements appear as matters of mainstream morality. When President Bill Clinton's sexual relationship with then-White House intern Monica Lewinsky hit the press, Clinton at first denied the affair. But as further evidence made such denials impossible, Clinton's confession to the American public—staged at a prayer breakfast—was immediately followed by meetings with spiritual advisors; the language of sin, repentance, and forgiveness; and the questions of commentators on whether Clinton's behavior paralleled America's own moral deterioration.[35] Rather than ask whether America (and Clinton) was encountering a moral crisis, there was a better question, Kathleen Sands remarks. It was:

> . . . why he should have been using the language of repentance in the first place, what bearing this sexual fling bore on his obligation as President or as citizen, what judicial machinations had to be deployed to drum these furtive genital acts into a constitutional crisis—these questions disappeared whenever religion descended into the discussion.[36]

The malleability of morality talk is an important ingredient when considering how rhetorical resonance enables CWA to hold a certain sort of moral authority in an otherwise religiously diverse public. Barthes notes that rhetorical mythmaking will fail if those who control the discourse cannot portray themselves as rightful authorities who have the expertise to gauge or evaluate the people and circumstances that their rhetoric involves.[37] By strategically juxtaposing its religious identity with generalized morality speech, CWA can avoid the risks associated with constant theological talk while simultaneously benefitting from the time-honored cultural connection between religion and morality. Through this rhetorical strategy, CWA can successfully portray itself as an organization with secular, ethical expertise.

Secular Rationales

In the name of such widespread appeal, CWA continuously constructs its moral stances by appealing to social authorities that unquestionably enjoy widespread legitimacy. These include, among others, appeals to quantitative data, science, health, nationalism, and logic. In most of the articles on the CWA website, numbers and other statistical data abound, traced carefully with footnotes and bibliographic sources. For more conversational articles, scientific data is still prominently featured, but logic—particularly in the form of "common sense" talk—is frequently employed.

In crafting its moral arguments, CWA relies heavily on a popular conservative Christian concept often called *the unity of truth*. This is the notion that if God is the author of all truth, truth must resonate throughout all of God's creation, which includes nature and social institutions alike. Beyond the negative spiritual impact caused by immoral behaviors, Christian proponents of this idea often point to other tangible, negative consequences of sin (such as disease, social disadvantage, or a compromise in security or safety), which, under this thinking, are the natural reverberations of sin working its way through the entirety of God's creation. This is why CWA is eager to point to examples of the physical risks of abortion or to higher rates of drug use among homosexuals: using this reasoning, poor social outcomes are almost always the result of moral failure.

While a general cultural respect for the "truth" of hard data is one reason for the Christian Right's emphasis on logic, statistics, and other classically "objective" measures, here again numbers are also used judiciously when groups like CWA need to caricature liberal intellectuals as out-of-touch elitists.[38] This is a particularly important tactic when controversies perennially arise regarding the objectivity of the facts to which CWA appeals, or to the validity of its interpretations of data.[39] To CWA, this critique does not pose an intellectual problem, for it operates on the assumption that the secular world of so-called objective facts is not really so. Because this world is run by liberals who, to CWA, deny the presence of God as the source of truth, the data produced by universities, liberal think tanks, or other non-Christian sources is already suspect. Thus, providing its own interpretation of the data or—just as often—relying on studies produced by conservative organizations resolves the issue. Under this reading of "fact" and "truth," objectivity can only be practiced when one first adopts the logical precepts that support CWA's worldview.

Medical facts have been a favorite feature of much of the group's rhetoric. Stylistically, note the presence of footnotes (original to this article) as well as the frequent references to mainstream medical sources:[40]

> According to a 1994 report by the Guttmacher Institute, 43 percent of women will have an abortion by age 45[2]; therefore the often unreported consequences of abortion affect almost half of the female population. Abortion has failed to offer a physically safe choice for women, and they deserve to know the facts.
>
> - *The Journal of Epidemiology and Community Health* stated, "Since 1957, evidence linking induced abortion to the later development of breast cancer has been observed in 27 of 33 studies worldwide.[3]" *The International Journal of Cancer* reported a higher risk of developing cervical and ovarian cancer after abortion.[4,5,6]
> - The *L.A. Daily News* quoted pro-choice Dr. Janet Daling stating, "I have three sisters with breast cancer, and I resent people messing around with scientific data to further their own agenda, be they pro-choice or pro-life. I would have loved to have found no association between breast cancer and abortion, but our research is rock solid, and our data is accurate. It's not a matter of believing. It's a matter of what is.[7]"
> - Research by the Royal College of Physicians and Surgeons reported 6 percent of women who have abortions are left sterile.[8] If a woman has an STD during an abortion, her risk for infertility increases.[9] A study by the *Journal of Infectious Diseases* found 87 percent of women carrying one or more STDs [sexually transmitted diseases] showed no symptoms.[10] [41]

Articles such as this hold a preeminent place in the organization's library precisely because numbers related to biological phenomena are often portrayed as more "truth-telling" than social scientific data that might be manipulated by liberal academics, something of which CWA often warns. Here medical statistics become a convincing mechanism through which abortion can be delegitimized without overt appeals to religion. The argument, offered both implicitly and explicitly, is that immoral ethical practices reverberate through many levels of human experience. To CWA, abortion is morally reprehensible because it kills a child. Yet the focus in the above article is to demonstrate how abortion also contradicts God's divine will for women's bodies—procreation—a transgression made explicit through more "secular" concerns like infertility and disease.

Although these issues pose important questions in a world where scientific accuracy is highly valued, the debate over CWA's use of objective data is something of a secondary concern. Remembering that social authority is better described as an effect rather than a discrete entity, what matters to CWA is that the majority of its readers find the information persuasive.[42] Perhaps this is why CWA often poses arguments that create a "both/and" appeal: the quantifiable data supporting its position is prominently placed, but is also sustained by many other layers of authority, including religion, populism (from whence most "common sense" arguments come), and logic, among others.

Consider, for instance, an article authored by Janice Shaw Crouse that describes why marriage is an important social institution. Crouse argues that marriage creates virtue in married individuals, which benefits society at large. The social reform policies of liberals, on the other hand, de-emphasize marriage and thus virtue (read as personal responsibility). Religion is not absent from Crouse's argument:

> God in His wisdom designed marriage to effectively serve both the unifying and procreative functions. A couple that pursues a great marriage lives in conformity with God's design, and thus, many virtues as well as great happiness arise naturally as a by-product of their respectful treatment of one another and others.[43]

Despite this overt religious rationale that opens the piece, the majority of the argument is devoted to sociological, statistically-based explanations of why virtue (which Crouse considers to be the byproduct of marriage), and thus marriage itself, is preferable. Citing a study that found that married males are more often employed than non-married ones, Crouse concludes that the virtue created in marriage also creates a good worker. But aware that some social scientists might question her interpretation of the data, Crouse prefaces her presentation of the study with this statement:

> Despite all the derogatory jokes about the oppressive, irksome nature of marriage, the data clearly show that married couples are healthier,

> happier, and live longer than those who remain unmarried. Social scientists try to parse out whether this association is the result of happy, healthy, positive people tending to marry with higher frequency or whether being married tends to make people happier, healthier, and more positive in their outlook on life. . . . Logic and common sense, however, face no such obstacle. To take just one instance, ordinary folks look at the following set of facts and draw the obvious conclusion that marriage does make a difference.

After asserting that married males make better workers, she goes on:

> Unlike social science researchers, people in business concerned with holding down expenses recognize which workers have not learned the habits that make them reliable workers. And so, when cut backs [*sic*] have to be made in their work force, they have no difficulty determining which are the least valuable workers and thus the ones they are going to lay off first.[44]

Here the overtly religious rhetoric is mentioned ("God in his wisdom") but is otherwise dismissed so as to highlight a more social-scientific perspective that appeals to quantifiable data. The logic can operate in two ways: one can embrace the theological argument, or the social commentary about economic productivity—expressed through statistics—can stand on its own as an adequate case in favor of heterosexual marriage. True to the resonance model, one need not adopt the theology behind the speech in order to embrace the greater message that people in traditional marriages are more virtuous (i.e., responsible) because of those marriages than those who are not.

But Crouse's persuasive work is not finished there. In order to put the "social scientists" who might interpret this data differently in their place (for Crouse acknowledges that it is impossible to tell whether more responsible people get married or if marriage actually creates responsibility), she appeals to "logic," "common sense," "ordinary folk," and "people in business" as other tiers of quantifiable authority. Crouse uses these figures to bolster her argument about the nature of objective fact further, arguing for causality where there may be only correlation. Her interpretation of the data might not be the same as a social scientist's, but in this context, an identical conclusion is unnecessary. Crouse has appealed to religion, social science statistics, and common sense as authorities that can individually or together support her argument, all while ultimately de-emphasizing its religious rationale.

Secular Experts

Secular argumentation is not the only method of achieving widespread appeal. In addition, CWA has placed extraordinary emphasis on the educational accomplishments and professional credentials of its staff. While CWA portrays itself in clearly Christian ways, on the whole, it emphasizes political, secular labels, as evidenced in its self-description as "the nation's largest public policy women's organization."[45]

The organization's president, Penny Nance, is described as a former congressional staffer, non-profit organization founder, and media specialist previously employed as a special advisor to the Federal Communications Commission (FCC).[46] Before CWA, she was an "advisor on media and social issues" who focused on "the protection of children, including broadcast indecency and the media task force on childhood obesity."[47] A graduate of conservative flagship Liberty University, Nance replaced former president Wendy Wright, one of the most vocal and public spokespersons for CWA during her tenure there. While at CWA, Wright "promot[ed] legislation and international policies that are beneficial to women and families, brief[ed] congressional and presidential staff on pro-family issues, and train[ed] grassroots activists."[48] In fact, with the exception of her expertise on "religious issues" (mentioned once) and her interest in "religious freedom issues" (also mentioned once), one could easily confuse Wright's work at CWA with any other political activist. She is described as a "United Nations Lobbyist," "Policy Expert and Activist," and "Author." In 2006, Wright was named among "The 100 Most Powerful Women in Washington."[49]

Janice Shaw Crouse, CWA's other most visible figure, is described in similarly secular terms. Crouse, a Ph.D. whose educational credentials are set prominently beside her description as the "Senior Fellow of the Beverly LaHaye Institute," is responsible for the bulk of the essays and articles that comprise the CWA website.[50] Like Nance and Wright, Crouse has few mentions of religion present in her biography. Rather, she is "a recognized authority on sex trafficking, the United Nations, U.S. domestic issues, as well as national and international cultural, children's and women's concerns." In addition, "she has twice served the President as an official delegate to the United Nations (2002 and 2003)." Her position as a presidential speech writer for George H.W. Bush, "authoring major presidential policy addresses," is emphasized, as is her former career in academics.[51]

With the exception of LaHaye herself, whose religious beliefs are cited as the reason for CWA, the organization on the whole is described as a *political* engine, complete with "institutes," "think tanks," and "PACs" (political action committees). It is staffed by "experts," "activists," and "legislative interns," all cast as committed and competent specialists who are also public servants. Far from the uneducated, backwards, and fringe reputation that dogged the early fundamentalists, CWA staffers are presented as highly educated, influential people whose expertise matters.

Controlling Sex

It seems clear, then, that religious rationales—from overt theological discussions to more oblique references to morality—are effective tools in the creation of chaos rhetoric insomuch as moral failure is often cast in the most catastrophic terms. But even one quick glance at CWA's chaos rhetoric reveals that the vast majority of its religiously inspired morality speech revolves around a specific issue: sex. As was discussed in the last chapter, the conservative cultural trend towards sexual regulation has an extensive history, and sex and its related issues (such as gender, sexual orientation, and reproduction) have long been considered the gauge by which one measures both cultural and individual morality.

Many modern critics of conservative social policy have questioned why conservatives spend time campaigning against more private, "personal" morality issues (such as homosexuality), which seem to pale in comparison to poverty, lack of affordable healthcare, and other social concerns that appear to more immediately impact countless Americans' lives. Yet many conservatives understand these latter concerns as issues often directly caused by sexual transgressions, as seen in the popular conservative claim that poverty is a frequent result of the financial burden caused by children born to people in non-marital relationships, which then creates government dependence. This idea has inspired articles from CWA (like Crouse's piece above), wherein heterosexual marriage is portrayed as the boundary within which sexual relations are acceptable precisely because it is construed as an imminently virtuous and responsible institution. Non-marital relationships are thus identified in just the opposite way.

Part of understanding the sexual nucleus of CWA rhetoric boils down to grasping the significance of sexual regulation. Nancy Fischer has observed that the public concern about sexual morality is not usually about controlling one's own behavior as much as it is an attempt to control the behaviors of others. Fisher notes that critiques of the sex acts (and, one could extrapolate, the gendered and reproductive choices) of others is a particularly effective way of creating social hierarchies insomuch as the critiquing person's evaluative act implies not only their own superiority, but also, in contrast, denigrates the critiqued, for "the implication of calling someone else immoral is the unsaid statement, 'I would never do that.'"[52] In this sense, Fischer observes (echoing Foucault) that sexual morality talk posits a world where one's sexuality becomes the core of one's identity, and thus one's capacity to be read as a valued member of society.[53] The treatment of sex as a special category that supposedly indicates one's innermost moral nature (and thus practically speaking, one's social worth) has not only led to rigorous controls over the conditions of its occurrence, but also to the careful regulation and proscription of individuals who transgress those conditions.[54]

Solidifying the relationship between sexual regulation and social hierarchy does not, however, explain why sexed, gendered, and reproductive acts have been the vehicle through which such hierarchies come to life. Put another way, why is sex the particular behavior granted such significance? Foucault's answer to the centrality of sex lies with the concept *biopower*, a term used to describe how the ability to monitor and influence the biological functions of a population (including its sexual practices) is simultaneously the ability to control many of the details of the lives of average people, including with whom they will live, whether they will be able to pursue education, whether and with whom they will have children, and so on.[55] Sex is, in a very literal way, the initiation of the social project and its many manifestations. Thus, practically speaking, the attention that sex receives has not been as much about the act itself, but its many implications.[56] When one uncovers the multiplicity of issues present in sex and related rhetoric, one is forced to see how conversations about sexual regulation make sense only in the wider context of regulation within other social institutions.[57] Foucault envisions sex not as an entity separate from law, economics, knowledge, or other social realms, but as a deeply embedded, discursive component of them. This is why it is difficult to find systems of sexual regulation that are not also closely intertwined with racial, ethnic, class, and gendered categorizations.[58]

For instance, Traci West's research on the rhetoric surrounding sex, race, and late twentieth-century welfare policy shows how poor black mothers who received government aid were "labeled a major threat that endanger[ed] the moral health of society" in those legislations.[59] This rhetoric took shape under the guise of federal welfare reform and its emphasis on the social dangers of "illegitimacy," a term used to describe the phenomenon of unwed mothers. The term "illegitimate" unfairly targeted poor black women, West notes, because it was never used to describe the men involved in the creation of pregnancies, nor did white women serve as the "poster children" for welfare reform, despite the fact that white women comprised a significant portion of the population served by such programs. Moreover, an unmarried woman and her offspring were not legally rendered "illegitimate" when they were fully, economically independent and thus did not use the welfare system. The use of the descriptor "illegitimate"—a term designating a sexual, then procreative, act that created an immoral state of being—was (and is) a racial, gendered, and classed rhetorical move intended to marginalize a certain population and deprive them of social legitimacy through the language of religious morality.[60]

If labeling certain members of society as sexual deviants who threaten the nation's future is a particularly effective means of rhetorical degradation, then sexual failure is a convenient trope to not only explain or express anxieties over national decline, but more fundamentally, to demarcate which groups can claim the right to speak for the country. As Janet Jakobsen notes, when sex is the symbol through which groups like CWA seek to re-Christianize America, then all those who violate its narrow understanding of proper sex and identity are not only construed as anti-American, but as living symbols of the death of the longstanding and deeply loved "Christian America" notion.[61]

Thus sex, gender, and reproduction are the acts that have been imbued with incredible moral weight because they are so fundamental to social control. Consequently, it is of little surprise that groups seeking cultural power do so by attempting to ideologically manage these realms. However tempting it is for people of all political stripes to view such groups or entities as "forcing" their agendas on others, Foucault's aforementioned model of diffused power undercuts this idea by implicating most of society's members for the perpetuation, repetition, and subsequent naturalization of such ideals even if only certain groups first popularize them.[62] While the groups that do the most to perpetuate these ideas (such as CWA) do so for their own political gain, these groups rarely invent the ideas that they promote as much as they use their power to increase their visibility.[63] CWA did not originally invent the notion of heteronormativity, nor the idea that abortion is murder, even though it has great political capital embedded in both claims. In this way, CWA is a part of "the public" that has consumed and embraced these ideas just as much as it readily reproduces them.

What this means, practically speaking, is that social power is synonymous with ubiquity. This is why CWA uses incredibly popular, mainstream symbols to forefront its political goals rather than supporting its views through theological minutiae that may hold only limited appeal. In this regard, there is no truly "private" realm in which sex, gender, and reproduction take place, for the norms that solidify common attitudes about these issues are very public realities.

Tactical Maneuvers: The Structures of Chaos Rhetoric

Chaos rhetoric has been described thus far as an emotionally evocative form of speech that manufactures a logic intended to create a sense of fear, outrage, or discomfort, which then pushes the reader or listener to resolve this negative emotion in ways advantageous to the group that first created the rhetoric. However controversial some topics may be, though, chaos rhetoric's persuasive value is also rooted in the use of specific structural tactics. These tactics persuade, in great part, because they attempt to incite a change in the identity of the reader or listener.

Identity shifts are central to the persuasion process. In her own study of evangelical rhetoric, Susan Harding describes religious conversion—itself a type of persuasion—not as a change of "heart" or "mind," as it is often described, but as a change of *language*, whereby the potential convert begins to adopt the religious language she hears as an accurate rendition of events compelling enough to cause her to redefine the world around her.[64] The narratives that comprise "witnessing" (that is, the process of telling emotionally compelling stories about the importance of conversion) are designed to prompt a commitment in the listener herself, who has been reading her own identity "into" these narratives and now must decide how she will respond. Calling a particular series of choices "sin," labeling the remission of cancer an "answered prayer," or contextualizing an act of violence as "evil" all involve adopting words that reflect the acceptance of a particular reality. This adoption is emotionally driven, for whether persuaded by images of fiery damnation or of God's accepting love and grace, being emotionally primed for the message is a critical step in determining whether it will be adopted, and thus whether the conversion will take place.[65]

While Harding's model closely parallels Burke's aforementioned terministic screen, Harding's focus explains the regenerative power (or more simply put, the popularity) of such rhetoric. In Harding's model, when the hearer (the "witnessee") acquires this new language and thereby successfully converts, he is transformed into a "witnesser," now ready to speak the new language to others and posit this new reality, just as was done to him. Adopting the language of the group and thereby accepting its terms as reality is thus not a simple process of logic, wherein a listener objectively considers the rationale behind an argument. Instead, conversions of all sorts (religious or otherwise) involve this careful manipulation of emotions through compelling language meant to be repeated.

Creating moments of rhetorical conversion thus involves employing language in such a way that its symbols and messages are at their most emotionally potent, a process enabled by four tactics endemic to most chaos rhetoric: first, chaos rhetoric demands the taking of sides, which both solidifies commitment and serves as something of a recruitment tool; second, chaos rhetoric enables and encourages defensive argumentation, thereby enabling tremendous symbolic flexibility while minimizing attention to the group's own cultural shifts; third, chaos rhetoric allows for the rationale behind an argument to be relocated, or refocused, onto another, more politically expedient overt threat; and finally, chaos rhetoric is a mechanism that incites activism.

Taking Sides

The success of most rhetorical projects depends on the audience taking sides, and so the discourse that a group creates is first and foremost designed to designate lines of social distinction. Political power—understood in terms of votes, community activism, rallies, and emails—is typically the result of strong feelings, not lukewarm sentiment, and thus a group's opponents are frequently caricatured in extreme ways. This is why feminists are often portrayed by CWA as women who categorically hate men, despite the fact that few feminists would likely support this view. However persuasive caricatured portrayals may be, though, their exaggerated nature can sometimes seem silly or unrealistic to the degree that they backfire, causing audiences to question the validity of their claims. More often, subtler forms of dichotomization are used that still maintain a diametrically oppositional (and thus persuasively divisive) world, but one that is less likely to be called into question.

Consider the employment application required of prospective CWA college interns, wherein applicants are asked to answer a true/false style quiz that engages their level of agreement with certain issues. These include statements such as "Women who stay at home to raise a family are missing out," and "The U.S. Constitution is an evolving document that must adapt to today's needs." There is no possibility for an essay answer to explicate the statements; it is fully suggested that a "T" or "F" is an adequate response. The irony is missed on another true/false question, which asks the applicant to respond to the following: "Right and wrong is never black and white; it is important to consider the shades of gray in any decision."[66]

Chaos rhetoric reinforces this dichotomous tendency through its assertion that the threat to the group's order is so great that there is no ideological space for "shades of gray." It is almost always constructed in such a way that the reader cannot identify with CWA's opponent while considering herself reasonable and moral. In the form of narrative internalization earlier described, readers take in the rhetoric and thus become a part of the story themselves.

This rhetorical practice comes to life in the following passage. Writing on the day of the decision legalizing gay marriage in Iowa, a CWA representative remarks:

> This case proves once again that the only way to assure that the institution of marriage is protected in Iowa is to pass a constitutional marriage amendment. Any legislator not willing to sponsor such a bill is proving their [*sic*] loyalty with political agendas and not with the people of Iowa or the intent of our Founding Fathers.[67]

Here the threat to marriage is so dire that one cannot waiver. Either the reader stands on the side of political agendas—read here as selfish politicking—or on that of the self-evident good of the average American and America's principles (as implied in the statements "the people" and the "Founding Fathers"). In this sense, "any legislator" does not function specifically as a comment on government officials, for it is the audience's role in this conflict to incite resolution: either the audience will choose to side with political whims, or it will follow true patriotism. When the audience communicates with legislators about this issue, their own advocacy of this position creates political force. Thus the reader narratively becomes the first part of the legislative process.

To CWA, one cannot support democracy ("the people") or claim patriotism while also supporting gay marriage. Note how Crouse critiques President Obama regarding the Defense of Marriage Act (DOMA), which defines marriage in strictly heterosexual terms:

> The Obama Administration is at it again; they are saying one thing while doing another. While the President defends marriage publicly, his administration is working behind the scenes to undermine the DOMA through legal action—filing court papers complaining that the bill discriminates against same-sex couples.[68]

In this exchange, the reader's own moral culpability is called into question: will he support the President, a secretive hypocrite, someone who is "at it again"? The self-evident goodness of heterosexual marriage is familiar and understood, juxtaposed with Obama's hypocrisy and "complaining." Within the terms of this chaos rhetoric, the reasonable reader cannot side with any position other than the one that CWA asserts and still maintain a sense of his own logical dignity.

Defensive Argumentation

Convincing an audience to take sides does not just create divisions between people, groups, and issues, however. As discussed earlier in the context of abjection, one of the ironies of a dichotomized worldview is that it is a prime example of social interdependency: delimiting the parameters of one group directly affects the identity of another, and this is why a group's opponents provide what is perhaps the most important criterion in crafting that group's identity (e.g., supporters of abortion rights are not, by definition, opponents of those rights). While this may sound simplistic, it is a point of utter importance, for there is no such thing as one-sided discourse. As such, chaos rhetoric is almost always, by definition, *wrought defensively*; that is, it centers more on the threat to a beloved symbol or sense of order rather than on that symbol or order itself. Because negative emotions often prove more persuasive than positive ones, this is the natural place for CWA to focus if it hopes to attract political attention.

Defensive argumentation is one of the most important functions of chaos rhetoric, if not its fundamental expression. If a group can deflect attention away from itself by focusing on its opponents, it can more imperceptibly smooth over ambiguities and inconsistencies in its own platforms, often by renegotiating how it uses certain words or concepts.[69] This is even more important for groups that highlight the eternal, absolute nature of their positions (like CWA), but that must nevertheless change their absolutist positions over time—sometimes in very fundamental ways. Although hiding indiscretions is an important part of the work that defensive argumentation performs, it also allows the group to deduce what its own positions should be; those issues that the public finds most persuasive are typically those that CWA defines as most urgent. Thus by re-creating the terms under which its enemy is defined, CWA can create the symbolic space where it can more subtly craft its own platforms.

For instance, early in her writing career, LaHaye argued that "feminism is more than an illness; it is a philosophy of death."[70] In the midst of the 1960s ERA battles, one of feminism's most prominent political acts was the fight to create equal working opportunities for women. Yet for a woman to desire money of her own was ultimately selfish, LaHaye argued, and compromised the order that God had created for human families: if "the feminists succeed in upsetting God's order, the result will be chaos and misery for the entire civilization."[71] Less than a decade later, LaHaye's newer writing reversed this position.[72] In this relatively short period, LaHaye went from strongly discouraging women to work outside the home to encouraging them to further their educations, professional lives, and financial standings.[73] Despite the change in perspective, feminism remained a prominent enemy a decade later, but one re-contextualized: "In their fierce independence, feminists want to shrug off all authority, regardless of the source. This includes, of course, men, government, culture, and God."[74] The dangers of feminism shifted towards the hedonistic, anarchist, godless lesbian at the same time as the conservative *working* mother, wife, and activist ideal emerged as an important symbol in conservative politics.

As a continuation of this defensive tactic, consider also the fact that, as recently as 2003, the CWA website was careful to point out that LaHaye's professional career did not begin until her children were older.[75] Today, this statement is no longer featured as a part of her biography.[76] The family lives of most of the central staff are but briefly stated; Nance's husband and children are mentioned in the last line of her bio, long after her professional achievements. Before Nance, the two most significant faces of CWA (Wright and Crouse) had or continue to have nothing in their biographies about their families, despite the fact that at other places on the website at least one of them explicitly discusses having a spouse and children.[77] Had the definition of feminism remained static since the 1960s, it would have described CWA's most prominent female figures. But through a renegotiation of terms, feminism is no longer synonymous only with "working woman," but with lesbianism, liberalism, and any other non-conservative gendered cause.

Another example of this defensive strategy was featured on the CWA website on the eve of the 2012 presidential election. In the days preceding the election, a pro-Obama ad campaign featuring popular Hollywood writer/actress Lena Dunham aired on Obama's website, focusing on the limitations that conservative social policy would have on women's reproductive rights. Dunham spoke to women about the importance of "your first time," a reference intended to humorously employ the *double entendre* of a first sexual encounter, portraying it as an experience not unlike many young women's first opportunity to vote.[78]

Like many conservative organizations, CWA took offense at the ad, but chose a rather novel way to respond. Although CWA has a long history of defining itself by its rejection of liberal reproductive health policy, it chose to bypass that discussion altogether in a race where conservative platforms on reproductive control were less likely to have helped its cause. To accomplish this, CWA first responded to the Obama campaign by criticizing its treatment of women as a monolithic entity:

> Responding to Liberal Hollywood's effort to convince women that this election is all about free birth control, Concerned Women for America Legislative Action Committee's (CWALAC) "Lady Smarts" ad campaign serves as a reminder that women will be thinking about jobs and the economy as they cast their ballots.[79]

CWA's legislative action arm (CWALAC) subsequently produced an advertisement that contained a series of images of young professional women, linking the dire financial situation of each to the Obama administration. Each woman's picture is superimposed with text describing her financial hardship ("If she worked at the Obama White House, she'd be earning 18% less than men"; and "Has an MBA—Is waiting tables"). A final image in the CWA ad campaign depicts a young conservative woman at her computer. The superimposed text reads: "Tired of letting others define what she cares about. Voting on November 6 for the first time."[80]

Through this juxtaposition of image and text, CWA responded to a competing advertisement on reproductive rights by almost entirely avoiding the topic of reproduction altogether. Despite the centrality of reproductive issues to its political vitality, CWA here attempted to separate itself from that discussion when such a portrayal was not politically advantageous. Instead, it tried to delegitimize the Democrats' advertisement by locating concern over reproductive health measures as an oversimplification of the political lives of women, steering them instead towards the troubled economy.

Rationale-Deflection

If re-negotiating or caricaturizing the identity of an opponent is an effective tool of deflection, another deflective mechanism is the relocation of a group's rationale. In this technique, CWA chaos rhetoric often appeals to the authorities of science, health, or another already-authoritative voice to shift the motivation for its arguments away from what appears to be its more fundamental concern, thus giving readers and listeners a more socially persuasive logic for their activist stance.

In the very recent past, CWA has conducted a focused campaign against Gardasil, a vaccine against one form of the Human Papilloma Virus (HPV). HPV is a sexually transmitted disease known to cause some forms of cervical cancer. As early as 2005, before the release of Gardasil, CWA praised the Centers for Disease Control (CDC) for acknowledging that HPV caused cervical cancer. That article included this statement:

> The facts about HPV once again reveal the wisdom in God's plan for faithful marriages: The only 100 percent sure prevention is sexual abstinence until one enters a mutually monogamous marriage with an uninfected person. Sex outside of marriage brings many health risks, including high-risk types of HPV. It's about time that the CDC has come forward and started to be honest with women about the connections among promiscuity, STDs [sexually transmitted diseases] and cancer.[81]

While CWA's praise of the CDC focused on its connection between promiscuous sexual behavior and cancer, the rhetorical tactic shifted when Gardasil was introduced to the market. CWA began a virulent campaign against its use, despite the fact that it had earlier described HPV as "high risk." Its complaint against Gardasil has been threefold. First, it asserts that mandated Gardasil vaccinations (such as those that were enacted in the state of Texas) have infringed on parents' rights to control their child's medical treatment. Second, it claims that Gardasil has risky side effects that may harm, rather than promote, the health of those girls given the vaccine. Finally, it argues that Gardasil provides a sense of false security because it cannot protect against all forms of HPV, the length of its efficacy is unknown, and it is not one hundred percent effective.

In almost every CWA article against Gardasil, a fourth concern is briefly mentioned: Gardasil will increase promiscuity among teens because it removes one negative ramification of extramarital sex. Despite the relatively small amount of press that this matter receives, this appears nevertheless to be the dominant rationale for CWA's opinion about the drug. Were CWA's true interest solely invested in parents' rights, risky side effects, and ineffective vaccines, then it seems only logical that it would have been a vocal contributor to the still-raging debate over the safety of other, much more common, and almost always mandatory vaccinations. These include customary childhood vaccines such as the MMR (measles, mumps, and rubella), the purported effects of which have resulted in thousands of medical studies and the worldwide formation of activist groups who have alleged that the vaccine is linked to autism and other debilitating health conditions. The fact that CWA has focused on Gardasil but has failed to comment on a series of other, far more controversial, vaccinations is an indication that its preeminent concern is neither safety nor parents' rights, but sexual regulation.

Race is another arena in which rationale-deflection has been heavily deployed. As discussed in the last chapter, the Christian Right and racial civil rights groups have long had a troubled relationship, in great part because conservatives have typically located the source of racial inequity in individual moral failure, whether on the part of individuals who choose racist behaviors or on the part of racial minorities who make poor choices. Large scale social injustices endemic to American culture are typically not identified as the source of racism and its related problems.[82]

Despite this history, CWA is like other Christian Right groups in its occasional self-depiction as an organization devoted to fighting racism. In 2009, President Obama nominated Latina Sonia Sotomayor to the Supreme Court, a move strongly criticized by CWA. The bulk of CWA's overt interest in Sotomayor was grounded in its claim that she was a racist, an assertion based on her ruling against a group of white Connecticut firemen whose job promotion was put on hold because racial minorities did not score as well on the firefighter promotion exam (a case later overturned by the Supreme Court on the grounds of reverse discrimination). CWA built its case against Sotomayor from her now infamous quote: "I would hope that a wise Latina woman with the richness of her experiences would more often than not reach a better conclusion [as a judge] than a white male who hasn't lived that life."[83]

During her nomination hearings, Sotomayor's words were featured on a graphic on the CWA homepage alongside certain phrases from the Bill of Rights. In the graphic, the phrase "We hold these truths to be self-evident; that all men are created equal" flashed on the screen, alongside a traditional Founding Fathers image featuring white men in powdered wigs. CWA replaced that image with Sotomayor's words (above) critiquing the life experiences of white males, this featured alongside an unflattering picture of her sneering. The graphic ended with the juxtaposition of partial quotes; "We hold these truths to be self-evident; that all men are created equal" appeared first, and was then set aside "white males who haven't lived that life." The reader was then presented with a link that read, "Help us defend Liberty! Click here!" Upon clicking the link, the reader was led to CWA's account of the Sotomayor confirmation hearings, where he was urged to oppose her nomination on the grounds of her racism.

In openly contrasting Sotomayor with the Bill of Rights (through text, image, and visual juxtaposition), the reader is compelled to reject Sotomayor's claims about race because these claims symbolically stand in opposition to liberty. Yet whether one agrees with CWA's analysis is secondary to the issue of whether CWA's proclaimed interest in racism is consistent with its wider cultural treatment of the issue. In most CWA chaos rhetoric, racism is used as a banner that generically describes what it perceives to be unfair social bias. However much this is often located as an individual moral problem, there are predictable moments when CWA references racism as a socio-structural phenomenon. Generally speaking, these are when CWA seeks to define acceptable minority status (that is, an innate identity) as a foil against which homosexuality (identified as a choice) can be delegitimized.

It is interesting that in the almost eight years that I consistently read the CWA website, only three times did I come across articles that spoke out vocally against racism. On two occasions, anti-racist rhetoric was used to defend white men against reverse discrimination. John McCain was the first, in his run for the presidency against Barack Obama; the second was the Sotomayor firefighter case, mentioned above. The third instance of CWA's anti-racist rhetoric involved a black Christian woman who lost her job after expressing anti-homosexual viewpoints at work. The article depicted the woman as the true minority doubly victimized by her conservative Christian and African American identities, contrasting her with homosexuals who claim victimization through illegitimate minority status.

If CWA's preeminent concern has been fighting racism, then it seems that it would have spoken out against many other moments of overt racism in American culture rather than focusing on the occasional reverse discrimination charge. Based on its rhetoric, one could make the case that CWA's interest in the issue has had more to do with using the arguments behind anti-racist activism to legitimize its own political positions rather than to actively campaign for an end to racial discrimination. The portrayal of some issues (at the expense of others) highlights the priorities of the organization's public advocacy.

Inciting Activism

Believing strongly in something is not enough to incite activist behavior. Rather, the shift from belief to action happens with a change in the perceived degree of threat, or the sense that one will meet greater success in battling that threat than was possible at other times.[84] The emotion-evoking power of chaos rhetoric creates a dire situation that demands response, while the institutions that craft such rhetoric often provide the organizational structures to make such activism possible. As such, a fourth tactic of CWA's chaos rhetoric is to create the perception of an elevated degree of threat sufficient to compel the reader to respond in ways that make a political impact. For CWA, prompting activism often occurs in overt ways, such as providing the reader contact information for a government official (often with a pre-written letter provided) or asking for a monetary donation. Yet despite these more explicit forms of engagement, CWA asks its supporters far more often for prayer.

Prayer is often portrayed by CWA as the most important power that it holds. Whether or not one believes in the efficacy of prayer, it still remains an important modality for CWA to emphasize if only because it is an easy entry into activism: unlike other forms of political involvement, it demands little to no sacrifice of time or money and can be performed anonymously, anytime, and anywhere. It is also the first step in more direct activism. Perhaps a reader has never prayed about the issues CWA engages. Deciding to pray (and thereby following the cues to pray provided by the website) represents a greater degree of activism than she had previously engaged. The level of commitment needed to sustain continual prayer may then make her more likely to entertain the possibility of a monetary donation, or a letter to a senator. This sort of "invisible activism" may therefore prime her for future opportunities in which she will decide to participate in progressively more obvious, direct efforts at political involvement.

Additionally, invoking blatant religious themes serves another important rhetorical function. If religious rhetoric is about drawing upon a perceived "ultimate" authority, there is perhaps no better time to employ this rhetoric than when those who are already committed to religious claims are straddling the fence and need to be convinced to act.[85] In a brochure that urges activism on behalf of CWA, former CWA president Wendy Wright recounts her arrest after protesting outside an abortion clinic:

> I mentioned that I had been jailed for praying. When I was in Houston, jailed for praying, the judge declared that I could be released from jail if I would simply agree not to do it again. If I promised that I would not pray in public at an abortion clinic again, I could leave jail. I couldn't do that. I couldn't promise that. Most of the people in the prison system knew why I was there. And they knew this condition on my sentence. One time when I was walking down a long hallway to my cell, a big prison guard yelled out at me, "Don't be discouraged—and don't give in to the judge!" That's our charge tonight. Don't be discouraged, and don't give in to those who would judge us for trying to keep our country free.[86]

Wright's words not only conflate prayer with sacrificial action but with freedom's very survival. The government is the agent explicitly depicted as an oppressive vehicle imposing inappropriate religious limitations (as seen in Wright's description of her crime not as blocking the entrance to a clinic—the actual violation—but as "prayer").[87] This is juxtaposed with Wright, who chose to break the law and face incarceration over the sacrifice of what she describes as her Christian principles. Throughout the CWA website, a prominent theme is that one cannot maintain her status as "upstanding patriotic Christian" without an activist response, as Wright continues:

> Everybody needs to call their Members of Congress to express outrage at the amount of money going to Planned Parenthood and other groups that are promoting comprehensive sex education and

> spreading falsehoods about the effectiveness of abstinence programs. We need to quit funding groups who give out false information that leaves our teens vulnerable in ways that affect the rest of their lives.[88]

The reader (part of the communal "we") is already part of the narrative, part of a morally reprehensible group that is responsible for spreading lies. Indeed, there is a strong sense that "true Christians" are separated from the lukewarm ones by their willingness to stand apart and act.

Despite the extent of Wright's activist sacrifice, it is enough for the average reader to become a moral hero through a simple click on a link, something CWA's website readily enables. A few keystrokes allow the reader to offer a donation, sign a petition, or contact a congressperson. For an extended time, CWA's homepage prominently featured the oft-quoted words of Edward Burke: "All that is necessary for the triumph of evil is that good men do nothing." As the reader watched, Burke's words faded, and were replaced by an invitation to subscribe to CWA e-alerts, which promised to send "briefings, news, and information on the issues that matter most to you and your family" directly to a subscriber's email. Such emails contained information needed to "impact public policy in Washington, at your state capitol, or in your own community."[89]

Receiving these e-alerts is thus commensurate with "doing something," to echo Burke, for in each message, urgency is always emphasized; timing is critical, for they are often sent out on the eve of important legislative decisions. The following email was sent to CWA members immediately after President Obama first addressed Congress and the nation regarding healthcare reform:

> Make no mistake about it; abortion **will** be funded by the government through the new health care plan. Planned Parenthood and the abortion lobby have been waiting for this day when abortion will be included as part of comprehensive health care reform. . . . This is why we are launching **today** the VOID THE ABORTION MANDATE virtual rally and grassroots campaign.
>
> President Obama and every single Member of Congress must continue to hear from **YOU**, their constituents. Your voice **IS** getting through! . . . We need **YOUR** help! Since all of you can't be together in the same place for this launch, we are asking you to please use every virtual tool at your disposal to help get the message out.

Here's what you can do:

- Please post our Void the Abortion Mandate logo and sample status messages on your Twitter, Facebook, MySpace and other social networking websites. Download the graphic, and copy the messages at www.StopTheAbortionMandate.com.
- Click on the Voided Check logo at www.StopTheAbortionMandate.com and send a voided check to your elected Representatives. Tell them you don't want the government funding abortion.
- Having a hard time explaining why abortion is covered under the health care plan? Download our new chart to show how it happens. Download it at www.StopTheAbortionMandate.com.
- Need more resources? Go to www.StopTheAbortionMandate.com/Coalition/Resources/ to learn more about the Hyde Amendment, government funding of abortion, and other important topics surrounding the abortion mandate.[90]

This particular piece of rhetoric starts with something akin to a crisis of authority. The reader should "make no mistake about it," for believing Obama's words on abortion amounts to believing a lie; there is an "abortion mandate." CWA thus establishes itself as a transparent agent of truth compared to liberal forces that seek to incorporate abortion into healthcare reform as part of an ongoing, covert plan (as seen in the phrase "waiting for this day").

Because of the way that Obama and Planned Parenthood are rhetorically linked and then fused with this act of deception, the reader must decide where he fits within the narrative. Either he sides with those who create deception, or he fights it. The grassroots campaign is CWA's response to those who identify with the latter, and who are encouraged personally of their individual efficacy in the process ("Your voice IS getting through!"). To identify with the narrative is not only an ideological commitment (should one identify with deception, or not?) but also an activist one (should one act with those who love truth, or not?). "Every single Member of Congress" and "every virtual tool" must be involved in this campaign. Following the links in the text is but one way that the reader tells the government that "you don't want the government funding abortion."

In this way, the reader can become an activist through a series of simple procedures ("post," "download," "copy," "click") that sends a symbolic "voided check" to government officials. The voided check image is a powerful one, for it reinforces the identity statement necessary to activism: namely, that the people (that is, readers) are really the ones in the position of legislative authority, as they hold the financial purse-strings and thus can command how the nation's finances are used. The physical and moral onus for activity is thereby placed on the reader, for if one believes Burke's comment that evil triumphs because of the complacency of the good, then failing to act is nothing short of condoning evil. That the audience may not fully understand the details of the email's rationale is presumed ("Having a hard time explaining . . . ?"), but this need not detract from activism. "Resources" and "charts" are available to remedy the information gap.

It is this focus on information that ultimately characterizes CWA's self-depiction. While it casts its own brand of objective data as the centerpiece of truth, this truth depends heavily on chaos rhetoric as its persuasive element. This must be so, because within CWA's worldview, facts are ultimately empty without activism, which is not spurred on without an imminent threat. By fusing the emotionally familiar with an unknown, dangerous element, CWA succeeds in making its arguments appear natural, logical, and timeless to a large portion of the population. Sex is the cornerstone of these arguments, for in its control through gender, reproduction, and other related platforms, the group not only manages the many social realms that sex impacts, but can also capitalize on the moral importance lent to sex, sexual identities, and gender. Chaos rhetoric thus allows it to engage culture through extremely potent symbols, but also incites activism, polarizes issues, changes "eternal" positions, and deflects the group's real rationale onto more persuasive agendas and themes.

What this means is that chaos rhetoric's most important trait is its plasticity, a sort of dynamism without which many social groups could not weather the political storms. As the next chapter will show, so long as it can consign its enemies to various realms of inaccuracy and immorality, CWA can flexibly reconstitute its image in almost any fashion needed, even in ways that may seem, on the surface, to contradict its own political positions.

3

All Things to All People: CWA as "True" Feminism

> *The left's feminists are perpetually in opposition to women of faith, a total partisan rejection of all things concerning Christian faith, the value of life, and family. They have an ideological agenda usurped by abortion rights and expressed through anger. It is wholly unattractive to most people.*[1]
>
> —JANNE MYRDAL, Concerned Women for America

EVERY FALL, I teach a course on feminist theory. I devote the first two weeks of the course to discussing the cultural uses of the term *feminism*. This may seem an extraordinary amount of time to give to a single term, but because of the pervasively negative connotation that the word still holds in American culture today, this conversation could easily go on the entire semester. This is not because of widespread antipathy towards the social advances of feminism, for like my students, most women are generally in support of the movement's push to create social equity even as they express disdain for the term itself.[2] Rather, such distaste is due to large-scale campaigns that have gone on for decades, waged by groups like CWA, that seek to describe the social shifts wrought by feminism as destructive. By the time they attend the first day of my course, most of my students are familiar with the stereotype of feminists as radical, angry women with a victim mentality; most also report being mocked by friends and family who ask why they are taking such a class.

Reflecting the cultural current it has helped to create, CWA devotes significant space on its website to demonizing feminists for being inherently anti-woman, anti-family, and thus anti-Christian, thereby attempting to render the liberal feminist movement something entirely outside of the mainstream of American life. Yet, despite CWA's role in creating this generalized antipathy towards feminists, its own website features several essays that use this same sort of chaos rhetoric to describe itself as the embodiment of "true," or conservative, feminism. CWA makes this claim by placing itself within a long lineage of nineteenth- and twentieth-century Christian female activist groups organized to clean up sin in American culture, calling these women the "original" feminists.

So which is it—or can it be both? It is not terribly surprising that such a paradox has emerged from a group whose own genesis has been equally paradoxical. After all, one can attribute the greater political visibility and power of modern women to the gains won by liberal feminism during the 1960s and 1970s; ironically, such empowerment has enabled CWA, in turn, to employ anti-feminist activism. Many liberal feminists and other contemporary observers have responded by describing groups like CWA as co-opting, or hijacking, otherwise liberal values, tactics, and rhetoric.[3]

Rather than claim that any one group "owns" feminism or female activism, this chapter will consider how CWA has used its identity as a women's organization to forward its political preferences, focusing specifically on how it deploys chaos rhetoric to identify as an anti-feminist organization while simultaneously touting itself as feminism's original, untainted expression. While I concur with other observers who remark that conservative women would not have nearly the same political voice were it not for the advances won by liberal feminism, I believe there is another dimension to consider, for how CWA deploys the term *feminism* in its rhetoric is hardly monolithic. As this chapter will show, CWA is able to manufacture the term in a wide variety of ways through its use of both logic and populist argumentation. Rather than attempting to recuperate a consistent claim about gendered inequity, and thereby form a cohesive feminist theory, CWA uses feminism as a tremendously elastic metaphor: it can relegate liberal feminists to an immoral realm of fringe illogic at the same time that it locates "conservative feminism" as a righteous, rational, and mainstream position.

This renegotiation of terms is achieved through one of chaos rhetoric's most basic tactics—defensive argumentation—which will be specifically highlighted in this chapter. Defensive argumentation was previously introduced as chaos rhetoric's hallmark; by focusing on a threat to the group's ideals, rather than those ideals themselves, the group can capitalize on the high persuasive value of negative emotion to undermine its opponents while also shifting attention away from its own dynamic changes and inconsistencies. In short, groups that use defensive argumentation manage their own personas by first managing the personas of their opponents.

What this means is that CWA has been able to craft itself into a powerful and righteous female subject, one that wears several different, flexible, strategically wrought faces, all through a series of linguistic strategies that relegate liberals generally (and liberal feminists, more specifically) to an ideological location inconsistent with logic and mainstream appeal. Once liberals have been portrayed in a negative light, CWA can then move freely between various identities that allow it to craft its own self-portrayal as the representation, protection, and embodiment of the true American woman, uniquely able to speak on matters of sex, gender, and reproduction.

Markers of the Righteous Woman

No matter whether describing itself as anti-feminist or the expression of true feminism, CWA can identify and speak against its enemies because it relies on the longstanding symbol of the righteous woman and her inherent moral sensibilities. As discussed in Chapter 1, enduring stories have been told throughout American culture that fuse together white female identity with religion and morality. These narratives locate a naturally nurturing, emotional, intuitive, moral woman as the arbiter of the nation's future, since it is through these characteristics that morality is passed on to her family. If these personal relationships do not define her identity, so the story goes, then morality cannot be successfully transferred throughout the generations.

This perception of women has formed the basis of many traditional gender role arguments, which typically cast women primarily as moral caretakers who must avoid the public spotlight (as well as competition with men) in order to let their "true natures" shine. Yet this thinking also sets up a "good mother/bad mother" dichotomy, one wherein women are either praised or blamed for the fate of the nation.[4] While it is tempting to think that this exalted status has granted women tremendous social influence, it has practically functioned as a mechanism of social restraint: in times of perceived moral decline, women have often been blamed for their failure to be "properly" female; in moments of national triumph, they have often been lauded through their revalorization as mothers, wives, and caretakers. This is a story with a tremendously long lifeline: it was told among the Victorians in their espousal of the "separate spheres" ideal; used by early twentieth-century conservative women fighting their own right to vote; publicized again during the middle twentieth century as tensions rose over America's world dominance; and is now recuperated in groups like CWA that claim that the liberal stances on sex, gender, and reproduction are a death grip causing a multitude of social ills. In every time period, a change in traditional gender roles has sparked a moral campaign warning of the unraveling of the social fabric.

With this historical context in mind, it is critical to understand how CWA crafts its own self-portrayal as a women's organization. It stands behind the traditional, essentialized image of the moral and nurturing woman, yet it must also find a way to tap into other identities that are more politically advantageous—that is, identities that will justify its own public, political involvement in a "man's world." In interviews conducted with CWA employees, Ronnee Schreiber notes that the organization's largely female workforce expended considerable energy addressing the importance of stay-at-home motherhood at the same time that all of them worked outside of their homes for CWA.[5] This very reality has required a reinterpretation of traditional gender roles in a way that can justify CWA's own political engagement.

What must be part of this reinterpretation? A first, critical concern is how feminism should be understood. In CWA's chaos rhetoric, feminism (whether positively or negatively rendered) almost always represents female identity, political activism, and radical social change. Because CWA embodies all of these things in its own politics, its audience must embrace these as legitimate goals in order to maintain the organization's credibility. But because these things are also characteristics of liberal feminism, CWA must strategically demonstrate how liberal feminism has twisted these elements for immoral aims. Accordingly, CWA must constitute itself as an entity with the morality and logic of a conservative woman, but the activist and gendered impulse more frequently identified with the liberal feminist.

This does not imply that CWA is a hybrid of feminism and conservatism, for the term *hybrid* often connotes the combination of two or more otherwise pure and stable entities. Rather than claim that CWA embodies any sort of authentic essence called "conservatism" or "feminism," I want to situate its rhetorical self-portrayal as a constant negotiation of labels that are produced in certain, politically expedient combinations, much like Judith Butler's description of the process behind the creation of social identity.

In line with her earlier discussions of identity formation, Butler observes that the labels used to identify persons and groups are not perfectly descriptive because they are, instead, political categories intended to highlight, favor, and normalize certain distinctions over others.[6] For instance, there are any number of traits that any one particular woman might hold; she might have traditionally "masculine" features such as a deep voice or great physical strength, all the while still remaining biologically female (if we measure this by reproductive organs and chromosomes). Butler's point is that while any one individual can have almost any imaginable trait while still being lumped under the auspices of a label ("woman"), the label nevertheless defines a set of common descriptors that are not intended to accurately describe each individual named by it. Instead, the purpose of the label is to politically standardize, normalize, and thereby constrain a suitable identity for the people classified in that manner.[7] Thus, many individuals who are biologically female (and who also have a deep voice and are physically strong) may nevertheless be deemed socially inadequate women (too masculine, "butch," or unattractive) because they fail to meet a certain "feminine" cultural standard.

This political renegotiation of labels is a critical part of understanding how CWA can paint its own self-portrayal as a conservative feminist organization, and as one that represents "real women" more generally. Part of its own identity-building revolves heavily around its use of *strategic essentialism*, the term that post-colonial theorist Gayatri Spivak has used to describe a group's deliberate deployment of essentialist identity tactics in order to effect the political changes it desires, even if the group may find such essentialist tactics undesirable in other situations, or even a generally poor descriptor of its identity altogether.[8] In her own examination of conservative women's groups, Schreiber, for one, has used Spivak's model to describe how groups like CWA may at one point distance themselves from gendered arguments but may later employ them when it is more politically advantageous, such as when they want to influence "women's issues" like childcare or reproductive policy.[9]

I want to amplify Schreiber's claim by suggesting that CWA's use of strategic essentialism has not only involved using female identity when it is convenient, but has also meant a constant renegotiation of the cultural meaning behind the so-called essence "woman" so that, ironically, this presumably stable essence becomes a continuously shifting rhetorical product. This means that CWA's deployment of the category "woman" has, in a Butlerian move, first involved taking the term "woman" and imbuing it with a set of cultural meanings (nurturing, reproductive, heterosexual, mothering, affable) while simultaneously imparting liberal feminism with its own set of adjectives (angry, irrational, lesbian, radical). In each case, the specific meanings behind both sets of symbols are shaped and honed to persuade at that political moment. The function of this ongoing naming process works to effectively render all liberals, but particularly liberal feminists, "non-women" who are thus unable to speak for "real women." As a result, when CWA appeals to certain traits and abilities that "women" hold, it is often doing so via chaos rhetoric that separates the true women from the counterfeit ones who illegitimately speak on the other's behalf. No matter which liberal group is the target of its attack, CWA's ability to claim ideological ownership of the symbol "woman" is largely responsible for the defensive maneuvers that permit its self-portrayal as uniquely rational, mainstream, and progressive.

Representatives of Reason

These self-portrayals start in the organization's most fundamental claim: that "real" women are rational. By portraying itself as an inherently logical engine, CWA can contend that it legitimately speaks in the name of morality, for it is with this sense that the world is an ordered place, filled with the intentions of a logical God, that CWA's own logic first starts. There are certain historical ironies embedded in this assertion, for one of the more persistent critiques against conservative Christian movements has been that their theologies represent an assault on reason. Whether rejecting evolutionary theory, warning of the coming apocalypse, or locating natural disasters as the outcome of God's wrath, some of the most spectacular declarations made by conservative Christians intended to persuasively garner public attention have also simultaneously alienated them from sectors of the public that find those claims logically untenable.

It would be a mistake, however, to argue that the history of the ACP movement has been dominated by a completely anti-intellectualist tenor, for while many ACPs have certainly drawn conclusions that run counter to much scientific knowledge today, they have done so by embracing certain attitudes towards science, objectivity that have resulted in a sub-culture very focused on facts. As George Marsden tells the story, the history of the ACP movement has long involved the use of explicitly scientific methods to approach the Bible as data that must be mined for God's message. In his discussion of the construction of the early theological contours of ACP,

Marsden notes, "When scripture was looked upon as the compellingly perfect design of God, every detail was significant. Hence, even though the Bible was not intended to teach science, God had guided even the poetic language so as to anticipate scientific discoveries."[10] This encouraged a general attitude that has endured for well over a century, that "Biblical interpretation [is] an exact science with precise conclusions."[11]

In kind, ACPs have almost always legitimized their own supernatural or other logically untestable claims in ways that appeal to logic or science; the issue is whether this logic has been grounded in the same set of philosophical presumptions as those adopted by the mainstream scientific community. As such, the Christian Right's emphasis on "facts and figures" is a continuation of its cultural predecessors' attempts to gain public status through appeals to reason. Rather than simply referencing scientific facts for the purpose of being publicly persuasive (as the last chapter discussed), an important part of CWA's self-representation has also involved depicting itself as an agent of truth uniquely able to create and assess objective data in ways that others are not. Claiming that its arguments stand strong in both the secular and religious worlds, those who reject CWA's platforms (and who thus shun "reason") stand accused of irrational, or at least biased, thought.

In truistic fashion, persuasively claiming that one is objective and rational lends legitimacy to one's own arguments. Yet the data provided by CWA functions not only to authorize its claims, but also serves as a rhetorical character in its own right, taking on a life of its own in the narrative. Numbers and statistics are themselves regularly presented as righteous protagonists fighting against agents of deception. In the following article on abortion, statistics from the Centers for Disease Control (CDC) and other government data are featured; note how CWA interjects itself into this chaos rhetoric as an organization with explicit concern for procuring "reliable abortion statistics":

> Discerning the risks of abortion has become tricky in the age of poor reporting and cover-ups. Reliable abortion statistics are hard to obtain. Today, 45 states have some sort of mandatory abortion-reporting requirement. But the negligent abortionist has little incentive to keep up with paperwork.
>
> In the 1997 publication "Abortion Surveillance—United States, 1993–1994," the U.S. Centers for Disease Control (CDC) reported that in 1991, 13 women died as the result of abortion. But in that

> same paper, CDC admits that, due to underreporting, its calculations are likely low.
>
> Other facts bear this out. Between the years 1981 and 1984, CDC reports 42 women died from abortion. However, former Commissioner of Health for New York City, Dr. Stephen Joseph, stated in a 1987 memo to doctors that during that same period 176 women died as the result of abortion in the United States—*30 in New York alone.*
>
> Risks of health complications can be quite high, according to Dr. Slava V. Gaufberg, research director at Harvard University Medical School. He noted in the online medical textbook *Emergency Medicine* that the rate of complications in second- trimester abortions is "up to 50 percent and higher." But tracking the complications is not easy in the current political climate.[12]

Using the defensive argumentation tactic so common to chaos rhetoric, this piece makes possible a reading of CWA that first depends on depicting its opponents in an unflattering light. If liberal activists are working to bend the truth to their political purposes, then "reliable statistics" are difficult to come by; the "current political climate" (one in which abortion is legal) created by the "negligent abortionist" demonstrates as much. The rhetoric invokes truth (as opposed to the negligent abortionist's "cover up") and science (as seen in the article's heavy use of statistics) to form an overall moral judgment (abortion practitioners are guilty of ongoing deception). Supporting abortion rights is transformed into support for negligent doctors whose "cover-ups" kill. By first presenting its opponents in this manner, CWA can then position itself as the agency equipped to uncover such deception and thus protect women.

Here and in many other articles, CWA represents itself not only as an agent of truth, but also "fact," a term often used to describe an unalterable objective essence that makes truth claims possible. Liberals are portrayed as simply uninterested in identifying real facts because they do not provide them political benefit, or, more often, they are incapable of identifying facts because they lack the morality that enables objectivity. Thus liberals exist in a state of permanent bias.

Claims of bias are utilized frequently in CWA speech, and like the aforementioned category "data," often become characters in their own right ("the biased" versus "the objective") that narratively vie for the public's support. CWA has attached these labels to specific subjects in interesting ways. "Bias" is treated as a self-evident category used to point out the selfish interests that influence the politics of CWA's opponents. In CWA's use of the term, however, what constitutes "selfish interest" can be anything from simply disagreeing with CWA to having a secondary interest in the success of a political position. This distinction is seen in an essay where CWA addresses statements made by the Sexuality Information and Education Council of the United States (SIECUS), an agency that it has long opposed for its outspoken support of comprehensive sexual education:[13]

> In a blatantly biased and a shamelessly self-promoting press release, the Sexuality Information and Education Council of the United States (SIECUS) announced the release of their "groundbreaking" publication, *SIECUS State Profiles: A Portrait of Sexuality Education and Abstinence-Only-Until-Marriage Programs in the States.* The publication is the result of two years of "research" and claims to be the "most complete" and "comprehensive" portrait of "what the nation's young people are, and in many cases, are not learning with respect to their sexual health. . . ."
>
> [A chief complaint made by SIECUS] "is that grants are mostly given to Southern states and to groups that "pose" as medical providers (crisis pregnancy centers and "anti-abortion" groups). 'These organizations,' according to SIECUS, 'run programs that consistently use medical misinformation, including anti-abortion messages, are religious in nature, and are biased against homosexuals. All lack oversight and evaluation.' This, remember, is supposed to be legitimate research and analysis—two years in the making—not biased propaganda.
>
> Krenin [SIECUS's C.E.O.] claims that 61 percent of young people have sexual intercourse before they graduate from high school and that "unproven" abstinence programs leave "too many of our kids at risk." The fact of having sexual intercourse, in her reasoning, is NOT the problem facing today's teens. [Her] conclusion is that funding for abstinence programs should stop immediately and that money, instead, go toward funding comprehensive programs "that work." Those programs are the basis for SIECUS' income and give a hint as to the source of the bias in the SIECUS report.[14]

CWA appeals to truth, accuracy (in contrast to SIECUS's biased propaganda), and logic (SIECUS's misapprehension of "the problem") to argue for the existence, and presumed immorality, of what it calls

SIECUS's anti-religious prejudice (here addressing SIECUS's critique that religious groups "pose as medical providers"). Under the terms of this chaos rhetoric, SIECUS cannot call its publication true "research," nor can it claim that its findings are "complete" or "comprehensive" because SIECUS has possible financial gain in such positions, reducing its stance into one of "shameless self-promotion." In this move, CWA can avoid addressing the statistical data and actual argumentation behind SIECUS's stance altogether by dismissing its report as "biased propaganda." By using this defensive position, CWA can symbolically assert itself as an organization capable of identifying "legitimate research and analysis" so long as it first delegitimizes SIECUS's ability to do the same.

Just as CWA contends that SIECUS has employed faulty logic in presuming that abstinence education programs do not work, CWA has used the "faulty logic" rationale to respond to a Connecticut State Supreme Court decision that a fetus is a part of a woman's body (and that, as a part of her body, may be aborted):

> Would the court agree that women don't have a male sex organ? This is not a trick question. If her fetus has one, then the fetus can't be part of her body or else the woman has a male sex organ. It's called logic, as in, "If elephants have monkeys on their backs and monkeys have fleas on their backs, then elephants have fleas on their backs". . . . The court concluded:
>
> "First, as with any bodily part, a fetus constitutes physically identifiable tissue. Second, implantation of the fetus occurs within the mother's uterus, and the fetus is attached to the mother via the umbilical cord and placenta. . . . Finally, the fetus is nourished and sustained by the mother; indeed, at five weeks of age, the fetus is incapable of survival outside the mother."
>
> Following this logic, a deep-sea diver attached to a ship by a tether and breathing apparatus, who is incapable of sustaining life without them, becomes a part of the ship. A submarine crew becomes a part of the sub, an airline passenger becomes a part of the plane (except for the nourishment part), a patient on life-support becomes a part of the hospital. (This would probably require approval from the Board of Zoning Appeals to remove life support. And, should the patient die, the court would probably order a building permit to remove him from that portion of the hospital.)[15]

Logic ("would the court agree that women don't have a male sex organ?") and science (the physiological status of the fetus) form the primary links in its argument, but they are accompanied by another linguistic strategy: ridicule. Many CWA articles use an acerbic or sarcastic tone through which to express righteous indignation. This is not merely a political emotion, for such displays further question the logic of the opponent by relegating its position to a realm of absurdity. Functioning also as a populist critique, strong emotion separates the reasonable and average person from the illogical extremist who endangers society at large. The opponent is portrayed as someone who has expressed something so indecent that the rational hearer automatically experiences both anger and disgust. In kind, consider this excerpt from Crouse, which addresses the ethics of liberals:

> It is bizarre how the left can howl about how inhumane it is to use the interrogation technique of "waterboarding" (which does no lasting physical harm) to extract information from terrorists, but they are just fine and dandy with death by dismemberment of unborn babies in the womb.
>
> To read their pious-sounding rhetoric about how essential the barbaric practice of abortion is to the health and well-being of women, one would be forgiven for thinking that abortion was the cornerstone of progress, that civilization only began to make headway when abortion became legal in this country. And naturally, feminists just want to share this priceless, newly-minted benefit with all the oppressed women of the world, who presumably have no other means of avoiding the Malthusian spectre [*sic*]: unending pregnancies and starving mouths to feed.[16]

Crouse's emotional response reinforces the rhetoric's dichotomy, which asserts that the logic of "the left" is so far outside the bounds of common sense ("bizarre") that it is synonymous with danger. As she responds to what she describes as a political position that protects terrorists but is "fine and dandy" with the "death by dismemberment" of babies, her highly charged words function to prime the reader to interpret liberals in a particular way: they are individuals who embrace a bizarre piety that protects the guilty and sacrifices the innocent. It is difficult to emotionally identify with Crouse's argument and still adopt the "liberal logic."

Rhetorically speaking, by consigning its opponents to realms of logical illegitimacy, CWA becomes the rational, moral agent capable of discerning truth, reason, and objectivity from the lies that liberals assert. This is a critical element in the success of chaos rhetoric, for CWA's own motives and truth-claims remain outside of the analysis and thus above the fray, allowing it to portray itself as an objective analyst and also an impassioned public advocate.

Representatives of the People

One of the most interesting aspects of an election cycle is witnessing otherwise powerful people claim that they're "just one of us," and certainly, politicians know that there is appeal in thinking that a candidate represents one's own values and understands one's daily concerns. Populist arguments are, in a sense, logical arguments in disguise, for the thinking behind them is that the common people are reasonable in a way that the powerful are not since those in power are blinded to the truth by their privilege. This is why it is so common for politicians to attack each other as "out of touch" or "extremists."

In a move to define its opponents outside of the boundaries of reason, CWA engages in the same sort of speech, calling out liberals on the grounds that they do not represent a mainstream voice that, the argument presumes, is inherently logical. CWA does this though charges of elitism. The elitist is one of the most persuasive and yet non-descript elements of CWA's chaos rhetoric, for talking about elitism is a way not only to identify an out-of-touch, yet powerful, enemy, but also to align itself as an entity that is on the side of the larger public. Although CWA repeatedly describes itself as little more than a network of average, ordinary women working together to incite grassroots change, it nevertheless remains an incredibly powerful political organization that, at times, displays the most salient qualities of elitism. As a result, it must defensively rework how it depicts elitists so as to exclude itself from the category.

Talk of the dangers of elitism has a long history within the ACP movement in arguments that tout the solidity of the average person's rational apprehension of the world. The "Scottish Common Sense" school, the nineteenth-century European movement that philosophically underpinned portions of early ACP thinking, argued that if the average person could apprehend the logic inherent within the world then they could understand the message of the Bible.[17] By this standard, complex doctrines that required arcane knowledge or years of schooling to comprehend had no place in standard Christian theology. Despite the popularity of this thinking, a significant tension has long existed among many conservative Christian groups regarding how to portray "the public" and its logic, for as certainly as the average person has found logic in the Bible, that person has disagreed with others like her on how to interpret that logic. Perhaps an even greater indictment of the reliability of the average Christian's "common sense" lies with past popular support for slavery by many white Christians (justified directly through the Bible).

CWA resolves this issue through its rhetorical control over how "the public" is defined. When polls and surveys show that most Americans do not agree with CWA's politics, CWA often marginalizes public opinion as something to be dismissed because the public has been poisoned by liberals. At these moments, it also often claims to hold minority status, portraying itself as an organization that is persecuted and oppressed because it preaches a truth that is unpopular in the larger culture. On the other hand, when public opinion aligns with CWA's positions, the public becomes an entity that embodies common sense, truth, and reliability. The people's words and convictions can be trusted as testament to the truth that elites cannot comprehend.

Because of this flexible positioning, CWA chaos rhetoric deploys charges of elitism in an extremely wide number of ways. The term is not necessarily used in its more traditional sense to designate the exclusionary activities of those who hold social power, but has become a wide descriptor of those who claim rights or resources that CWA opposes. Most often, CWA's charges of elitism revolve around the notion that rights are in short supply, and thus when one group has them, another group does not. Since rights are cast as limited and oppositional, judgments of legitimacy are necessary.

To this end, the category "special rights" has been frequently used in CWA chaos rhetoric to describe illegitimate claims for special legal protection inspired by personal choice rather than by immutable identity. Under the auspices of "special rights," CWA argues, morally improper choices are elevated to the realm of civil rights. Homosexuality is the most frequent topic discussed as a part of "special rights" advocacy. Consider this article supporting a marriage amendment in Missouri that defines marriage in strictly heterosexual terms, and which describes those who oppose the amendment as "elites." Their opposition to "the mainstream" earns them such a label:

> All major news media, the universities and even some corporations opposed the amendment, and you begin to see that the elites who embrace the homosexual agenda are far, far out of the mainstream," said Robert Knight, director of the Culture & Family Institute (CFI), an affiliate of Concerned Women for America (CWA). "The average person understands that weddings involve a bride and a groom, even if the elites don't get it.[18]

Here CWA sides with "the public" by reviving the argument on the inherent strength of the "average person's" sense of morality. This not only serves a logical function (the people have "common sense"), but a qualitative one as well—"most" people find gay marriage unreasonable. In a similar piece, populist arguments are used to assert that homosexuals are holding the public morally and economically hostage. The fact that "the public" is described as an entity that experiences discomfort is used as evidence to declare its powerlessness in the face of the homosexuals who dictate its decisions:

> The Center for American Progress is urging Congress to include special coverage for transgender individuals in health care reform legislation. They complain that most insurance plans do not cover medical procedures to change a person's sex. Adding these services would only raise premiums by an insignificant amount, they claim. (Which, by the way, is not because the services are inexpensive, it is because only a few people want them. Taxing the many to benefit the few, anyone?)
>
> Yet if you were to object to your loved one being placed in the same hospital room with someone of the opposite sex or to paying for someone's sex-change operation, you would be labeled "insensitive" and "homophobic." You will have done the unthinkable. You will have dared to question the golden calf of "sexual rights". . . . So why should I be forced to share a hospital room with someone who is biologically male? Why should I be forced to subsidize my co-worker's desired sex-change operation, even though I think it is immoral? Because transgender individuals have rights! Everyone has rights! That is, everyone except straight people.[19]

The chaos rhetoric employed here asserts that if one group has rights, another must lose them; at its core, this is an economic argument that portrays a scarcity of rights unevenly distributed throughout the population. In its comment that, "transgender individuals have rights! Everyone has rights! That is, everyone except straight people," CWA uses the boundaries of elitism to create the image of a powerful minority (gay people) that has coerced a majority (straight people) into following its treacherous whims ("the golden calf of 'sexual rights'"), thereby undercutting the majority's rights. According to the logic of the piece, so few people want a sex-change operation that the changes to insurance plans will "force" the average person (defined by their non-transgender status) to "subsidize" operations that they deem immoral. To CWA, this becomes a violation of the terms of its members' citizenship, since it is "taxing the many to benefit the few."

Objecting to the coverage of such surgery on the grounds that it violates not only the people's constitutional rights, but more vividly, their moral comforts, permits CWA to bypass the issue of whether more popular minority groups that receive benefits through taxation (such as veterans, or the elderly, for instance) might deny the majority their economic and moral rights as well. Instead, the rhetoric crafts the impression that an unpopular, and thus illegitimate, minority wielding tremendous social power has the ability to rob the majority of an important component of its citizenship. Transgendered individuals are symbolically sealed with coercion, causing injury to the "patient" who is the "mainstream" CWA reader. From this negative depiction, CWA is then able to define itself as the voice of "the people" who will not stand such intimidation.

This emphasis on the experience of pain, suffering, or coercion as an indicator of one's minority status is a trope frequently used in CWA speech, most often to portray itself or its allies as those who have been victimized by elites in the arena of civil rights. Those who experience disempowerment (as specifically defined by CWA) are frequently depicted as those who deserve to be legally recognized. This distinction is critical to Lauren Berlant's argument that two competing images of citizenship have been repeatedly juxtaposed in American nationalist rhetoric. The first invokes a relatively vague and ideal model of inalienable rights in which all people who are citizens receive cultural protection and value regardless of their perceived characteristics. The second model disrupts the first by highlighting how certain groups' citizenship has been withheld—literally or symbolically—through dominant interest groups' politicking and self-interest. However, this is not citizenship in the abstract, for Berlant concludes that a marginalized group will fail to be recognized or valued by the larger culture until it can prove that it has experienced significant physical or social injury.[20]

Demonstrating Berlant's point, CWA repeatedly juxtaposes homosexuals with African Americans to argue that homosexuals capitalize on the suffering of others by choosing to create their own discrimination, thereby taking rights away from "true" minority groups. Since, like many Christian Right groups, CWA defines sexual orientation as a matter of moral will and not immutable identity, its simultaneous focus on homosexuals as economically powerful individuals even further rhetorically distances them from the ability to claim minority status. In another essay on the Employment Non-Discrimination Act (ENDA), which would prohibit discrimination based on sexual orientation or gender identity, CWA argues that while gay people claim they are victims of discrimination, the ENDA describes discrimination, in part, by "lack of ability to obtain economic income, adequate education, or cultural opportunity."[21] In an argument construed in specifically economic terms, CWA claims that homosexuals cannot be considered a protected class under the ENDA because "homosexuals have an average household income of $63,100.00 versus a general population income of $36,500.00. By contrast, the average income of a disadvantaged African-American household is somewhere between $12–13,000."[22]

Money is not the only category through which one gains protected status; cultural oppression is measured as well. In making this argument, CWA also consistently compares homosexuals with African Americans to prove that the former do not experience cultural oppression. In an article drawing on the common trope of hijacking, entitled "Homosexuals Hijack Civil Rights Bus: Claiming A 'Civil Right' to 'Marry' the Same-Sex Demeans a Genuine Struggle for Liberty and Equality," CWA writer Janet LaRue features the words of an African American man opposed to gay rights:[23]

> When has a multitude of gays been kidnapped and made to be slaves for 400 years? When was it illegal to teach gays to read and write? When were there ever any gay Jim Crow laws? When were gays required to say "sah" or "ma'am" to straight people? When were there separated gay and straight water fountains? In public buildings, when were there separate entrances for gays and straights, the gays going out the back? In theaters, have gays been forced to sit

> in the balcony while the straights sit on the main floor? When were there segregated lunch counters based on sexual preference? When was a gay required to give up their seat on a bus to a straight person? Who was the gay Rosa Parks? Were gays at the bottom of the economic social structure for decades? Where were the poor gay ghettos? When have gays gotten worse jobs and lower pay than straight people? When were there separate-but-equal schools for gays and straights?[24]

The goal of this chaos rhetoric is to create a symbolic equation wherein true minority status is read through the lens of the history of African American oppression. If one's suffering does not mimic the form that African Americans have experienced, then no oppression has actually transpired. This is a claim with great irony, for as earlier mentioned, the Christian Right has largely resisted acknowledgement of socio-structural oppression (such as racism or sexism) because such conversations stray from the classic conservative depiction of social problems as the result of poor individual morals instead of systemic social problems. Yet, in this case, invoking socio-structural oppression is an advantageous rhetorical move for two reasons: it can situate racism as a more widespread and heinous sort of oppression against which homosexuals cannot compare their own suffering, and it can also locate such systematic oppression as the artifact of a bygone era that no longer exists in modern American culture.

If the symbol of elitism works in part because it crafts an opponent who benefits at the expense of a wounded minority, then one of CWA's most frequently invoked arguments is that Christians, themselves, are a group suffering at the hands of liberal elitists who attempt to discredit them. The injury here takes the form of ridicule and unfair caricature, as in Crouse's remark that "Amazingly, the old stereotypes still exist . . . Today's pseudo-sophisticates view Biblical orthodoxy with disdain and/or hostility."[25] Writing immediately after the re-election of George W. Bush in 2004, Christian Right pioneer Paul Weyrich weighed in on the CWA website about his frustration with "the liberal establishment" by again drawing on this sense of unfair caricature. Speaking about Democrats and what he believed was their repudiation of "values voters," he writes:

> The left hates tax cuts. They do not want people to be able to spend their own money. Since we are stupid, only they, the leftist elites, can know best how to spend it for us. Hillary Clinton suggested that

> Democrats go to church for a time to learn the language. Who is stupid now? (Although they might benefit from spending some time in church.) Do liberals really think that by being able to quote a bit of scripture or to understand Liturgy they are going to be able to win over the values voters? I guess she really thinks we are stupid beyond belief. The reason George W. Bush appears sincere when he invokes the Almighty is because he is sincere.[26]

In this piece, the attempt to deceive Christians into giving over their votes by the use of Christian-friendly language is not the only troubling aspect of leftist thought, since it is prefaced by Weyrich's initial statement of who the enemy is. Couched in primarily economic terms, the left is comprised of tax-cut haters who "do not want people to be able to spend their own money," a statement fusing conservative economic policy with Christianity. While Weyrich goes on to discuss what he perceives to be leftist antipathy for Christianity, it is not Christianity that is at risk of being sacrificed, for Weyrich speaks time and again of "the people" and "Christians" as if the two are one and the same. Thus by symbolically merging "left" with "elite," "insincere" with "anti-Christian," and, in the same breath, "Christian," "sincere," "churched," and "people," leftist elites not only threaten Christianity but the whole of America. Antipathy towards Christianity becomes the rhetorical vehicle through which the terms "Christian" and "people" can be collapsed into a powerful symbol of nationalist righteousness that stands against the political deception of the "leftist elite."

With this elasticity of symbols in mind, it is interesting to see CWA's sense of its own power juxtaposed against the chameleon-like elites. As with the term *logic*, what constitutes elitism must be carefully proscribed to protect CWA's own elitist tendencies. While CWA and the elitists might both be powerful, CWA defines itself as non-elitist because of its ability to identify and call out the deceptive logic of its opponents; in other words, its own moral righteousness saves it from such charges. In one of the most overt examples of this rhetorical deflection, CWA discusses the reasons why so many ACPs became part of the political process in the recent past. Note, again, the hijacking speech:

> "It's like when the hijackers took over those four planes on September 11 and took people to a place where they didn't want to go," State Rep. Cynthia Davis (R-19th) of Missouri told *The New York Times*. "I think a lot of people feel that liberals have taken our country somewhere we

> don't want to go. I think a lot more people realize this is our country and we're going to take it back". . . . But the elites in Hollywood, academia and government got too used to pushing the envelope. Consumed with building their bridge to where they envisioned America should be—a land of irrepressible individual freedom—they didn't realize that we see where it really leads—more and worse than what they've already given us. Pornography in prime time, broken marriages in the elusive search for happiness, and couples longing for children they can't naturally conceive because of infertility from sexually-transmitted diseases. Their promises of utopia have proven painfully unrealistic: that abortion will eliminate child abuse, or that easy divorce will strengthen marriages.[27]

If elitism is one of the most effective tropes within CWA chaos rhetoric, the repeated use of hijacking language is perhaps its most emotionally volatile expression. As earlier mentioned, hijacking imagery has been repeatedly deployed by CWA since September 11, 2001 as a metaphor used to pit the righteous, pure, and innocent against the forces that both commandeer power and embody evil. While CWA has been openly and bitingly critical of others who have invoked 9/11 for what it sees as political gain, its own ability to feature hijacking imagery is, no doubt, linked to how it defines itself out of elitism while in many ways displaying its most striking characteristics. In passages such as this, the events of 9/11—the ultimate attack against the nation in recent memory—are fused with the sexual sin of "the elites," which CWA claims to have the expertise to both identify and resolve. CWA thus symbolically becomes *the* anti-9/11, *the* ultimate anti-terrorist organization, and thereby transforms its own use of the image into an apolitical and populist act. In its own self-portrayal its political righteousness is not abstract, for it knows how to both represent and protect the people, broadly understood.

Representatives of Real Women

As the preceding examples show, the ability to manufacture logic and populist arguments in specific ways that exclude its ideological opponents has been critical to CWA's ability to define itself as both reasonable and mainstream. While CWA uses its identity as a women's organization to claim the expertise needed to draw these distinctions, it sharpens these arguments when speaking specifically about (and against) liberal feminism. As another symbolic category critical to its chaos rhetoric, feminism functions for the organization as both a generic insult that designates disagreement with CWA's political platforms, but also as an entity with specific meanings that CWA uses to its favor. CWA most often speaks of feminism negatively, contrasting what it portrays to be the poor morals, nasty dispositions, and flawed logic of feminists with the level-headed, rational, caring, conservative women who comprise its membership. At other points, however, CWA speaks favorably of feminism, reviving the theme of illegitimates (liberal feminists) who have hijacked an otherwise legitimate or noble institution (feminism), leading it far astray from its moral, conservative Christian beginnings. In a move unlike how it treats most of its other opponents, however, CWA often attacks feminists in relational terms, describing them as mean, angry, or rude; as will be discussed, this effective tactic remains gendered to its core. No matter its usage, CWA's deployment of the term *feminism* remains constrained by the boundaries of logic and populist appeal, for proving that liberal feminists are dangerous (and that conservative feminists are not) first depends on relegating liberalism to a realm of illogic and radicalism.

The Cure for Feminism

CWA chaos rhetoric typically casts liberal feminists in three ways that feed strongly into the negative feminist stereotype. First, feminists are often portrayed as psychologically damaged individuals because, presumably, they have denied themselves the relationships and experiences (marriage, childbirth, etc.) that "whole" (conservative) women have. Second, feminists are frequently rendered as lesbians, who, under CWA's reading, are both sexually perverse as well as non-nurturing, since heterosexual, reproductive motherhood is the setting in which the organization contextualizes the ability to care for others. Finally, because of these other shortcomings, CWA often represents feminists as women who perceive the world in a fundamentally flawed way, for they see gendered oppression where there is none. As such, liberal feminists are construed as a group that employs a victim mentality to claim "illegitimate" or "special rights," the aforementioned category used by CWA through which to discuss groups that claim discrimination but do not actually experience it. Just as it handles arguments about anti-gay discrimination, CWA typically holds that gender discrimination is an individual moral problem (wherein certain individuals act in sexist ways) rather than one with socio-structural causation (wherein the entire culture operates in sexist or patriarchal fashion). Because it understands itself as an entity that uniquely comprehends the nature of rights, CWA can become an agent of "women's rights" in a way that counterfeit rights advocates (i.e., feminists) cannot.

Historically speaking, the presumed moral authority of women has usually been lauded only when women do not use this authority to challenge patriarchal structures. When they have done so, their moral insights have often been drawn into question or presumed absent altogether.[28] In a similar move, CWA often removes the terms "heterosexual," "Christian," and "reproductive" from descriptions of liberal feminists so as to delegitimize their female identity, and thus presumably, their moral abilities. By crafting the feminine ideal as the God-fearing Christian mother, the feminist can be defined in the negative as not only less than moral, but also less than female. This symbolic separation of "feminists" from "women" is exhibited in the way that CWA portrays its 1978 beginning:

> Beverly LaHaye watched a television interview of Betty Friedan, founder of the National Organization for Women. Realizing that Friedan claimed to **speak for the women of America**, Beverly LaHaye was stirred to action. She knew the feminists' anti-God, anti-family rhetoric did not represent her beliefs, nor those of the vast majority of women.
>
> The first meeting to educate and alert Christian women on the **Equal Rights Amendment** (ERA), led by Beverly LaHaye, occurred in San Diego, California. More than 1,200 attended. This was the springboard to beginning Concerned Women for America as a national organization.[29]

Through its use of bolded typeface, "the women of America" and opposition to "the Equal Rights Amendment" are fused into a symbiotic relationship out of which each, in opposition, is given a specific identity. In a few short sentences the basic anti-feminist rubric of CWA is worked out: feminists, a category of women who are against the most basic relationships in life ("anti-God" and "anti-family"), delegitimize themselves as women insomuch as they stand against "the vast majority of women." This majority must be "educate[d]" and "alert[ed]" to the activity of feminists, for the latter are not merely philosophically confused but pose a valid threat to the aforementioned categories "God" and "family." In most every way that matters, feminists are cast as fringe.

In 2005, CWA published an essay on a new conservative student organization on the University of Virginia campus that further highlights this theme of the radical, out-of-touch feminist. The organization's name, NEW (which stands for "Network of Enlightened Women"), is presumably a play on the name of the feminist organization NOW (the National Organization of Women). The article describes how NEW represents the redemption of what feminism has twisted:

> The glory of feminism, which engulfed waves of young women in the 1960s and '70s, has increasingly lost its luster with today's generation, many of whom have observed its radical swerve to the left. Today's feminists have embraced an increasingly hostile and denigrating view of the male half of the species, bitterly viewing them as a hindrance to female liberation. Not surprisingly, radical feminists today also devalue the institution of marriage (after all, empowered women don't need men), and view motherhood with contempt. . . . Many collegiate women have observed the detrimental effects of such attitudes, and just aren't buying them. Being feminist is as out-of-style as crimped hair and big bangs; conservative college women are exposing today's feminism for what it is: entangling ideology that needs to be toned down.
>
> [Notes N.E.W. founder Karen Agness] "We embody the most dangerous threat to the feminists because we engage them intellectually. Instead of using feminist tactics such as protesting, rudely interrupting, or writing inaccurate commentaries, we develop leadership through education. . . ." Agness believes the discussion is valuable for college-age women who are often surrounded by feminist influences that devalue the virtues of motherhood and elevate a career. "Conservative women aren't being suppressed by a patriarchal society, as feminists allege," she says. "Women will be happier when they recognize the need for balance and realize the importance of the family is just as valid as having a career. Both are great choices."[30]

Here feminists are mainly defined by their rejection of both men and marriage, understood as normal things that "most women" want. This rejection of normalcy has left them blinded to the degree that they cannot see the counterproductive nature of their own tactics, and thus they represent something even more radical ("a radical swerve to the left") than the feminism of the 1960s and 1970s that CWA is usually so quick to denigrate. In short, feminists' delusions (countered by NEW's "intellectual engagement") account for their irrelevance and unhappiness. Logic and reason are the primary authorities referenced here, but they appear in many different forms and degrees of assault: the feminist attacks reason with her irrational anger and contempt for motherhood; educated college women reject feminism on the grounds that its "entangling ideologies" are absurd; and NEW founder Agness appeals to the reasonable balance pursued by "most" women to have both career and family.

CWA's tendency to engage in personal attacks on individual feminists is an interesting strategy. In several different articles across the website, the private lives of feminist leaders are heavily analyzed for instances of abuse, abortions, broken relationships, or psychological damage that would explain their turn to feminism, much as one would pinpoint a trauma used to explain alcohol or drug abuse.[31] References to the unsightly physical appearance of liberal feminists and their supporters is also not out of bounds, as in Janice Shaw Crouse's remark that "unlike Nancy Pelosi's surgically induced gash of a smile, which is hard to endure, [Sarah] Palin simply lights up the room when she enters it."[32] In a speech delivered at Princeton specifically targeting feminism, Crouse equated feminism with feminist pioneer Betty Friedan, noting: "Even her friends describe Friedan as difficult, ill-tempered, disagreeable, ego-driven, rude, nasty, self-serving and imperious."[33]

On one level, these tactics can be read as nothing other than *ad hominem* attacks (which, while rather simple, are often effective), since engaging in personal critiques of specific feminists enables CWA to depict the entirety of feminism as unattractive, irrational, and reactionary precisely because it is the outcome of defying traditional gender roles. This might explain why CWA still insists on frequently invoking Friedan decades after her public prominence: she symbolically operates as something like a rhetorical time machine through which CWA can transport its membership to a moment when feminism was not mainstream, and was defined by a leader known by some for her unlikeability. At the same time, focusing so heavily on individual feminist leaders and others in the spotlight allows CWA to sidestep the question of whether most women's lives (feminist and non-feminist alike) reflect the same traumas, or whether the "average" liberal feminist really resembles its descriptions.

Such arguments also operate as gendered markers that allow CWA to build upon female identity when it is politically expedient to do so. If women's moral capacities have been traditionally associated with emotional sensibility and a concern for relationships, then CWA must itself heavily capitalize on the image of the emotionally stunted and relationally inept feminist if it hopes to represent itself as both "truly" moral and "truly" female. On the other hand, there is an additional gendered argument implied by the portrayal of the irrationally angry feminist. Her degree of negative emotion allows CWA to employ the longstanding stereotype that men are capable of emotional objectivity in ways that women are not, thereby allowing CWA to take on a "male" role that renders it more politically level-headed than liberal feminists.[34] This is not a counterintuitive move, for in the claim to rationality is also the claim to power. Thus CWA can prove its own special sense of morality by becoming symbolically "male" in its logic, but remaining reliably "female" in its moral and relational character.

A deployment of this frequently used tactic occurs in a specific piece of CWA rhetoric that warns that feminists are looking for "converts" to victimize with their illogic. In an article critiquing "Take Our Daughters to Work Day," a program that was first sponsored by feminist publication *Ms.* magazine, CWA warns that young children (especially boys) are particularly at risk from its message. Although she admits that the program "sounds like a good idea at first glance," the author concludes that it is really "feminism class for young girls."[35] Because the Ms. Foundation encourages participating adults to point out workplace inequities, particularly those involving gender, CWA claims that participating promulgates a victim mentality: "It seems doubtful that most young girls would note such 'inequities' unless an adult pointed them out. What a great way to begin indoctrinating young girls into feminist thinking and to perpetuate the war between the sexes."[36]

But this indoctrination is not the only harm. The author remarks that favoring daughters over sons for such programs is destructive, since boys, more than girls, are actually the ones in need of the sort of individual role modeling that such "take your child to work" programs advocate. Why? Boys' naturally more rambunctious natures are misunderstood by "the establishment," which equates good behavior with traditionally feminine characteristics. Thus boys are doubly harmed by a program that not only favors girls, but that sees girls' inherent qualities as superior:

> Boys are different from girls, and they need to be socialized differently, in ways that account for their natural aggressiveness and boisterousness—characteristics that can become assets if channeled in the right direction. . . . . But professional educators and child development experts still tend to regard such natural differences as pathologies, and one method of 'treatment' is attempting

> to get boys to act more like girls. The Ms. Foundation, it seems, is only too happy to go along with this attempt to feminize boys.[37]

The author ends her critique with the warning that the most "insidious" aspect of such programs is that they send the message that a person's worth depends on money and career. This is not problematic from a materialistic perspective *per se*; rather, the real hazard is "age-related infertility. This is a fancy-sounding name for a very simple truth—that while women are focusing exclusively on their careers, the so-called 'biological clock' is ticking."[38] Thus, CWA reduces "Take Our Daughters to Work" Day to programming that creates victim mentalities, feminized boys, and unhappy, infertile women, three dangers that the organization often associates with feminism. As the entity capable of detecting the real agenda behind the program, CWA adopts the caretaker role by becoming an agent of protection that secures the welfare of children (particularly boys), reproductive women, and thus the larger culture.

The career woman continues to stand as one of the most conflicted symbols used in CWA chaos rhetoric. As earlier mentioned, CWA has had to morally justify the existence of working women in order to align with a changing culture, as well as to explain how it employs the women who give life to its own organization. At the same time, however, it borrows so strongly from motherhood and reproductive imagery that it must warn of declining fertility and compromised personal relationships so as to support the logic that shapes how it renders the ideal woman.

This is why the "true" conservative woman is distinguished from the feminist in CWA speech not necessarily by the former's decision not to work, but in her ability to work *and* balance family life. The organization openly presumes that feminists do not have families, a presumption backed by the stereotype that feminists do not want such balance and are willing to sacrifice everything for their careers. CWA often lauds powerful conservative women with families, for their success is not only a sign that balance is possible, but that sexism does not exist. If it did, CWA argues, women would never experience such public empowerment. This line of argumentation is nowhere more clearly seen than in the overwhelmingly positive response CWA has had to Sarah Palin, the 2008 Republican vice-presidential candidate, mother of five, and self-proclaimed born-again Christian.

Palin has been an enduring character in CWA's discussions on feminism. From articles that tout her attractive appearance, to others that celebrate her courage in mothering a child with a disability, Palin herself symbolically functions in CWA rhetoric as the best of conservative values.[39] Here Crouse uses Palin's identity to demarcate legitimate female power:

> All women who have perfected that balancing act feel satisfaction that "one of our own" would be the first woman to break through to the highest ranks of political leadership in this country the world's most powerful democracy. It is so gratifying that it won't be a radical feminist with her extremist agenda who sacrificed everything else, including her own self-respect, for political power, like the feminists who defended Clinton's "indiscretions" in the Oval Office. In fact, Sarah likely has pounded the final nail in the coffin of radical feminism. The choice of Sarah means that providing opportunities (not quotas) is the key for women's empowerment. Her success means that a woman with intelligence and inherent leadership abilities, who is hard working and has a family willing to work together, can reach the highest levels of professional attainment and exude (as well as exert) natural authority with a feminine touch.[40]

In an overt populist claim, Crouse calls Palin "one of our own," someone who has pledged herself to *both* mothering and career, all the while eschewing feminism. Crouse is not the origin of this sentiment, for "*all women* who have perfected that balancing act" celebrate Palin's political success.[41] As a basic rhetorical move, this claim strikes a dichotomy for the reader: Palin is opposed to radical feminism *because* she is powerful, self-respecting, intelligent, hard-working, professional, authoritative, and feminine. By collapsing the vast diversity of feminisms under the moniker "radical," CWA successfully alienates feminism as something far from mainstream. Palin's achievements "[pound] the final nail of the coffin of radical feminism," because they refute the feminist claim that society is an essentially inequitable place, but a place where, critical to CWA's political mantra, one's moral decisions are almost entirely responsible for determining one's destiny. Palin is proof that one need not adopt radical feminist ideals in order to secure social power.

The True Feminist

Only after the organization portrays liberal feminists as illogical, angry women does CWA's own feminist identity become possible. If feminism as a technical term has undergone significant renovation from the time when LaHaye first warned against the feminists and their dangerous aspirations, there is no more paradoxical turn than in CWA's most recent assertions that it is itself an agent of true feminism and, in turn, progressivism. In a dramatic portrayal of rhetorical flexibility, CWA uses the term *feminism* in its chaos rhetoric to suit its political needs: female power for the cause of conservative social values is positive empowerment (and thus called "conservative" or "true" feminism), while female power for the cause of non-conservative social values is read as liberal, or radical, feminism (and is thus illegitimate).

Why would an organization that consistently warns of the unpopularity of and social disdain for feminism openly seek to adopt the label as its own? One answer lies with CWA's concern to appear progressive and yet simultaneously traditional, a move perhaps motivated by its need to recruit and maintain younger members as well as to prove its political relevance. As earlier mentioned, even if the term *feminism* often suffers from a public relations problem, the social advances of feminism are generally well accepted by the public, and this is a fact with which CWA must grapple. This is why CWA can argue that its real opponent is not feminism as a philosophy, but the *feminists* who have twisted it into something foreign and unfamiliar to "real" women. In this distinction between feminism and feminists, the "pure" and the "illegitimate," CWA can claim the progressive agenda of the former while rejecting the negative connotations it associates with the latter. In yet another article embracing hijacking imagery, entitled "Hijacking A Noble Cause: How Feminism Has Abandoned Its Founders," a CWA writer asserts that "early feminism and modern feminism are two different movements":

> Unlike the early feminist goals, modern feminism's agenda is based on a foundation of separation and anger rather than equality and fairness. Today's feminists wrongly claim kinship to feminism's founders, thereby cloaking their radicalism in the early movement's popularity and moral authority.[42]

CWA's central argument here is that Christian principles of justice motivated the early feminists, epitomized in the persons of Elizabeth Cady Stanton and Frances Willard. Women like these "asked only for equality, with no special treatment."[43] By contrast, modern feminism is something that has been led astray in its portrayal of women as victims.

The article's pinnacle lies in the following list, which dichotomously denotes the differences between the two:

1. Early feminists looked at the world through reason; modern feminists see everything through a gender prism.
2. Early feminists did not view men as the enemy; modern feminists believe that men are their constant oppressors.
3. Early feminists saw marriage and motherhood as privileges; modern feminists see the family as a prison.
4. Early feminists saw abortion as exploitation of women; modern feminists see it as a solution to the problem of exploitation.[44]

In establishing this particular form of chaos rhetoric, CWA equates "early feminism" with reason, tolerance, family, and the social and physical protection of women. Modern feminists cannot link themselves to this early movement because, using this logic, they oppose almost all of its terms. Stanton and Willard thus become symbols of the ideological gap between the earlier and later movements, the "true" feminists whose otherwise noble ideologies have been "hijacked." Because the two are commemorated in CWA speech as pro-family, anti-abortion, and pro-religion, they become the founders of a lineage of both morality and progressivism through which CWA can trace its own existence. Despite the fact that historians familiar with the lives of these early feminists would be likely to strongly dispute CWA's depictions of Stanton and Willard as conservative, traditional women, CWA nevertheless fashions itself as an historical extension of their work.[45]

So long as the term *feminist* refers to women who support conservative or traditional values, Palin, who was earlier depicted as proof of the foolishness of "radical" feminism, can also be portrayed as feminism's true epitome. While Palin was a confusing vice-presidential choice to many liberals who read her relative inexperience and frequent gaffes as a sign of a poor candidate, CWA suggested that she was an ideal choice because she stood for all that is "true": feminism, faith, and family:

> The presence of Palin in the public square as a true feminist with values is simply attractive. Palin stands unwilling to give up faith, family and life, and that sure sounds like most of us women out here! She believes not only that America is exceptional, but that the women of America are as well! Palin represents the continuity of

> true feminism, no excuses nor apologies needed. It is not perplexing at all, it is just plain and simply someone to whom we can relate and in whom we can believe! The perplexity comes from the left, in their total lack of understanding mainstream America. . . . Gov. Palin is successful, and her message is well received. The liberal feminist's is not. Palin gives voice to the silent majority of women, conservative and moderate; the liberal feminists do not. As Mrs. Beverly LaHaye once noted during the public battle over the Equal Rights Amendment, "They (liberal feminists) do not speak for me." And out of that statement grew the nation's largest public policy women's organization, Concerned Women for America, the organization President Reagan praised for bringing the "reinforcements" to his conservative policies in the 80's. . . .[46]

Once again creating a selective lineage that "represents the continuity of true feminism," Palin's political family tree includes LaHaye and Ronald Reagan, who are both presented as bastions of conservatism. Liberal feminists cannot replicate the appeal of Palin because they are hopelessly out of touch with the larger culture that she embodies. In her own engagement with the very sort of activism in which LaHaye participated decades earlier, Palin is transformed into a symbolic incarnation of LaHaye. Thus, when CWA describes LaHaye as a "Recognized Women's Rights Pioneer,"[47] this need not be read as an impossibility, so long as one understands feminism as a tradition devoted to the preservation of conservative values.

On the surface, this seems to be the only way that CWA can coherently talk about its own feminist tendencies, for the alternative involves adopting liberal feminism's claim that society is institutionally sexist and thus perpetuates widespread oppression. In light of this conundrum, CWA's self-depiction as a feminist organization has involved a careful dance that, once again, engages the issue of whether to acknowledge socio-structural oppression. While CWA has frequently embraced the notion of social oppression to describe liberal antipathy towards conservatives or to discuss the co-optation of legitimate rights by morally illegitimate individuals, contests over classic "women's issues" (that is, issues that overtly involve sex, gender, or reproduction) are another area where the group often deploys arguments of widespread sexism so long as it can locate responsibility for this oppression with liberals.

CWA employed this tactic in responding to a meme (a virtual "postcard" intended for widespread internet replication, often of a humorous or witty nature) released by Democrats on the eve of the 2012 presidential election. The meme, which visually resembled many others circulating at the time, featured an illustrated picture of an early twentieth-century flapper, alongside the caption, "Vote like your lady parts depend on it!"[48] The meme referenced the pro-choice record of the Democrats, as well as recent moves by the Obama administration to push for the mandatory coverage of birth control by insurance companies. Whether or not CWA understood that the humor behind the campy speech and image was an intentional part of this communicative genre is unknown, but CWA responded to the meme with the following attack:

> So the top of the Democrat ticket does not think women care about national security, border security, the economy, education, religious freedom, or anything else. The Obama/Biden campaign portrays women as thinking exclusively with their nether regions. Of course, when they run their national convention as abortionpalooza, what should we expect?
>
> Hey, Obama/Biden campaign, why are you objectifying women and portraying them as one dimensional—with that dimension located in the pelvic area? Do you not respect women? The Democrats have shouted from the rooftops for months now that the Republicans launched a "war on women." This e-card says the Democrats are waging war on women's sense and sensibility.
>
> Democrats don't recognize and, more importantly, appreciate the complexity and intelligence of women. Evidently, they think women are only good for one thing. The Obama/Biden campaign should get their minds out of the gutter and out of women's underwear. Our foremothers did not fight for the right to vote so that the Democrats could reduce them to their "lady parts."[49]

In a swift reversal of political stereotypes, CWA blames Democrats for objectifying women for their own political gain. The critique hinges on the claim that Democrats have oversimplified women, for this is the first rhetorical step in a parallel assertion: that the Democrats' entire political platform can be simplified to abortion (and thus "abortionpalooza"). In the rhetoric, President Obama is not only guilty of misunderstanding women (a recurring accusation lodged against liberal feminists), but also of treating them in the same way as have other agents of female objectification, such as pornographers and abortion providers, who, in CWA speech, are frequently portrayed as opportunists who are interested in women only to the degree that they can profit from the use of their bodies.[50] CWA attacks the Democratic campaign from both symbolic angles, first from its "abortionpalooza" comment, and next from its scolding description of the Obama/Biden campaign having its "mind in the gutter" and "in women's underwear." Describing the president through images of sexual degeneracy and female objectification further permits the reading of CWA as an agency that can detect how the real agent of systematic oppression—liberalism—creates sexism.

By painting itself as the epitome of logic, true feminism, and legitimate popular sentiment, CWA has positioned itself as a force with the right to command American society. It has done so by constructing chaos rhetoric about its opponents that defensively relegates them to realms of irrationalism, destruction, and immorality. From this act its own superior nature is inferred; it becomes not only the opposite of these categories that promise destruction, but the entity with the special expertise to discern the difference between the two. The symbol of the lesbian radical feminist who denies her own female nature provides the foil against which CWA's conservative readership can reinforce their claims to a true female essence and their preservation of the family. Similarly, by relegating liberal feminists to realms of psychological damage, irrationality, and fringe status, CWA emerges as the only truly progressive alternative that American culture offers women.

This extensive use of defensive argumentation is not only critical in rendering a flexible self-portrait, but by extension, an equally malleable understanding of the nation and its interests. As the next chapter shows, how CWA rhetorically depicts the nation is critical to its ability to exert cultural control over it. Christian Right groups have long claimed to bear a unique sort of righteous acumen necessary to detect the immoral agendas of irrational elitists, feminists, and other liberals who threaten the American enterprise. As will be shortly discussed, when CWA rhetorically renders the "nation" and "religion" in such a way that the two become inseparable, the result is that the nation's citizens are redefined and thereby judged on their conservative Christian moral worth.

4

Sex and Cultural Salvation: CWA and Nationalist Rhetoric

> *If we don't hang together we'll hang separately, I mean, that's what my father believed when he formed [the] Moral Majority, [it] was an organization of Mormons, Catholics, Protestants, Jews, people of no faith. And there are bigger issues now, we can argue about theology later after we save the country.*
>
> —JERRY FALWELL JR. Interview with Glenn Beck[1]

IN THE EARLY 1980s, Christian Right powerhouse and fundamentalist preacher Jerry Falwell famously remarked that the goal of his newfound organization, the Moral Majority, was threefold: to get people saved, to get them baptized, and to get them registered to vote.[2] As his son would recount decades later, his father's first goal could not be theological quibbling, for there was no time for such details when the nation's very survival was at stake. While Falwell Jr.'s remark struck many evangelicals as blasphemy, prioritizing the nation above all else is an idea that has been central to Christian Right activism, one expression of which has been this impulse to equate religious and political conversion with each other.[3]

This chapter considers how the entity called "the nation" is rendered in CWA chaos rhetoric, once again treating CWA as a case study on the workings of the larger Christian Right. Theologically speaking, Christian Right leaders have provided an assortment of responses to explain why they seek to transform the nation into their own Christian likeness, ranging from the sense that changing culture will cause mass individual conversion, to fulfilling a divine master plan, to concerns over their own spiritual contamination. From a socio-critical perspective, however, the nation is a subject of particular importance for several reasons, three of which I will address in this chapter. First, nationalistic speech that can double as patriotism is simply more popular and accessible to the general public than is religious speech, the particularities of which can often make as many enemies as friends. It thus makes far more sense to discuss one's political platforms in less controversial, more attractive terms so as to reach the widest audience possible. Second, the architecture of the nation—its politics, its legal system, its social mores—is where CWA's real cultural power lies. The organization's ability to determine the structure of national politics is directly tied to its skill in realizing the sort of physical, moral demarcations of which it frequently speaks, such as bans on abortion or gay marriage. Finally, CWA's rhetorical rendering of the nation as an entity dependent on a certain type of religion for its survival reveals the very specific ways in which the categories "nation" and "religion" are deployed (and, I will argue, conflated) by the group. As will become apparent later on, CWA does not describe religion as a thing it seeks to preserve on its own merits as much as it employs it as a tactic to transform the nation in specific ways.

To explore how the idea of "nation" (and with it, "religion") is used by the group, this chapter will specifically focus on how CWA uses the Six Core Issues, the name it gives to the organizational framework through which it stages its advocacy. These six issues are labeled "Family," "Sanctity of Human Life," "Education," "Pornography," "Religious Liberty," and "National Sovereignty."[4] While all of the excerpts featured in this book could be grouped under one or more of these headings, in this chapter I will consider each excerpt using at least one of the headings deliberately chosen by CWA in order to more fully consider how it intentionally constructs its public image.

CWA uses these categories together to create something like a symbolic constellation through which it forges an image of the nation. No single political platform is sufficient to generate the image of the nation that it needs to gain political support; only together do these issues create that representation. By examining instances where the nation is overtly discussed in the context of these topics, this chapter will show how CWA has crafted a narrative that positions itself not only as the nation's savior, but also as the nation itself.

To achieve this self-portrayal, CWA draws upon two sets of powerful, recurring symbols that are continuously threatened in its chaos rhetoric. The first symbol set involves child and parent imagery. Talking about the nation's decline through chaos rhetoric that highlights the image of the exploited child as a symbol of innocence, virtue, and vulnerability crafts an innocent, exploited nation by association. Political references to children are rarely about children themselves, but are indirect ways that a culture can express its values, preferences, boundaries, and fears.[5] This also explains why moral failure—particularly the sexual kind—is of such tremendous focus in CWA chaos rhetoric, for to combine the symbol of the child with the risk of sexual moral failure permits the group to use the highly evocative metaphor of child sexual exploitation through which to describe the nation's own corruption and exploitation by liberals.

But to render the child synonymous with the innocent nation is only partly useful, for the nation's strength must also be underscored lest it be viewed as ineffectual or naïve. Thus, the nation is also depicted as a beloved parent whose moral fortitude and wisdom are responsible for the sustenance of the entire cultural enterprise, and whose wisdom transcends the folly of its children. This is seen overtly at several points in discussions about the will of the Founding Fathers (who function not merely as historical characters, but also as symbolic *double entendres*). More often, though, the parental language operates in related, but more generic, protectionist speech. This occurs when CWA portrays itself as a watchdog group whose duty is to warn citizens that the government's antics lead down the path to trouble. It also takes place when CWA represents itself as the protector of religious liberty, which, under this reading, must remain relatively absolute if any other right or freedom is to exist.

The protective parent image is enabled by a second, and perhaps more fundamental, set of commonly used symbols: the government and the nation. Whereas the first set involves two beloved symbols, the second set engages the diametrical juxtaposition of what are portrayed as two opposing forces. "Government" often stands symbolically apart from "nation" in CWA rhetoric; the former describes a morally blind aggressor, while the latter depicts the innocent, always righteous, and yet still powerful, victim. This is a common tactic among moralist groups, for governments are all-purpose villains that can be blamed for almost every problem.[6] By separating the two, CWA can claim to engage in politics to preserve the righteous nation but never act as an entity of the intrusive government. As will become clear in this chapter, CWA often forges its own identity so closely with the nation that, in many instances, it is impossible to distinguish one from the other.

The Six Core Issues represent the rubric through which CWA deploys the complementary images of the innocent child and the wise parental figure as the icons of the nation under constant attack by a misguided government. In the narrative it constructs, CWA portrays violations of "proper" sex, gender, and reproduction as acts that destroy the nation through the degradation of the liberties that its founders created, as well as the corruption of the morals of the nation's children (and thus the nation's future). How society's agents use sex thus becomes a clear barometer of national health or decline. Beyond allowing the reader to locate national vitality through sexual issues, such rhetoric also interprets the nation as an entity continually generated by CWA activism. There are few moments in CWA chaos rhetoric where the innocent child or the wise Founding Father is not paralleled with CWA itself; the organization becomes the entity that represents moral innocence, strength, vigor, and wisdom. The resulting symbolic constellation delivers an image of the CWA reader as one whose own political activism not only sustains, but also literally creates, the righteous nation.

Manufacturing a Nation

Before turning to the Six Core Issues directly, it is important to consider the rhetorical function of nationalist rhetoric, and more specifically, how the nation as a discrete entity is symbolically represented.[7] In order for CWA to create a coherent sense of national identity, it must first restrict the descriptors that it includes, for not everyone's image of the nation can reign supreme and still support the organization's political narrative. This process of constraint requires the formation of what Butler calls a "signifying chain," a discursive mechanism that strings together a series of accepted social authorities that create the contours of identity by pushing the listener to interpret powerful symbols in specific ways.[8] While the signifying chain is a concept that closely parallels other theoretical concepts discussed earlier (such as the terministic screen, mythmaking, and discourse, more generally), my interest in using this particular model lies in its ability to reveal, in greater detail, precisely what symbols must be fused together to render a very distinctive, conservative understanding of the nation suitable for CWA's political agenda.

Butler describes the signifying chain by invoking the Lacanian image of a judge, a person who wields authority because he has been granted the authority to interpret the law. Significantly, the judge's job is not to bestow the law with authority personally, nor is he the origin or creator of the law. Rather, the judge's authority comes from his ability to claim that the law itself has authority; because the judge is tied to the law through his interpretation of it, the law creates the judge's own authority by association. The judge reinforces the authority of the law by citing a long corpus of legal precedent (here symbolizing the signifying chain). It is only through this repeated performance of accepted conventions—repeating past legal decisions, and using those rationales to create current interpretations of "law"—that the judge holds any power.[9]

Butler uses this metaphor to argue that there is no original, *sui generis* authority to which all social constraints and thus identities might be traced, but only the multi-layered repetition of past claims, values, and identities reorganized and reinforced in ways that create the "acceptable" identities that can exist in any culture.[10] The judge is not an agent of creativity, in other words, but simply reiterates what has been previously deemed acceptable. If one applies this same rationale to how the concept "nation" is presented, it becomes clear that CWA crafts its own signifying chain by operating as the judge who grants authority to certain concepts, ideas, symbols, and values (such as logic, science, populist appeal, children, and freedom, among others already discussed) to fashion an identity for the nation that declares liberals unacceptable citizens. CWA's most basic rhetorical act is thus the repetition of many popular and frequently invoked mantras, such as the notion that America is a Christian nation, and that the nuclear, heterosexual family is its ideal. The discursive boundaries of the nation's morality are formed by publicly repeating and connecting these ideas together.

Lest one conclude, however, that the signifying chain that shapes the law is naturally authoritative, Butler argues that the real power behind signifying chains is that they are constituted "precisely through the infinite deferral of authority to an irrecoverable past."[11] Butler uses the term "irrecoverable past" to reference a vision of history wherein the values held by a group are seen as a continuation of some long-enduring, if not eternal, essence deemed good and pure by the culture at large, this despite the fact that such claims are usually unproveable.

Stephanie Coontz highlights the making of such an irrecoverable history in her book aptly titled, *The Way We Never Were*. In this study of American family life, Coontz demonstrates that the 1950s ideal of the smiling, nuclear family epitomized by Ward and June Cleaver was never a widespread reality. "Leave it to Beaver was not a documentary," Coontz notes, but was largely an imaginary arrangement that was rarely realized by most families even as it has been continuously drawn upon in later decades as a reality from which American culture has fallen.[12] In this way, the "irrecoverable past" that marks the signifying chain not only works as a claim to the longevity (and thus authority) of the particular ideal, but in the Foucaultian sense, involves creating a version of reality that depends on a certain degree of anonymity since the source of these claims has no origin to be adequately questioned.[13] Butler argues that this authority's influence is magnified precisely because of its "obvious" and yet hidden construction: the source of the idea cannot be located to be refuted, but at the same time, its refutation seems unnecessary because the symbolic relationships established through it are so popular as to appear perfectly natural. Rather than a call to historical fact-checking, though, Butler's point is that "the past" is not an objective state that can be restored if only enough effort is devoted to its recovery. Instead, it is itself a medium that is always flexibly reconstituted by a culture to justify its present political positions.[14]

A critical component of CWA's signifying chain is the claim that a specific brand of moral righteousness is a precondition to effective political activity. By making this claim, CWA is cast as the entity that embodies moral insight; as Butler notes, those groups that set the particular discursive standards by which identities are constructed often establish themselves as the ideal or norm.[15] This rhetoric becomes increasingly important to the operations of many modern nation-states, one of the central functions of which is to create "proper" citizens willing to compliantly subjugate their own interests to those interests of the public at large.[16] The "public interest" is thus not a self-evident thing, nor is it actually in *everyone's* interest, but it is always determined by moral claims made by those who control the political reigns.

In the infamous Tuskegee Syphilis Study of the mid-twentieth century, for instance, hundreds of poor black men who sought medical care were neither informed of nor treated for their syphilis infections because the US federal government determined that there was a significant public interest in examining the untreated progression of the disease. Considered utterly expendable, countless numbers of men and their infected wives and partners became ill and died, and many children were born with congenital deformities and other disorders related to their parents' infections. While the Tuskegee event was certainly extreme, the underscoring principles behind it are rather ubiquitous to political contestation. Those values that privilege a powerful group and its specific set of interests are often transformed into "national" values and the "public interest," even when significant sectors of that same public are devalued in the process.

If the law is commonly understood as something that is supposed to reflect and preserve the public interest, then the degree to which the Christian Right creates persuasive signifying chains directly determines what shape the law takes, as in Jakobsen's argument that the rhetoric of "sexual respectability" (and with it, "family values") has worked to "[reassert] Christianity as the defining discourse of the nation."[17] To this end, legal scholar Catharine Cookson notes that despite the public's perception that laws are impartial social parameters, legal decisions frequently favor certain groups over others—even when the groups are engaged in virtually identical acts—simply because of their existing power dynamics. In a 1990 case ruling against the legitimacy of drug use in certain Native American rituals, Cookson details how the common use of peyote was not unlike what many Christians do when they drink communion wine. Rather than an all-out ban on the use of mind-altering substances in religious ritual, the decision was more about a blanket social fear of drug use and an admonition against a non-mainstream moral authority (Native American religion). Christians (even minors) can drink communion wine without penalty while Native Americans are jailed on drug charges because of the normalization of certain power arrangements that call the former group's acts "sacramental," but that nullify and demonize the latter's as substance abuse.[18]

Yet if the evidence required in judicial proceedings often skews in favor of dominant groups, the legislative process is even more tenuous, Cookson notes, for it is "driven by politics, not evidence." She continues:

> Unlike the courtroom situation, nothing need be factually proven or even factually probable before Congress enacts a policy measure or proscribes an activity. Popular opinion, even if uninformed, propels the lawmaking process, and unless the enactment is challenged as unconstitutional, there is no accountability other than back to that same popular consensus."[19]

If the law itself is determined by those values that are created and reinforced through public discourse, then the issue at hand is how groups like CWA can create signifying chains through their rhetoric that become so popular that they are rendered self-evident in the public's mind. Convincing the public that its opponents are destructive, immoral, and ultimately un-American is a first, critical ingredient in CWA's attempts at creating public persuasion.

The Six Core Issues

CWA achieves such persuasion through chaos rhetoric that takes shape under The Six Core Issues. It asserts that its focus on these topics is based not only on their importance, but also because these are issues upon which it can make a meaningful public policy impact. At the same time, it is quick to note that these are not merely political platforms, for "at its root, each of these issues is a battle over worldviews."[20] With this imagery of an embattled, urgent threat in mind, these six constellation points (along with CWA's summary of them) include the following:

> **Family**
> CWA believes that marriage consists of one man and one woman. We seek to protect and support the biblical design of marriage and the gift of children.
>
> **Sanctity of Human Life**
> CWA supports the protection of all innocent human life from conception until natural death. This includes the consequences resulting from abortion.
>
> **Education**
> CWA supports reform of public education by returning authority to parents.
>
> **Pornography**
> CWA endeavors to fight all pornography and obscenity.
>
> **Religious Liberty**
> CWA supports the God-given rights of individuals in the United States and other nations to pray, worship and express their beliefs without fear of discrimination or persecution.
>
> **National Sovereignty**
> CWA believes that neither the United Nations nor any other international organization should have authority over the United States in any area. We also believe the United States has the right and duty to protect and secure our national borders.[21]

If the primary threat employed in CWA's chaos rhetoric is typically sexual or gendered in nature, it may seem difficult to reconcile how some of these issues are at all sexual at first glance. While "Family," "Sanctity of Life," and "Pornography" are all platforms used by the Christian Right to target sexual and procreational norms, others such as "Religious Liberty," "Education," and "National Sovereignty" are not so obviously pertinent.

Nevertheless, Kintz has argued that most conservative claims are intrinsically sexed insomuch as they depend on an ideological structure that sees proper sexual identity as the basis of all other aspects of morality. This structure, she notes, "might be visualized as a closed set of concentric circles stacked one on top of the other and ascending heavenward: God, property, womb, family, church, free market, nation, global mission, God."[22] This results in a "moral and emotional universe" that is "glued together both by the symbolic figuration of the proper woman and her activism."[23] As will soon be clear, not only does this mean that almost all Christian Right issues can be construed through a sexual lens, but it also suggests that anyone who disagrees with the Christian Right or CWA's understanding of traditional sexual morality will almost automatically have their other political views delegitimized. This worldview of sameness and conformity takes shape within conservative realms in ways true to the emotional mechanics of chaos rhetoric, wherein those things that mirror the conservative social and economic ideal are deemed safe and legitimate, and everything that strays from it is considered dangerous and illegitimate.[24] Rather than presume that the appeal of familiar, safe concepts is something unique to conservatives (which Kintz implies), perhaps it is more accurate to see these as qualities that almost all people find attractive, and thus persuasive. This is why CWA has such a vested interest in making its values the public's values, and its fears the public's fears.

The Family

In recent years, many American political contests have been lost and won in the fight over "family values." Defining what makes up a family—and what leads to its demise—has been a political enterprise of almost unequaled proportions. CWA's own list of concerns regarding the family reads as follows. Note what issues create its vision of the family and the things that threaten it:[25]

We are concerned about:

- The disrespect for family and for the unique contribution of fathers and mothers. The attempt to eliminate natural distinctions between men and women.

- Sexual promiscuity, cohabitation and sexually transmitted diseases, including HIV/AIDS.
- The alarming increase in violence in American households, including same-sex and opposite-sex partner assaults, spousal assaults, and child and elder abuse.
- The growth of prostitution that feeds the sex trafficking industry worldwide— endangering the well-being and lives of thousands of girls, boys and women.
- The fiscal responsibility of government and its impact on our nation.
- The prevalence of drug and substance abuse in our country.
- The detrimental effects of gambling on the family.

With these concerns in mind, CWA responds with its goals:

We are working to see:

- The family esteemed as the bedrock institution of society consisting of individuals related by blood, marriage (the legal union of one man and one woman), birth, or adoption. The respect for the distinctiveness of men and women.
- Society value and respect marriage, encourage sexual abstinence before marriage and educate on the dangers of promiscuous sexuality; HIV/AIDS treated as a public health epidemic and not as a civil rights issue.
- An end to violence within households, especially the sexual abuse of children, while reinforcing the importance and autonomy of healthy families.
- An end to prostitution, the demand for prostitution and sex trafficking.
- The reasonable appropriation of government monies and the fiscal responsibility of balanced budgets.
- An end to drug and substance abuse.
- The elimination of gambling in all its forms.[26]

This portrait of the family is not unique in conservative social policy, yet CWA's list reveals in greater detail the complicated facets of its formation. The family is rendered legitimate when it is legally acknowledged (through marriage), heterosexual, and gender-distinct. Yet "family" here also includes seemingly disparate topics such as prostitution, government fiscal practices, public health concerns (STDs and HIV) and gambling. Given the amount of time that CWA spends talking about the importance of marriage in preventing poverty and other social ills (such as government dependence, which is high on the list), this reference to "fiscal responsibility" is likely a statement discouraging public assistance programs for poor, single-parent families that do not embody the nuclear family norm. CWA has long held out marriage itself as a solution to social problems, presuming that marriage creates personal responsibility and virtue.[27] It has also maintained the popular conservative claim that so long as the government provides economic support to single women, they are unlikely to marry or pursue their own economic independence.[28] Gambling is often included in lists of social ills that cause financial degeneration, another problem that creates impoverished families. It seems likely, then, that these references to the traditionally gendered, nuclear family are not just statements on gender roles, but also involve fiscal judgments that create a signifying chain connecting improperly executed gender with poverty with immorality. Under this reading of the family, its moral success can be measured, in part, through its economic stability.

However, there remains no issue more frequently invoked in CWA's chaos rhetoric about the family than gay rights and gay marriage, for acknowledging the legitimacy of homosexual relationships dismantles the linchpin of traditional gender roles and the supremacy of the nuclear, heterosexual family on which its rhetoric so fundamentally depends. For this reason, CWA is adamantly opposed to acknowledging homosexual couples with children as "families." As is typical with CWA rhetoric, homosexual relationships are rendered illegitimate not because of an explicit theological argument, but primarily to the degree that they are fused with disease, abuse, and the absence of morality altogether. While extramarital sex in all of its forms is problematic to CWA, the organization can explain non-marital heterosexual sex as the poor control of an otherwise healthy (i.e., heterosexual) impulse. Frequent claims made by the gay rights movement that explain homosexuality as an immutable characteristic fly in the face of how CWA renders the heteronormative, nuclear family as "natural." This is why the disease most often associated with homosexuality (HIV/AIDS) receives specific mention under CWA's "family" umbrella; HIV/AIDS has been so conflated at several points with homosexuality that it serves as its own chaos rhetoric to rhetorically fuse disease and death with homosexual identity. It is intriguing that the contextualization of HIV/AIDS as a "public health" rather than "civil rights" issue (as echoes CWA's language) directly mimics the Reagan administration's wording of its AIDS prevention platform during the mid-1980s. The platform was crafted with significant help from, and in an effort to please, conservatives angry over the possible elevation of homosexuality into an acceptable lifestyle.[29]

As previously mentioned, then, the longstanding conservative alarm over HIV/AIDS thus should not be understood mainly as a concern over public health, for instead, the significance of HIV/AIDS in CWA rhetoric lies more in the disease's ability to serve as a barometer of national morality. In kind, consider the following excerpt from an essay that links gay marriage with social deterioration. In an essay entitled, "Gay Marriage Is Not Only Wrong; It's Socially Destructive," author Robert Knight, one-time director of CWA's anti-gay rights think tank, portrays homosexuals as sexually promiscuous individuals unable to sustain committed relationships of any sort. Claiming that the institution of gay marriage in Holland neither stopped nor slowed the spread of AIDS (as gay men continued to have promiscuous sex, he notes), Knight concludes that the legalization of gay marriage has no known benefit, for unlike in heterosexual marriage, gay marriage does not create virtue. His argument culminates in a claim about the nation:

> As for the moral argument [against gay marriage], it's easy to make to those who have not shut their ears to self-evident truth. But even if marriage were not created by God Himself as the fountainhead of human life, a powerful case can be made on purely sociological grounds. Sanctioning "gay marriage" would, among other things:
>
> - Further weaken the family, the first and best defense against an ever-encroaching government.
> - Encourage children to experiment with homosexuality. This will put more kids at risk for HIV, hepatitis A, B and C, "gay bowel syndrome," human papillomavirus (HPV), syphilis, gonorrhea and other sexually transmitted diseases.
>
> . . .
>
> - Put more children at risk as adoption agencies abandon the current practice of favoring married households and begin placing more children in motherless or fatherless households.
>
> . . .
>
> - Pit the law and our government against the beliefs of tens of millions of people who believe homosexuality is wrong.

- Create grounds for further attacks on the freedoms of speech, religion and association.[30]

Knight's signifying chain depends on threats of big government, corrupted children, disease, and the violation of civil rights. Here Knight explicitly links the homosexualized child with national decline. It is bad enough that innocent children face a future of corruption and disease because of the normalization of homosexuality, yet their immediate physical danger is juxtaposed with a larger cultural hazard. The real risk lies with the homosexual's ability to compromise the nation's (here read as CWA's) values. Because homosexuals are portrayed as naturally promiscuous, and promiscuity is caused by immorality, gay marriage cannot, by definition, create the moral stability that is essential for the nation to flourish. Focusing on damage to the family is an equally critical trope, since the heterosexual nuclear family is portrayed as the force that keeps the unjust government at bay. Other sorts of families naturally breed disease, abuse, and other social harms, according to CWA, and thus necessitate the intervention of the government to rescue them from the social ills caused by their own poor moral choices. In short, illegitimate families create social burden.

In this sense, the legitimate family's values function as the just nation's values, if simply because they are extensions of one another. This is also why, under Knight's terms, gay marriage makes democractic society impossible. Knight's argument contextualizes gay marriage as breaking down "the first and best defense against an ever-encroaching government," "pit[ting] the law and our government against [us]," or "creat[ing] grounds for further attacks on the freedoms of speech, religion and association." The legalization of illegitimate sex would plow a direct path towards familial destruction, opening the floodgates for government intrusion against the righteous family, and thus the righteous nation.

The equation of the nation's welfare with anti-gay rights activism is depicted in another article authored by Knight, this one attacking a topic that has been ubiquitous to the CWA website, the Employment Non-Discrimination Act (ENDA). Here Knight links gay rights with national decline in even more explicit ways:

> If enacted, [the ENDA] will destroy any chance of restoring long-term fiscal sanity because it will sunder marriage and family, where self-governing, productive citizens are born and raised.

> ENDA is profoundly dangerous. It turns private sin into a public right and brings the force of government against morality itself. Any such law is a violation of our unalienable rights as proclaimed in the Declaration of Independence. To put it more simply, a statute that directly contradicts God's moral law is illegitimate. Laws embody and reflect morality, or they are not laws. They are tyranny. That's why so-called same-sex "marriage" laws are absurd and treacherous. Forcing citizens to accept a counterfeit as the real thing is an act of despotism.
>
> ENDA adds not only "sexual orientation" but "gender identity" to federal workplace anti-discrimination law. Thus, it takes an axe to the idea that sexual behavior has a natural normalcy or any relation to morality. It falsely equates a changeable condition (sexual desire) with race and ethnicity. Worse, it turns traditional values into a form of bigotry punishable under the law.
>
> People who like to describe themselves as "fiscal conservatives but social liberals" are fooling themselves. Without morality, you cannot have a sound economy, as Adam Smith pointedly observed.
>
> The left has long been at war against sexual morals for good reason. People conditioned to think as short-term opportunists instead of as members of the family tree are easy to manipulate. Just give them the false promise of a painless future free from individual responsibility. . . .
>
> Societies that lose respect for marriage eventually lose creative energy derived from the delayed gratification that strengthens families. Instead, people strive for immediate, sensory pleasure, and societies become less dynamic and fertile. Government grows bigger to pick up the pieces and create grounds for even greater hegemony.
>
> Our very survival is at stake, not just our economic well-being.[31]

The complexity and fullness of CWA's argument against homosexuality is here on display: forcing a population to follow something immoral is not law, but despotism. As long as the country's politicians are contemplating the inclusion of sexual orientation in the ENDA, they are several steps closer to delegitimizing the democratic process. That homosexuals attempt to compromise the legitimate rights of other groups ("race and ethnicity") to produce their own "absurd" and "treacherous" platforms is an example of the "tyranny" that such legislation will enact.

But this is, at its core, an issue of economic vitality, for beyond violating the sanctity of law, Knight argues that society itself will cease to be a productive engine if such legislation passes. If heterosexuality is the site from which springs responsibility, procreation, and "creative energy," those motivated by the "false promise of a painless future free from individual responsibility"—that is, liberals generally, and homosexuals specifically—will derail the entire social enterprise. The "los[s] of respect for marriage" that results from sanctioning homosexuality promises to create a host of social problems that will lead the country to financial ruin.

To be clear, this is not Knight's argument in favor of gay marriage as an institution that might make homosexual relationships stable, "responsible," and "legitimate," for gay marriage has already been defined as a moral impossibility. Repeating the argument in his earlier essay, because Knight presumes that homosexuals are hedonists, and thus by definition "strive for immediate, sensory pleasure," they cannot provide the hard work and self-control necessary to create any social institution of worth. Homosexuals are thus not part of the "family tree," with "family" understood both literally in heterosexual, procreative terms and, metaphorically, as the nation.

It is interesting that in its "Family" platform, CWA never uses the term "homosexuality." Instead, it relies on images of an idyllic heterosexual, nuclear coupling to describe its social ideal in positive, rather than negative, terms, referencing the "one man and one woman" arrangement as the intention of "biblical design." CWA may find more persuasive value available in this rendering of the superiority of the "unique contribution of fathers and mothers" and the "natural distinctions between men and women" than overt attacks on homosexuality, attacks which have invigorated a movement of fiscal conservatives who nevertheless find social conservatism negative and exclusionary.[32] This is the same group to which Knight alludes, reminding them of the moral impossibility of what he regards as their contradictory political positions.

Homosexuality thus remains the most prominent antagonist of the nuclear family if only because it is portrayed as the adversary of nationalist strength. Through speech that warns of the breakdown of law, morality, and productivity, CWA can maintain a sense of its own progressive vision of a moral nation concerned with the rights of its legitimate citizens, thereby divorcing gays and lesbians from membership in the national "family tree."[33] The nation thus becomes a place that needs not acknowledge homosexuals, for they cannot, by definition, contribute to its sustenance. The heterosexual, nuclear family becomes the entry point for moral, and thus civic, value.

Sanctity of Human Life

There are few legal events in recent history that challenge CWA's respect for the nation's institutions more than does *Roe v. Wade*, the 1973 decision that legalized abortion. As with the "Family" platform, CWA uses the topic to separate and juxtapose the nation from the government, and in so doing locates abortion as an issue that distinguishes those who willingly violate human rights (abortion supporters) from those who preserve and protect the rights of innocent citizens at all costs (abortion opponents). Despite the centrality of the fetus in these discussions, CWA's "Sanctity of Human Life" platform describes other innocents destroyed by the procedure, highlighting women as another population that incurs its harms. CWA also implicates embryonic stem cell and fetal tissue research as morally reprehensible practices that debase the sanctity of life, which CWA defines as something that begins at "conception" and ends at "natural death," a position in line with most traditional conservative social platforms.[34] The value, or sanctity, of life is defined not only by the parameters of time but also by the relative moral status of this life—it is innocent:

> We are concerned about:
>
> - The protection of innocent human life—including protecting the unborn from abortion, fetal tissue experimentation, and embryonic research; and society from euthanasia, cloning, population control and human genetic engineering.
> - The physical, emotional and spiritual harm to women, men and their families resulting from abortion.
>
> We are working to see:
>
> - Laws passed to protect our society from practices and policies that endanger or debase innocent human life.
> - Public awareness of the harm of abortion to women, men and their families; and the promotion of pregnancy care centers and post-abortion counseling services.[35]

CWA's decision to highlight the frightened and desperate pregnant woman over the murdered fetus in its anti-abortion advocacy reflects the same move made by many other Christian Right groups. This shift in focus reflects the growing sense that talking about pregnant women as murderers is both distasteful and judgmental. While a good public relations move, this also allows CWA and similar groups to focus their rhetoric on a more persuasive subject. Whether or not fetuses are humans whose life should be protected at all costs is a tremendously controversial issue, but few doubt the value or humanity of pregnant women.[36] Because it is typically pregnant women themselves who ultimately decide to abort their fetuses, however, CWA must shift the moral blame elsewhere so as to locate an enemy. It accomplishes this by placing the moral responsibility for abortion on others external to the pregnant woman, transforming her into the innocent victim of abortion providers (who promote abortion for their own financial gain) and liberalized society (which denigrates motherhood in the name of female empowerment). In this way, pregnant women are morally innocent, like the fetuses they carry:

> Abortion propaganda tells women they need abortion so that there are no consequences to their behavior and choices. The propaganda tells them that abortion is necessary so that they can remain on an equal level with men. Abortion sends the message that fighting discrimination is more important than a woman's health. Yet society's focus on equality gained at the cost of a woman's physical and psychological well-being diminishes all women and further blinds them to their own self-destructive behavior and choices . . . Women deserve better than being told that their career is more important than their child. Women deserve better than being told, "A baby will ruin your life." Women deserve better than the lie that a risky and dangerous surgery offers a solution to their situation.[37]

"Propaganda" about abortion is responsible for luring women into believing that their equality with men and quality of life depends on their childlessness. This façade comes with a price: their "physical and psychological well-being." CWA does not dispute that a child can hamper a woman's ability to gain "equal status" with men, but in a move that reflects CWA's frequent self-portrayal as a women's rights organization, it claims that abortion is really a source of female oppression. Women are cautioned that the trade-off for this false equality is so steep and in some ways so damning that the act of abortion invalidates any positive returns; not only do women forfeit their true destinies as mothers, but they put their bodies at great physical risk. Thus, abortion cannot be read as a form of liberation since it "diminishes all women" by morally blinding them to the ways that they sacrifice their most important priority: motherhood. Those who believe that their priorities lie elsewhere are simply victims of the liberal forces that have led them astray.

For all of the attention given to the women victimized by abortion, CWA continues to use traditional pro-life speech that describes aborted fetuses as the primary innocent victims. This rhetoric works on many levels, but the most frequently used tropes describe fetuses as citizens robbed of their lives, and thus their basic rights. In this way, the Supreme Court's ruling in *Roe v. Wade* represents how the government's sense of morality has gone terribly astray. Representatives of the righteous nation, however, can right that wrong.

The following piece of chaos rhetoric is couched in the public and highly emotional circumstances that led, in part, to the passage of the Unborn Victims of Violence Act (UVVA), a law that permits fetuses to be regarded as legal victims whose injury or death can be prosecuted.[38] The UVVA was created primarily in response to the 2005 murder of Laci Peterson. Peterson's husband, Scott, was convicted of first-degree murder in the death of Laci, then eight months pregnant, and their unborn son, Connor. As the nation watched the sordid details of the case, which involved, among other things, a mistress and a getaway plan, public opinion was strongly fixated on its more vivid horrors: a young husband murdered and dismembered his pregnant wife, presumably because of his affair with another woman.[39] Drawing from this reservoir of public revulsion, CWA here capitalizes on the criminal act of Scott Peterson, who thrust the fetus into the context of criminal victimization through the simultaneous death of his wife:

> George W. Bush was firmly convinced that the rights of all human beings, regardless of size or so-called "viability," should be fiercely protected. That's why he signed The Unborn Victims of Violence Act, also known as "Laci and Connor's Law." This law was introduced following the murder of Laci Peterson, who was eight months pregnant with her son Connor when their bodies were found washed up on the San Francisco Bay. Fetal protection laws such as The Unborn Victims of Violence Act help bring justice to unborn children, who have no voice. A *Newsweek* poll released in

> May 2003 revealed that 84 percent of Americans echo this sentiment of serving justice and believe that when both the mother and unborn child die the attacker should be charged "for two murders instead of one."
>
> In 2004, Concerned Women for America (CWA) worked to move people to action and help give unborn children legal protection and justice by lobbying for Laci and Connor's Law. Wendy Wright, then-CWA senior policy director, pointed out that "*Roe v. Wade* stripped all unborn children of being recognized in the eyes of the law. Legislation like Laci and Connor's Law helps to right this wrong by bringing justice to little victims of violence."
>
> The most poignant statement on the matter comes from Sharon Rocha, Laci's mother. . . . Mrs. Rocha finds it difficult to understand "why groups and senators who champion the pro-choice cause are blind to the fact that these two-victim crimes are the ultimate violation of choice. . . ."
>
> Choice is a loaded concept. What would the child choose? Life, definitely. And, when life is taken away, justice. For the sake of unborn children, justice must be served.[40]

This rhetorical fusion of the death of a fetus with crime is enabled through the rhetoric of choice. The essay argues that "choice" rhetoric is "loaded" unless it situates the unborn child as a human who would choose to preserve its own life, and in the absence of that choice, to choose "justice" through which to handle the circumstances of its death. Critically, this logic works only to the degree that it speaks from Laci's perspective. As the being whose value remains undisputed, Laci's identity takes on new meaning because, like the fetus, she also died. In the logic used in this rhetoric, Laci is paralleled with the fetus insomuch as she was an innocent whose own choice was stolen in her death.

Innocence, here, is thus measured in nationalist terms. Although they are laws that describe two different situations, the fact that author Wendy Wright is able to consider *Roe v. Wade* and UVVA in the same breath is precisely because whereas the former "stripped all unborn children from being recognized," the latter returns the fetus to the status of victim. Fetal homicide laws do not explicitly apply to abortions, but Wright situates such laws as legal moves to overturn *Roe v. Wade*. *Roe v. Wade* "stripped all unborn children" of legal recognition, Wright argues, yet UVVA brings "justice to little victims of violence." Consequently, when the "little victims" cannot have life, the nation has a legal responsibility to provide them justice. In this signifying chain, the rhetoric fuses the fetus with moral innocence with rights with justice insomuch as it is also able to parallel Laci Peterson's identity with the fetus. If Laci became a victim by being denied choice and life through criminal acts, so too, ignorant and desperate pregnant women become victims when they are pushed to abort by another sort of criminal, the abortion advocate, who, like Scott Peterson, is the real focus of moral blame.

At the center of CWA's anti-abortion rhetoric is the claim that the morally inept have co-opted the nation's controls in ways that falsely portray "true" rights and liberties. In a pamphlet intended to train pro-life activists, CWA provides a history of abortion that situates the practice as a longstanding social problem, one that has arisen from the decline of social morals. The pamphlet's historical narrative begins with the assertion that while all American states banned abortion in the early days of the republic, this ban weakened in the face of nineteenth- and twentieth-century figures who were interested in using abortion as genocide against African Americans, or who promoted unbridled, consequence-free sexuality.[41] While many historians would dispute this rendition of abortion's past, the issue, once again, is not historical accuracy as much as it is persuasive value. Within this narrative offered by CWA, the immoral have taken over the national reigns. As a result, "the quiet consciences of those who stand for the sanctity of all life understand this is an assault on the most vulnerable—those who are too weak to defend their rights—as well as an exploitation of women."[42] Drawing strongly on the symbols of motherhood and the innocent child, women who undergo abortions cannot be demonized as moral failures in the same way that homosexuals can. The pregnant woman considering abortion is herself an innocent aggressed against by an abortion industry that cares only about her money, and by a culture that has fed her nothing but lies. If persuaded of "truth" by the right people, she will have her chance to realize her moral self in her future motherhood. The protective nation has a responsibility to see that happen. If it does not, it compromises its claim to stand by and for the innocents and their rights, and in this way, is indistinct from a fascist state.

Pornography

If the nation is defined as something separate from government in part by the former's firm embrace of traditional morality, the issue of pornography is an excellent example of how CWA aligns itself as an agent of the nation. Once again, this happens primarily through talk of the dangers that pornography poses to innocent children. While the term "pornography" holds a generally negative label in popular culture as the sensorial violation of a self-evident obscenity standard, the consensus among scholars and free speech advocates is far from clear.[43] The self-evidence of this standard is certain to CWA, however, which understands pornography as the use of sexually explicit images to incite sexual arousal and/or activity outside of the married Christian heterosexual context. Because of this broad definition of pornography, CWA employs some interesting and flexible rhetorical turns in this platform.

CWA's strong rhetoric against pornography must, in the legal sense, attempt to show harm to be at its most persuasive. Once again turning to secular authorities rather than religious ones, CWA locates "moral deterioration" as the outcome of pornography, the instigator of almost all of the social problems it cites. These problems can be resolved by strong enforcement of law and increased government regulation of sex industries as well as the transformation of the entertainment industry into a "more positive moral influence":

> We are concerned about:
>
> - The ever-increasing prevalence of pornography, sexually-oriented businesses, and prostitution, and the lack of enforcement of existing laws.
> - The morally deteriorating impact of the entertainment industry on our country and the increasing emphasis on violence and sexual exploitation.
>
> We are working to see:
>
> - The consistent strict enforcement of laws regulating the use and distribution of pornography, and raising public awareness about the harm of pornography to men, women, children and society.
> - The entertainment industry become a more positive moral influence on society.[44]

The dangers of pornography are only vaguely spelled out here, but the message remains that the "ever-increasing prevalence" of pornography and the general ubiquity of sexually exploitive images are dangerous. In a model that treats sexuality as a wild, animalistic urge, CWA approaches healthy sexuality as something that is domesticated precisely because it is confined to the act of heterosexual marriage. But when exposed to pornography or other sexual obscenities, sexuality becomes untamed, uncontrollable, and ultimately, harmful. The slope, indeed, is slippery, for CWA has often suggested that the innocent person uses pornography out of sheer curiosity but is soon drawn into an addiction that ends in child abuse. As one article puts it, "Imagine your sexuality is so damaged you crave images of babies being raped. Keep on celebrating porn and indulging in what the Internet has to offer and you may soon find yourself in that situation. This is the darkest corner of those seeking to be uninhibited with their sexuality."[45]

The logic behind CWA's definition of pornography is critical, for if sex is fundamentally dangerous when uncontrolled, then any influence that promotes the removal of sexual inhibitions is pornographic. This is why, for instance, an article on the death of the founder of *Cosmopolitan* magazine, Helen Gurley Brown, appears under the website's "pornography" heading.

In the article, CWA's Janice Shaw Crouse describes Brown as one who "was the embodiment of the worst female stereotype as a master manipulator . . . Everything that Gurley Brown wrote . . . promoted the idea that women have to look out for themselves, make their own rules and work the system in order to get ahead."[46] Brown's offense is not only selfish feminist ambition, but a message of female sexual liberation for which *Cosmopolitan* remains famous. In a move to denigrate the value of that message, Crouse spends considerable time talking about how Brown was eventually happily married later in her life, a move contextualized as Brown's own realization that sexual liberation is a bankrupt personal philosophy. Crouse ends the article by mourning Brown's "terrible legacy," which warrants a paragraph on the spread of STDs and the proliferation of abortion. "American women are paying a very high price for living the "Cosmo" lifestyle," Crouse concludes.[47]

The entertainment industry is an equally pornographic entity under these terms, and CWA has launched several campaigns to support the Federal Communication Commission's (FCC) efforts to limit foul language and nudity during daytime and primetime television.[48] Here CWA engages in a rather classic conservative approach to government wherein it rejects government intervention in economic matters as "big government" but welcomes such intervention in obscenity/decency legislations that it deems vital to the nation's welfare. This is an important dichotomy to strike, for if all government regulation fell under the "big government" umbrella, then groups like CWA would have no legitimate governmental entity to influence.

Pornography thus becomes a matter of consequence precisely to the degree that it can be construed as fundamental to the nation's interests. CWA is explicit in the following essay that it has the legal right to determine the cultural boundaries of moral decency. While this is first explained in a signifying chain that connects pornography with the breakdown of the family, then with the exploitation of children, and then ultimately with child abuse, the final link is situated in explicitly legal terms:

> The naïve argue that what someone does in private is nobody else's concern. Research shows, however, that pornography and obscenity are very much everyone's concern. Pornography has become a multi-billion dollar industry—$5 billion *annually*—that victimizes both those who are involved in its production as well as those who consume the products. We have documented evidence today that pornography affects us all; it harms its users and the impact spreads to all who are connected with those individuals: the wives or husbands, boyfriends or girlfriends, and the whole family. We should be especially concerned about the nation's children. The National Center for Missing and Exploited Children reports that they receive more than 1,000 complaints annually about online obscenity affecting children.
>
> For some people, magazines like *Playboy, Hustler* or the free online adult pornography sites serve as a gateway to more graphic and perverted images. For certain ones, an addiction to violent and sadistic images is linked to sexual assault. The Federal Bureau of Prisons issued a study last year reporting that 85 percent of prisoners convicted of possessing child pornography admitted to abusing at least one child.
>
> The ill-informed argue that they have a First Amendment right to view pornography, but nothing could be further from the truth. Our free speech rights do not extend to pornography, which, if allowed, would give one person the "right" to abuse and debase another person. The Supreme Court ruled in 1973 that "obscene material" is not protected under the First Amendment. Thus, obscenity

> is illegal and has been since 1973. . . . The Supreme Court has been clear that there are "legitimate governmental interests" at stake in stemming the tide of obscene materials; such actions directly impact public safety, public morality, family life, and lead to a decent society.
>
> As citizens, we need to complain when we see violations of the obscenity laws. As concerned citizens, we need to ask state and local legislators to act responsibly regarding sexually-oriented businesses; they end up costing the community in numerous ways that harm citizens far beyond the real money expended in policing and regulating. As the saying goes, "If you do nothing in the face of evil, evil prevails."[49]

In an important boundary marker, CWA designates matters that include "such actions [that] directly impact public safety, public morality, family life, and lead to a decent society" as "legitimate governmental interests," which are "everyone's concern." CWA transforms itself into an agency whose special knowledge of morality and decency warrants its involvement in the "private" sphere, for rights and liberties that the country grants end where safety, morality, family, and decency start.

As is often the case, CWA makes this argument against the existence of a private realm by discussing the damage of pornography in terms of national welfare. This works on many levels. In the most basic sense, criminals abuse children because of child pornography, thus violating both individual children and the nation's moral welfare. Beyond this, though, is the matter of fiscal health, for the nation must expend its precious resources on policing child abusers as well as curbing the other negative ramifications that result from the national, moral damage caused by unrestrained sex. As in other chaos rhetoric, the sexually exploited child becomes the image of how "evil" acts through seemingly innocuous channels. In a recuperation of the idea that the country's citizens have misunderstood the boundaries of the rights and liberties bestowed upon them by the nation, CWA has the right—and duty—to intervene.

Education

The exploitation of children is not isolated to the issue of child pornography, however. Because education is the process of training and socializing children, anything that involves, compromises, or devalues the process of

Christian value transmission becomes an educational issue within CWA rhetoric. With this definition in mind, CWA approaches education as an eminently national concern, for what children are taught about morality will determine the future morality of the nation's citizens. Morality is portrayed as something transmitted through both classroom content and school culture, and because of its perceived failure in both realms, CWA warns that liberalized education creates corrupted youth who are unable to embrace the moral strength needed to sustain the nation. The government/nation dichotomy is pivotal to this assertion, for while the government often mandates the teaching of certain topics in the name of cultural diversity or science, the representatives of the nation's true values recognize that Christian principles, instead, should underscore all educational pursuits:

> We are concerned about:
>
> - The declining quality of education, the deterioration of parental rights and authority, the increasing emphasis on Godless philosophies, and, in particular, the unbalanced presentation of America's founding, of evolution, and of sexual education.
>
> We are working to see:
>
> - The quality of education restored to a level of excellence in academic achievement without governmental mandates that are detrimental to parental rights.[50]

When CWA describes the "declining quality of education," it both creates and echoes a growing sentiment within mainstream American culture critical of institutionalized education, as seen in part by the significant upswing in homeschooling in the United States. In 2001, a US Census Bureau publication indicated that while there were a variety of reasons that many families homeschooled, most did so because they felt that the quality of the education that children received in schools was poor. Up to one-third of those surveyed reported that religious reasons were behind their decision.[51]

Most CWA articles that attack the quality of American education express concern about the "godless philosophies" that compromise its excellence. Such philosophies can include anything from the teaching of evolution to normalizing non-traditional gender roles. CWA repeatedly suggests that not only is the content taught by schools disturbing, but so is the very climate that they produce, for schools over-discipline and humiliate boys for their naturally "male" behaviors (aggressiveness, physicality, etc.) and are thus gender-biased.

This is why Crouse can describe the growing visibility of women on college campuses as "the crisis of the disappearing educated male," a crisis brought on by colleges that denigrate men, their needs, and their experiences.[52] Males naturally need physical activity, she argues. Moves to cut men's sports are the residual effects of Title IX funding (a legislative act that denies federal funding to any educational institution that discriminates on the basis of sex), which appears to create gender equity. However, Crouse argues, what it really does is create female-centered cultures on college campuses. The result is that women, who are "encouraged to 'be the best' and to excel in order to 'make it' in the workplace" will ultimately dominate men in terms of academic performance and career/professional growth.[53]

If colleges now make it "harder for men to succeed and . . . the loss of educated men in the workplace will be incalculable," this is problematic not only from a professional stance. Crouse contextualizes additional damage in terms of marriage. The gap between educated women and an increasingly uneducated male population "is showing up in the declining marriage rates as well as in the divorce rates" as women are beginning to gain the upper hand. Physical education and gendered learning differences aside, Crouse argues that colleges are also becoming outright hostile to men because of radical feminism:

> Is it any wonder that men are avoiding today's college campuses? Hostility toward men and masculinity begins in daycare and increases each year thereafter. Sexual harassment training and policies have created an uncertain environment, if not a hostile one, where men have to watch their every word and action lest it be misunderstood or misinterpreted. Some experts criticize a campus "worldview that sees things only in terms of oppressors and the oppressed." Typically, the few campus men's studies programs are designed to push an anti-masculinity agenda.[54]

Through this critique of American higher education, Crouse redraws the lines of what counts as legitimate minority status, a theme visited in the last chapter. This is but one glimpse at CWA's overt campaign to protect and privilege masculinity as the source of national stability. Critical theorists have documented how the dismantling of inequitable social systems is often experienced by the powerful as a sort of reverse discrimination. Feminist theorist Marilyn Frye, for one, has famously drawn the distinction between oppression and discomfort, noting that just because men experience distress in the midst of the growth of women's rights does not mean that society constrains them in ways that they cannot control (which is how she defines oppression). More simply, their discomfort does not necessarily mean that men have lost access to avenues of social influence.[55]

With this context in mind, the fact that Crouse and other CWA representatives so frequently cry foul over the treatment of men in American society reveals the gendered anatomy—literally—of almost all of CWA's platforms, which necessarily depend on a model of male empowerment that exceeds female agency. Here the possible decline of the power of the heterosexual male makes male disadvantage significant enough that Crouse introduces the idea of a conscious restructuring of college admission quotas that would favor male applicants, a conclusion she reaches later in the article.[56] This is ironic in light of conservatives' longstanding opposition to affirmative action and other similar quota systems. But rather than a logical misstep on the part of Crouse, this is more likely an example of using classically liberal platforms in what conservatives might consider a "legitimate" way, unlike their "illegitimate" uses by liberals who claim oppression that CWA perceives does not socio-structurally exist. CWA can interpret the educational system through a signifying chain that configures radical feminism with an anti-male gender bias with the decline of marriage, and with these the institutional lifeblood of the nation, only insomuch as it first presumes that society depends on the triumph of masculinity.

In addition to its concerns over discrimination against males in American education, CWA education rhetoric is also focused on the harms involved in comprehensive sexual education curricula. Christian Right groups often see such information as causing teen sexuality and pregnancy, poverty, and a generally unclear sense of moral boundaries. CWA strongly refutes a variety of studies that indicate that abstinence-only education is largely ineffective in preventing teen sex, claiming instead that comprehensive sexual education promotes sexual activity:

> . . . the leading comprehensive sex ed curricula discourage the most effective way to reduce teen pregnancy and sexually transmitted diseases (delaying sex until, and restricting it to, marriage)

> by explicitly describing various sexual activities, encouraging role playing of sexual acts in the classroom and field trips to buy condoms, and downplaying the risks of pregnancy and sexually transmitted diseases with contraceptive use.[57]

This fear of moral relativism allows CWA to fully explore the topic of "parental rights," the term often used to describe a diverse movement (both within and outside of the Christian Right) that calls for greater parental control over the topics discussed in the public school setting. In a multitude of articles touting the importance of parents in keeping schools factually accurate and morally righteous, mothers are often portrayed as the heroines who demand the removal of sexually obscene curricula, who argue against the teaching of evolution, who promote a telling of American history that forefronts the idea of America as a "Christian nation," and/or who otherwise work to improve what is considered to be a degraded and liberally-imprisoned school system.[58] One such essay features a mother who objected to the content of a math textbook because it focused more on the process of problem-solving rather than arriving at an absolute, right answer, an approach she viewed as a sign of the infiltration of moral relativism. The woman subsequently took up a campaign to reform the state math curriculum; CWA describes her activity as evidence of how "an everyday citizen can be a patriot."[59]

If CWA's longevity is the result of its grassroots base, then such portrayals of the activist mother are key to its survival, for she demonstrates exactly how the common person can fight the forces of corruption.[60] But what about those children whose parents remain uninvolved? Or unaware? For this particular population, CWA redefines "education" not as something that takes place within a classroom, but the experiences gleaned from all influential life encounters. One particularly emotional article revives the signifying chain that links poor educational quality with the spread of homosexuality with child endangerment. The article describes an adolescent boy, Josh, whose own inadequate educational experiences doom him to an early death.

Josh's troubles start with his parents' deficient conservatism, for "like many American adolescents. . . . his family has only casual ties to a church, and his parents consider themselves moderate politically, when they have time or interest to think about it."[61] Josh concludes that he is a homosexual largely because of media exposure to the idea, which has reinforced and wrongly labeled the discomfort he feels around girls as well as the attention he craves from other boys. He has been exposed to stories of same-sex interactions in the books he has read at school, which have normalized homosexuality in his mind. To make matters even worse, his emotionally distant father has left him without a strong masculine role model to whom he can turn to place him back on the right path. In his naïveté, Josh is unable to understand the psychological impact of his relationship with his father nor the one-sided information he has received: "Josh has no significant barriers to exploring homosexuality, because *he has never heard or read an opposing viewpoint*. Not at school, not on any TV sitcoms, not on the Internet (because relatively few sites exist), and not at his church."[62]

If education is about "hearing opposing viewpoints," then Josh has remained uneducated. There has been nothing in his life that has provided an alternative to how he interprets his present situation. The fact that Josh is in this position during a time of vulnerability is evidence, the author argues, of "deliberate exploit[ation]" by many forces, including public schools, liberals on all fronts, and psychologically dysfunctional families that ultimately encourage kids to "convert" to homosexuality. The essay ends with an emotionally charged depiction of the impact of Josh's liberal "education":

> Josh's future probably holds a revolving door of sexual contacts, with his first visit to a clinic to be treated for a sexually transmitted disease at around age 17. . . . He's turned into a drop-dead gorgeous young man, but he has no interest in the appreciative glances of young women. He's too much in demand at the "gay" bars and bathhouses. He is already drinking heavily, smoking and doing recreational drugs. Somewhere along the line, he'll have several longer-term boyfriends, and may even move in with one or two of them. Their break-ups will happen after six months or a year, and be spectacular events punctuated with drama, screaming fights and threats of self-harm, contributing to the high rates of domestic violence cited for "gay" males.
>
> He will go to a counselor for treatment of depression, anxiety or an eating disorder. Seeking some peace and stability, he'll join a "gay"-friendly denomination like the Metropolitan Community Church. Along the way, he may well become HIV-positive. In his 30s, he will start to have relationships with boys who are 16 and 17, just as someone did when he was a teen. He may even transmit the

> HIV virus [*sic*] to one or more of them. Josh is likely to die early, probably before 55 and very likely in his 40s. His grandmother will cry at his funeral, knowing he would have made a great father and even grandfather. But it won't happen for him.[63]

In line with the constellation effect of CWA's politics, this particular piece of chaos rhetoric draws from a variety of the group's political platforms to create the most evocative image of moral failure: one boy's poor education becomes a tale of immoral sexual exploits; the danger of the compromised, dysfunctional family; and the threat of a nation whose culture is dying with every lukewarm, indifferent citizen. The very fact that naïve children can actually believe themselves to be "gay" (a term delegitimized by its persistent inclusion in quotation marks) is its own sort of victimization-turned-perpetration, since children who are convinced of this by liberal culture may well grow up to sexually abuse other children once like them. Those who fail to restore the educational system to its godly basis are thus not only accessories to private sexual immorality, but to the public specter of child abuse. Once again, the homosexual threatens to compromise the hopes and dreams of innocent children, and thus the core of the nationalist enterprise. Within the boundaries of this rhetoric, only the righteous parent who represents the nation's true values can create offspring who, if properly trained, productively contribute to its survival.

Religious Liberty

If the image of the nation works as a symbol apart from government because of the former's presumed innocence and justice, it is the "Religious Liberty" plank where this innocence-justice dyad reaches its highest form. Here the term "religious liberty," rather than describing both the establishment and free-exercise clauses of the First Amendment, instead provides a very broad reading of the liberties to which religion is entitled. CWA stands explicitly by the notion that religious liberty does not imply freedom from religion, but freedom *for* religion, and specifically, Christianity:

> We are concerned about:
>
> - The trend of government to diminish and disregard the God-given inalienable rights of individuals.

- The erosion of religious liberty and the legal and cultural imposition of anti-Judeo-Christian philosophies upon our society.

We are working to see:

- Our government strengthen and renew its commitment to respect and protect each individual's exercise of his God-given inalienable rights.
- The protection and preservation of religious liberty as provided in the United States Constitution.[64]

CWA often maintains that the government is determined to rob conservatives of their religious liberties by forcing religious people to commit acts that they believe are immoral. In an article that juxtaposes the government with the nation, President Obama becomes the agent of the government, identified here by his determination to undermine Christian ethics on matters involving abortion:

> President Obama has proceeded to eliminate regulations protecting from discrimination those health care providers who object to committing abortions or other acts contrary to their consciences.
>
> No one should be forced to participate in an immoral act. Conscientious objectors are exempt from combat. Physicians opposed to the death penalty are not forced to administer lethal injections. Likewise, doctors should not be forced to do procedures they believe are immoral.
>
> This totalitarian effort to purge the medical community of those who value life will corrupt the medical profession. Doctors should heal, not kill. Forcing doctors, nurses and pharmacists to violate their consciences will push qualified, ethical people out of the profession, worsening the crisis of fewer health care workers in an already diminishing field.[65]

In this piece, Obama actively corrupts the good intentions of the nation by forcing otherwise ethical medical practitioners to perform abortions. The sexual realm signifies the ideological border wherein the nation's essential rights are truncated or maimed, for in this piece, the right to object to other immoral behaviors (which, interestingly, include military action and the death penalty) has been preserved.[66]

If the sexual realm is where morals are made, then that is also where rights become religious entities, something "God-given." Painting proper rights in this way, the organization can claim concern for the protection and exercise of each individual's rights so long as these rights and the larger "preservation of religious liberty" coincides with the values of "Judeo-Christian philosophies." As one article notes:

> This nation was founded as a refuge from state encroachment. God was always a part of that search for freedom and worship. There was never any idea, otherwise, of building colonies apart from free religious expression, freedom to worship, building a just society upon the principals [*sic*] of the Bible and the idea that God was a part and parcel of it all. And so it has been from the beginning. In that sense the roots of our country are in the Bible. Biblical principals [*sic*] gave the ideas that sparked the building of this nation. This idea of a secular state, hostile to the Christian Faith (as we have to endure today) would never have entered the thinking of our early founders.
>
> That God directed our forefathers to this land to plant this country here, I have no doubt. God was active in the lives of the people that settled this land. They did what they did in response to the call of God to come here and plant a new nation. . . . They were building a new nation, under God. The pledge to [*sic*] allegiance honors both our history and our present attitude (which is like a prayer) that we believe that God is the Lord of this nation and we want to honor this fact with both our lips and our lives.[67]

In CWA chaos rhetoric, there is no proper telling of the nation's beginnings that does not start in a biblical context, literally founded by God through the forefathers. In fact, the Pledge of Allegiance, a nationalist/religious utterance that features so prominently in American civic life, is described as something "like a prayer"—a profession that "we believe that God is the Lord of this nation." To align the planks of CWA's "Religious Liberty" platform to this understanding of American history means that "inalienable rights" and citizenship are legitimate only to the degree that they are read through a specifically Christian lens. Any perspective oppositional to a totalizing Christian worldview (and CWA's interpretation of it, more specifically) constitutes an attack on religious liberties.

One particular freedom that receives significant attention is, as CWA puts it, the "freedom" to oppose homosexuality. Over the past several years, CWA has been extremely concerned about the passage of various hate crimes legislations that punish offenders with a more severe penalty if their crime is against a protected class. While race is one of those classes, sexual orientation is another often included, particularly in light of the brutal beating death of gay college student Matthew Shepard in 1998. CWA has opposed this legislation on the grounds that Christians who want to speak out against homosexuality will be denied the right to free expression out of fear that their comments might be construed as a hate crime.

But even more than its concern over free speech, or even being labeled an organization that "hates," CWA rejects the notion of a hate crime on the grounds that it unfairly creates a special class of citizens who receive extraordinary treatment because of their chosen identity, returning again to the "special rights" argument discussed in the last chapter. In this sense, hate crimes legislation is simply unnecessary since all people are already guaranteed equal protection under the law. Interestingly, however, CWA does not use this argument to speak out against the inclusion of the other groups mentioned in hate crimes legislation:

> The Hate Crimes Act constructs a ranking of victims based on actual or perceived "sexual orientation" and "gender identity." This legislation flies in the face of the 14th Amendment, which guarantees "equal protection under the law" for all citizens—regardless of their sexual preference. Such legislation would require the government to investigate the sexual history, behavior, and identity of victims, and invest more resources into the prosecution of those who are perceived (by whom is not clear) to engage in particular sexual behavior over and above crimes committed against other victims such as grandmothers, former homosexuals, military members, police officers and victims of prior crimes.
>
> "Hate crimes" legislation also represents an overreach of the federal government into state authority. . . . A federal "hate crimes" law would signify that if the Department of Justice did not like a verdict in a state they can intrude to trump a state's ruling. Yet there is no evidence to suggest that states are discriminating against any particular victims.

> Furthermore, expanding "hate crimes" to include "sexual orientation" and gender identity could put people with traditional values directly in the crosshairs of official government policy. "Hate crimes" laws place us on a slippery slope toward religious persecution. These laws are already being employed as a tool in Brazil, Europe, Canada—and even right here in America—to intimidate and silence people who honor natural human sexuality and who value the sanctity of marriage as between one man and one woman. If a person speaks out against various sexual behaviors, that person may be accused of "hate speech," which could lead to an accusation of associations with "hate crimes."
>
> Please do not pass legislation that subverts our national foundation of equal justice for all by granting special treatment to a class of citizens based on a perception of an individual's sexual preference.[68]

CWA's first defensive move is its claim that hate crimes legislation enables preferential treatment for an illegitimate group at the expense of other victims. The list of those affected might initially seem puzzling. But when read through the lens of CWA's symbolic lexicon, those who experience persecution because of hate crimes laws are "true" victims who are more symbolically moral or vulnerable than the homosexual. The innocent grandmother, the law-abiding and nation-building soldier and police officer, and the "former" homosexual (that is, someone who has rediscovered morality) all suffer by this "victim ranking." So do those who have been repeatedly victimized ("victims of prior crimes"). According to this rhetoric, the moral and the most vulnerable stand to lose substantially if "hate crimes" legislation is passed, for while they were victimized despite their innocence, homosexuals experienced victimization because of their sin.

Because hate crimes legislation is here discussed as a federal policy (the Hate Crimes Act), CWA introduces the risk of federal intrusion into state affairs. Christians may find themselves "in the crosshairs" of governmental policies, not unlike what some conservatives have experienced in Canada, Brazil, and Europe (where recent hate crimes legislations have prohibited certain forms of public, conservative Christian speech, in particular).[69] Within the symbolic constellation constructed through CWA chaos rhetoric, conservative Christian speech on homosexuality can never be synonymous with harm or civil rights violations, as homosexuality is not a civil right, nor do homosexuals experience harm that they did not self-perpetuate through a chosen identity. Thus hate crimes laws reinforce CWA's sense that the government and nation exist as separate entities: in this signifying chain, the government, through the Hate Crimes Act, is linked with inequality, the victimization of innocents, and the undermining of religious liberty. In parallel fashion, the nation, under the auspices of the Fourteenth Amendment, is fused with essential human equality. In almost every one of CWA's portrayals of the nation, the nation's inherent justice and goodness are structured such that the sexually variant cannot profit from its institutions or its policies, assuming a conservative reading of law and rights.

National Sovereignty

CWA's final platform, "National Sovereignty," is in many ways the natural outcome of the "Religious Liberty" platform before it, as liberty is often portrayed as the necessary foundation of national sovereignty. What is different about this platform is the awareness of the United States as a global force. Whereas previous rhetoric has remained rather inwardly focused on the nation and its internal political struggles, the "National Sovereignty" platform widens the lens of the organization, recognizing a new series of threats from both inside and outside the country's borders that might weaken the nation's international standing:

> We are concerned about:
>
> - The loss of national sovereignty to international organizations and other foreign powers through judicial and administrative decisions.
> - The lack of border security to protect America from terrorists and all illegal immigration.
> - Judges who exceed their authority to interpret law by intruding on the authority of the legislative and executive branches of government.
> - The security of our nation and the increasing pressure to weaken the country's defenses.
>
> We are working to see:
>
> - A reaffirmation of the independence of the United States and protection of the right to self-government without legal

recognition of any foreign authority as to the interpretation of the U.S. Constitution.

- Our nation develop and maintain strong border controls to protect us from foreign terrorists and the flow of illegal immigration. We welcome legal immigrants, especially those fleeing government persecution because of their religious beliefs or other basic human rights.
- The nomination and confirmation of highly qualified individuals as judges who have demonstrated a commitment to the limited role of the judicial branch, the rule of law and respect for the text of the state and U.S. Constitutions.
- The United States deploy the strongest national defense system in the world as a deterrent to foreign aggression.[70]

In most conservative social policy, the threat of the international "other" has usually taken the shape of the illegal immigrant or the terrorist, and CWA is deeply concerned about these figures. However, CWA most often construes sex as a violation of national sovereignty by referencing the intrusive reach of outside powers such as the United Nations. This is most visible in its opposition to the United Nations' Convention on the Elimination of All Forms of Discrimination Against Women (CEDAW) Treaty, which CWA has attacked for several years. CEDAW asserts that because of restrictive gender ideals, women in some cultures are unable to control the terms of their reproduction, are often limited by social norms of "homemaker" and "mother," and are regularly prohibited from opportunities for economic, political, and cultural independence. Using many of the same arguments on abortion, prostitution, and gender discrimination as it has employed against American liberals, CWA has opposed CEDAW because it "urges governments to interfere and exert pressure in personal and cultural issues."[71] More explicitly, CWA has objected to the sense that women's traditional roles might be interpreted as restrictive.

That CWA understands there to be a "personal and cultural" realm that should be free from government intervention may seem ironic in light of the fact that its own work in the American context attempts to exert governmental control over such a realm. But here again is the rhetorical dividing line between government and nation. As the self-proclaimed representative of the latter, CWA's work is neither inappropriate nor interventionist because it portrays its position as morally superior, and as such, in the best interest of women.

This self-perception explains a banner at the top of the website's homepage in the spring of 2010, proclaiming, "Save Mother's Day!" The article connected to the banner referenced the concern voiced by some conservatives that CEDAW might be used to outlaw Mother's Day, because the holiday reinforces traditional gender roles.[72] From this, CWA construed CEDAW as the "hidden weapon" of radical feminists that, if adopted by the United States, "would devalue and harm American women, just as it has already done to women in countries which have ratified CEDAW." Among its many harms, "CEDAW will pressure us to decriminalize prostitution, put infants in government day care, revise our textbooks to reflect non-stereotypical gender roles, criticize the influence of religion on our society, and—unbelievably—to stop celebrating Mother's Day."[73]

Despite its ongoing work against CEDAW, most of CWA's recent national sovereignty work is domestically focused, arguing that American citizens can do as much, if not more, to threaten the nation's sovereignty as can foreign enemies and organizations. As long as judges redefine the legal contours of the country in ways that CWA finds unfavorable, the judicial branch is portrayed as a force that damages the nation like a terrorist, or one that saps its precious resources, much as illegal immigrants are often depicted. Apart from its concern over "activist judges," as it calls them, much of CWA's concern as of late has focused on the Obama administration's healthcare reform plan. While on the surface this seems to be a domestic matter having little to do with national sovereignty, CWA has described healthcare reform by invoking the popular trope of socialism as the "other" infiltrating the nation, claiming Obama's plan will favor the agendas of illegal aliens, liberals, and homosexuals, all the while using federal money for abortions.

Under this reading of the threat to national sovereignty, otherwise domestic affairs can threaten the nation's independence and vigor insomuch as they are influenced by predatory philosophies that threaten a conservative interpretation of democracy. Repeating the government/nation divide, the threat from Obama comes through a government healthcare plan that will truncate the nation's liberties. Liberty is not the only thing at stake; life, as well, is at risk. The sanctity of life argument is here revived, for the following article asserts that "Obama-care" is really after the quick deaths of the inconvenient through abortion and euthanasia. In this excerpt, the author's remarks are contextualized in specifically patriotic, and beyond that, militaristic, terms:

Here's the bottom-line of Obama-care. Take an 85-year-old man who fought for his country in World War II or Korea, who paid taxes and obeyed the law all of his life, who built a home and raised children who themselves grew up to become productive citizens, and who started a business that eventually employed dozens or even thousands of people.

He doesn't get end-of-life treatment, so those resources can be redirected to illegal aliens and taxpayer-funded abortion. He's given a few drugs to die on quickly and quietly, so Nancy Pelosi can have her Botox treatments and Rosie O'Donnell will get liposuction. . . .

Do you think that those who are pushing the Freedom of Choice Act—who want to eliminate any restraints on abortion—and who let Terri Schiavo die of dehydration—do you think they will really have any qualms about pulling the plug on Granny? . . .

What then must we do? What is our assignment?

You who have gathered here today are the Minutemen. You are the soldiers of the Continental Army leaving bloody footprints in the snow during Washington's retreat across New Jersey in December of 1776. You are the 5th Corps of the 20th Maine Infantry charging the Confederate lines at Gettysburg. You are the Doughboys of the Argonne. You are the boys of Easy Company dropping behind enemy lines on D-Day.

But what can we do, you ask? The party of death controls the White House, has super-majorities in Congress and owns the media (news and entertainment).

I'll tell you what you can do: You can take to heart the words of Winston Churchill to the students of Harrow School in 1941: "Never give in—never, never, never, never, in nothing great or small, large or petty. . . . Never yield to force; never yield to the apparently overwhelming might of the enemy."

And you can draw strength from the last stanza of The Star-Spangled Banner: "Then conquer we must, when our cause it is just, And this be our motto: 'In God is our trust.' And the star-spangled banner in triumph shall wave O'er the land of the free (*Do you hear that, Mr. Obama, 'the land of the free'*?) and the home of the brave!"[74]

CWA symbolically merges the fight against the Obama administration ("the party of death") and its healthcare plan with several of the major military battles in which the nation has engaged, and which, importantly, have generated significant nationalist pride. Uniting the two leads to their equation: what conservatives are up against is yet another battle of epic proportions where the nation's life and liberty are on the line. Thus when the author asks "But what can we do?," the answer is couched in militaristic language. Put most simply, an attack on the nation requires the nation to defend itself.

What the "troops" must defend is certain vulnerable populations that Obama and his allies wish to see "die . . . quickly and quietly" so that their own political problems might be alleviated. The ethics of the opponent are portrayed as unquestioningly absent, for these issues do not even pose a moral conundrum to Obama and other liberals. Rather, the left represents a coldhearted attempt to push aside the inconvenient. CWA becomes the populist conscience, the voice of the oppressed.

Thus when the author invokes Winston Churchill, whose World War II speeches are widely known, he equates the Obama administration with Nazi Germany, and thereby secures one of the most salient contemporary symbols of evil with Obama's work, which he has already described in terms of the death of innocents. This transpires in great part when CWA asks the reader to situate himself as a soldier, one who crosses both time and place, a symbolic figure who self-sacrifices for the nation. By drawing on the symbolic reservoirs of the Revolutionary and Civil Wars as well as World Wars I and II, the author manages to collapse all four of these conflicts, culturally imbued with great patriotic pride, power, and images of American moral fortitude, and to equate them with the battle against Obama, who, through his portrayal as a menacing force, is symbolically consigned to a position external to the nation. The reader-turned-soldier's metaphorical "bloody footprints" are signs of the sacrifice needed to fight Obama, for this is not a simple war of words but demands "dropping behind enemy lines."

It is this ability to abstract and then divide the government from the nation, empowered by a strong sense of American exceptionalism, which drives CWA's National Sovereignty platform. Indeed, exceptionalism might well be the central, enduring theme of the signifying chains active in CWA speech, although its use is multi-layered. Wherever there is a strong thread of American exceptionalism there is an equally robust strain of CWA's own ideological supremacy, which allows it to portray its own political activity as something that can rightfully disappear behind the banner of the "Christian nation" that gives it the authority to speak.

Whether and how America really is or was a "Christian nation" is perhaps the most important question with which CWA must grapple in order to sustain its rhetoric, and thus its political legitimacy. In one article addressing this matter, the author poses the question, "Was the American Revolution an act of rebellion against God and the Bible?"[75] This inquiry is contextualized in light of the debate within conservative circles about the degree of deference that Christians should show the government. Part of this dispute is linked to a biblical passage (Rom 13: 2) in which the apostle Paul directs the Christian church at Rome to support governmental authorities, viewing their right to rule as something willed by God. Quite obviously, this position creates problems for CWA, for under this reading of the passage, the organization's activist efforts would be unbiblical anytime its political opponents are in office.

By contextualizing this issue in terms of the Founding Fathers and the American Revolution, the author refutes the notion asserted by some that the Bible was willingly ignored or at least misunderstood by these early Americans. Instead, "the Founders clearly believed that they were not in rebellion to God's ordained institution of civil government; they were only resisting tyranny and not the institution itself."[76] Reviving the division between the upstanding nation and the tyrannical government, the author quotes Declaration of Independence signer Francis Hopkinson (who, he also notes, was a "church musician and choir leader"). Hopkinson is portrayed as the person answering the following questions:

> *Q. It has often been said, that America is in a state of rebellion. Tell me, therefore, what is Rebellion?*
>
> A. It is when a great number of people, headed by one or more factious leaders, aim at deposing their lawful prince without any just cause of complaint in order to place another on his throne.
>
> *Q. Is this the case of the Americans?*
>
> A. Far otherwise.[77]

CWA has removed the uncomfortable burden that a rigid biblical literalism might create by fashioning a caveat through which the Founding Fathers can operate as agents of justice rather than rebellion. The motives of the Founding Fathers always remained pure:

> Reflective of the Founding Father's belief that they were not rebelling against God or resisting ordained government but only tyranny was the fact that the first national motto proposed for America in August 1776 was "Rebellion to tyrants is obedience to God." . . . According to the Founders' biblical understanding, the fact that they were engaged in a defensive action made all the difference; they believed that they could boldly approach God and sincerely seek His aid and blessing in such a situation. In fact, so cognizant were American leaders they that they would account to God for their actions, and so convinced were they that they would be held innocent before Him, that the flag of the Massachusetts Army proclaimed "An Appeal to God," and the flag of the Massachusetts Navy likewise declared an "Appeal to Heaven."[78]

The author asserts that both biblical and national fidelity were preserved by the Founding Fathers when they resisted "only tyranny" and not "ordained government"; what distinguishes tyranny from lawful rule is the special sense of justice with which they were enabled, thus resulting in a "revolution" rather than a "rebellion."

This is precisely how CWA can portray "defensive action" against the government as the will of God. For so long as their exceptional principles guided them, there was no such thing as an unjust, unwarranted, or ungodly act committed by the Founding Fathers. Correspondingly, so long as the category "ordained government" exists, groups like CWA can describe their political activity as something entirely apolitical, and the activism of their opponents as simple politicking. CWA thus uses the image of the Founding Fathers to create an interpretive lens through which its readers might understand their own advocacy. Equipped with an exceptional and unique insight into justice, sure of the blessing of God, and aware that they are under attack, CWA's members can move confidently to transform American culture.

A Holy Union: The Marriage of God and Nation

Each of CWA's six political planks is a statement on the identity of the nation and its legitimate inhabitants, identities defined and demarcated at various points through specific rhetoric on sex. Each core issue depends on, and is mutually reinforced by, the other. To CWA, there is no private sphere so long as agents of liberalism and moral relativism seek active, public representation. Because it stands as a uniquely knowledgeable entity on what rights the Christian nation should bestow, its job to protect the nation is aligned with its task of political domination.

Like a constellation, the nation is thus only visible when all of these planks coalesce. This totalizing vision communicates to the CWA reader that by protecting the nation through activist work, she is engaging in nothing less than national self-preservation. For it is in the context of American culture, through the avenues of its legislation, and in their own American identity that CWA readers assert the superiority of their social positions. If CWA can portray itself as something like a vital, living foundation on which the nation depends, then CWA's own agents—its grassroots base—provide the activism that makes the nation possible.

The one enduring character throughout CWA's chaos rhetoric is thus not God, nor the Bible, but the nation. In the scheme of CWA's speech, appeals to God are useful only to the degree that they preserve the patriotic enterprise. Likewise, the vision of that which is ungodly is also often that which is un-American. If the "religious" quality of religious speech is its ability to claim authority beyond human critique, it seems entirely possible to assert that there is no distinction here between God and nation, for both are positioned as equally unquestionable, and mutually reinforcing, entities.[79] Sexual regulation is the vehicle by which the nation proves its exceptional, godly status, leaving no realm in CWA's universe that can—or should—remain untouched by its advocacy.

5

Lonely Messengers? The Ubiquity of Chaos Rhetoric[1]

For a nation of spin doctors and bloggers, Americans are remarkably naïve about the deeper forces in language, especially religious language. We pride ourselves on our cynicism about manipulative speech even as we credit it with magical potencies. We laugh about those gullible enough to be deceived, but too rarely ask how exactly they fall under the spell of their deceivers—unless we are interested in producing similar effects ourselves. . . .

—MARK JORDAN[2]

THE CULTURAL STORY of CWA, and the larger Christian Right of which it is a part, is a narrative with many renderings and many storytellers. The version of that story that has filled the preceding pages reveals how CWA uses words and symbols to craft a chaos rhetoric that can create the widespread cultural sentiment needed to generate national, political support for conservative causes and platforms. Because the self-stated goal of the Christian Right is to impact American politics, the ability to identify and describe the mechanisms through which this impact becomes reality is a critical part, if not the central expression, of explaining the components of Christian Right identity.

But many others have also participated in the discursive construction of the Christian Right—from their liberal activist opponents, to media representatives, to the scholars who study them—and assessing how to gauge and integrate these voices is certainly a challenge. While this final chapter offers no simple, decisive answers, it does aim to shed light on the murky and often hotly contested ways in which the Christian Right has been understood. As the previous chapters have shown, members of the Christian Right often claim that their activism is the fulfillment of true democracy and religious freedom. At the same time, others often regard it as something antithetical to the country's values altogether. One rather common account argues that the chaos rhetoric employed by CWA and the larger Christian Right is a dangerous force that manipulates the public, blurs the separation between church and state, violates the religious liberties of those who oppose the Christian Right's cultural dominance, and with these, thwarts any sense of true democracy.[3]

Yet to construe groups that use chaos rhetoric as synonymous with social danger and moral degradation is not a necessary connection, for almost all groups that seek to persuade the public use similar rhetorical techniques.[4] Rather than offering an opinion on whether chaos rhetoric is morally appropriate, or on the "proper" political role of CWA (both things far outside of both the scope and intentions of this book), in this final chapter I consider whether the chaos rhetoric at the center of CWA and the Christian Right is at all exceptional, and if not, what this tells us about the significance of such groups to American public life.

To approach this question demands looking at whether this technique so fundamental to CWA's political success is actually at all unique. This chapter thus begins by examining excerpts of activist rhetoric from two different liberal advocacy groups that have directly opposed CWA's work: the National Organization of Women (NOW) and People for the American Way (PFAW). Despite their clear ideological differences with CWA, both NOW and PFAW are concerned with many of the same topics (such as gay rights and abortion), and as will become evident, also employ the recognizable structures and emotions of chaos rhetoric to publicly transmit their views. If the speech used by these classically liberal organizations shows that chaos rhetoric is nothing other than a rather mundane or routine tactic that groups use in the process of public persuasion (albeit an effective one), this forces the question of whether the Christian Right is an altogether unique phenomenon, and what it means when one group critiques another for using the very tactics that it also employs.

The second part of this chapter further probes this issue by considering the qualities that some scholars use to describe, distinguish, and contextualize the Christian Right and the ACP movement, more generally. The point of this exercise is not only to consider the movement's social significance, but also to ask questions about the presumptions that underlie particular strains of scholarship. More explicitly, I examine how certain scholars who study evangelical Christianity have crafted their own brand of chaos rhetoric to disenfranchise the Christian Right (and ACPs more broadly) from the political or religious mainstream, a move in line with many of the dominant political commitments of the academy. This has happened not only in more obvious chaos rhetoric that appeals to the dangers of the Christian Right, but also in more subtle examples that create differentiation and opposition where such distinctions need not be obviously rendered. This final chapter thus demonstrates the ubiquity of chaos rhetoric across many different sectors of public discourse and considers, more specifically, the role of certain types of scholarly chaos rhetoric in the creation of popular social perceptions of Christian conservatism.

Mirror Opposites

CWA understands itself as an agency of righteousness that, along with other Christian Right groups, is uniquely able to determine the proper moral course of the nation. This is a necessary self-portrayal, in part, because of the competitive nature of its activism. Liberal advocacy groups vie with the organization for the public's attention, but in the true style of chaos rhetoric, they also operate as a foil against which CWA can defensively craft its own image. In fact, one might remember from earlier chapters that the first line of CWA's own institutional history invokes NOW, the self-described "largest organization of feminist activists in the United States."[5] LaHaye claims to have founded CWA in part as a response to NOW's portrayal of women's rights, which she interpreted as extremist, offensive, and counter to the sensibilities of the average American woman.[6] Although NOW's activism is multi-faceted (including reproductive rights, gender equity, economic concerns, and an end to a number of identity discriminations), CWA most typically situates NOW as a primarily pro-abortion organization, as seen in CWA president Penny Nance's remark that NOW members are "out of their minds" and "completely blinded by ideology and a searing lust for a woman's right to choose to abort her child."[7]

PFAW is also a liberal advocacy group and is usually invoked by CWA as an example of liberal corruption on the fronts of gay rights and an "activist judiciary," although like NOW, PFAW's political platforms are actually much more broadly wrought. PFAW was founded in 1980 by television executive Norman Lear, who was "concerned about the growing influence of radical religious evangelists" and who consequently sought to create "a non-profit organization designed to speak out for Bill of Rights guarantees and to monitor violations of constitutional freedoms."[8]

Advocating classically liberal platforms, PFAW openly opposes groups from the Christian Right and has labeled one of its core issues "Fighting the Right." Also similar to NOW, PFAW's activism is often described by CWA as both misguided and unnecessarily partisan, if not outright un-American. PFAW was famously mentioned in Jerry Falwell's post-9/11 comments as one of several groups responsible for angering God and thus provoking the terrorist attacks.[9]

Despite the seeming opposition between the political interests of these groups and CWA, a comparison of their rhetoric shows some striking similarities. Remember that CWA's chaos rhetoric operates by deploying specific symbols designed to create a heightened sense of social chaos and threat. As earlier discussed, themes of nation, logic, populism, and science (among others) all typically weigh heavily in this chaos rhetoric as authoritative symbols that are aggressed upon by elitists, feminists, and other sorts of liberals whose moral worth is deemed questionable, if not altogether absent.

With these qualities in mind, consider the following excerpt from NOW, which responds to the media portrayal of the death of Kansas abortion provider George Tiller. Tiller was shot during a Sunday service at his church in May 2009 by a man claiming to act on behalf of the pro-life movement.[10] In the piece, author and then-NOW President Kim Gandy implicates in Tiller's death conservative political commentator Bill O'Reilly and his FOX news show, *The O'Reilly Factor*, which at that time was the most watched American news program on television.[11] Concerned with the possible violent implications of O'Reilly's rhetoric, Gandy offers the following commentary:

> Unsurprisingly, right-wing blowhard Bill O'Reilly was one of the most vocal opponents and antagonists of Dr. Tiller. From the first time Tiller's name surfaced on The O'Reilly Factor in early 2005, the show host brought up the doctor on 29 different episodes, typically including the blatantly false and inflammatory characterization of him as "the baby killer." Hate speech such as this littered O'Reilly's commentary: Tiller's medical services were referred to as "Nazi stuff," and Tiller had "blood on his hands." On his radio show in 2006 O'Reilly appeared to begin a threat, only to catch himself: "And if I could get my hands on Tiller—well, you know. Can't be vigilantes. Can't do that. It's just a figure of speech."
>
> Many have pointed to O'Reilly's loathsome jargon as a possible catalyst for the murder. O'Reilly and those like him will claim that

> their hateful rhetoric is nothing more than free speech and has no bearing on the actions of the man who murdered Dr. Tiller. But make no mistake, hate speech of this kind sets the stage for those who carry out the dirty work of the anti-abortion movement.
>
> Extremists like O'Reilly aren't the only ones furthering their anti-women agenda. Mainstream news sources like NBC often repeat right-wing terms, such as referring to Tiller not as the OB/GYN he was, but as an "abortion doctor," even an "abortionist." The website Slate asked the question 'Is it wrong to kill an abortionist?'
>
> I probably don't need to tell you this, but "abortionist" is not a real medical term; and this type of language diminishes health care professionals like Tiller, a highly-skilled and well-respected physician who used his medical training to lawfully assist women in dire need of medical treatment.
>
> And he was murdered in public—not just to punish and halt Dr. Tiller himself, but to send a message to anyone who assists women in exercising their full reproductive rights. This was an act of domestic terrorism, and any terminology suggesting that Dr. Tiller may have had it coming is shameful. On the bright side, we applaud "CBS Evening News with Katie Couric" for calling Tiller's murder a "hate crime" on its June 10 edition, comparing it to that day's killing of a security guard at the Holocaust Museum, apparently by a white supremacist.[12]

Just as CWA has done many times before, here a *liberal* speaker claims that the media is an entity that destroys truth. While CWA is prone to equate "media" with "elitists," Gandy reworks this equation in similar ways by equating certain forms of media with an affront on American liberties. In short, Gandy's claim is that conservative speech cannot be rendered legitimate ("free speech") because it is "hate speech." Here again, claims to "truth" or "fact" are crucial, for Gandy's aim is to render O'Reilly as not only misguided, but specifically, deceptive. As she will contend, this brand of deception compromises core national values, foremost among them, life.

Gandy creates this scenario by situating O'Reilly's speech as the filter through which one might interpret conservative speech as a whole. She argues that his rhetoric was fundamentally illegitimate because it produced "loathsome jargon" and "blatantly false and inflammatory" characterizations of Tiller, which reflected on the larger pro-choice movement of which Tiller was a symbol. Yet this is not just "talk," as Gandy is quick to note, for O'Reilly is explicitly portrayed as a catalyst of danger. He "caught himself" in a public threat when he unintentionally exposed his true motives, rendering his already illegitimate speech a "possible catalyst for the murder." She is careful to argue that this is not protected or "free" speech precisely because it endangers others. Gandy's assertion that "hate speech of this kind sets the stage for those who carry out the dirty work of the anti-abortion movement" thereby links "hate speech" with conservative rhetoric with the "dirty work" (murder).

But perhaps the most telling symbol that Gandy produces is the image of Tiller's killer as a "domestic terrorist." Appealing again to the values of the nation—and opposing what may threaten the nation's very core—Gandy contends that the conditions of Tiller's murder (namely, in public) also represented an assassination attempt on civil liberties. As an act not only of terrorism but, more locally, of intimidation, Tiller's death was intended to stop what Gandy describes as a fundamental piece of American citizenship: the fulfillment of a legal right.

While Gandy has already established that O'Reilly's comments are egregious on their own, she continues on with an argument on the extent of the damage wrought by his words. Gandy claims that the harm is not limited, but, rather, contagious. Conservative commentators like O'Reilly (who is a "blowhard") infect other media outlets—and the American mind—with unfair renderings of abortion providers, undercutting their honorable characteristics (as seen in Gandy's critique of the term "abortionist"). Despite being an agent of "lawfulness," Tiller was killed. As an agent of dangerous, contagious speech, O'Reilly perpetuates the forces that killed Tiller through his contamination of the airwaves. O'Reilly and like-minded others thus bring about the death of the law through their speech as well as the demise of objective, cultural sensibility.

These arguments culminate in what is probably Gandy's most powerful rhetorical turn in her speech. She applauds CBS for its comparison of Tiller's death with the death of a security guard at the Holocaust Museum by a white supremacist. This is a final, crucial symbol in Gandy's assertion: an agent of "legitimate" order (the security guard), employed by an organization that exists because a violent, unlawful, and illegitimate act occurred against an otherwise innocent people (the Holocaust), was killed by an agent of hate, bias, and illegitimacy (the white supremacist). In praising CBS for its equation of Tiller's death with that of the Holocaust

Museum security guard, Gandy can symbolically declare the danger of an irrational ideologue (O'Reilly) against order, the law, and innocence.

The chaos rhetoric produced by Gandy thus echoes many of the same structures, symbolic juxtapositions, and even terms used in CWA chaos rhetoric, despite the opposition in political platforms. In another instance of chaos rhetoric, liberal advocacy group PFAW draws upon similar themes in its claim that conservative religious groups like CWA have used illegitimate methods to attack gay rights:

> Politically, Religious Right groups use the disease or addiction model to assert that civil rights protections should not be afforded to gays and lesbians.[13] According to this "logic," public policy that treats gays with equality and dignity actually inhibits individuals from seeking to be "cured." In Maine earlier this year, "ex-gays" were featured in one of the television commercials run by Religious Right groups during the successful campaign to overturn a statewide anti-discrimination law.
>
> The recent ads also attempt to equate homosexuality with AIDS and other diseases; one of the recent ads was titled, "From Innocence to AIDS," cleverly alluding to Religious Right myths about gay recruitment of children and promoting Religious Right efforts to portray homosexuality as a "death-style." Typical of such rhetoric was a recent Chuck Colson article about Billy, a doll being marketed in the gay community. Colson suggested that all Billy dolls should come with a plastic coffin, asserting that most gays are "men whose lives are tragically marked by disease, addiction, misery, and early death."
>
> Dr. Robert Garofalo, a Boston pediatrician who authored a health study of gay teens last spring, complained to the Boston Globe that the recent ad campaign, was "a complete misrepresentation" of his research on substance abuse and other high-risk behavior. Garofalo told the Globe he believes the disproportionate risk of gay youth for substance abuse and suicide are the result of alienation gay teenagers face in a "culture that is often unaccepting." Religious Right groups attributed the problems to homosexuality itself, which Garofalo calls "the complete opposite conclusion of what the paper actually concluded."
>
> Misrepresenting ideology as science is a favored tactic. Paul Cameron is a virulently anti-gay "researcher" whose methods led to his being ousted from the American Psychological Association. Although Cameron has been thoroughly discredited, his "research"

> continues to be a favored source of ammunition for the Religious Right. William Bennett, Chuck Colson, and others continue to repeat Cameron's conclusion that the life expectancy for gay men is 43 years, a statistic based on his reading of obituaries in gay newspapers. (Cameron's statistic was effectively demolished in online magazine Slate). Bennett's trumpeting of this statistic last year on ABC's This Week and in the Weekly Standard was picked up by National Review and continues to circulate as the kind of "truth" that the Religious Right wants to tell America.[14]

Like Gandy, the PFAW article claims that truth-twisting is the primary rhetorical enterprise of the Christian Right. Using quotation marks freely so as to delegitimize its terms (much like what CWA does in the production of its own chaos rhetoric), the author undercuts the Christian Right's understanding of "logic," "gays," and "research," transforming them, instead, into propagandist moments of deception rather than objective fact. In particular, quotation marks are prominently used to undercut the terms "ex-gay" and "cured" so as to situate homosexuality as an acceptable, essential identity rather than part of the "disease or addiction model" to which the Christian Right frequently appeals.

This notion of a "disease or addiction model" is formative to the rest of the article. PFAW asserts itself as something of an epistemological agent, an identity confirmed later in its location of the Christian Right as a producer of "rhetoric" that employs certain "tactic[s]." It (PFAW) is familiar with this "model" and has the vocabulary and knowledge to talk about, identify, and situate it politically. With this authoritative mechanism in place, the PFAW article proceeds to delegitimize the Christian Right's characterization of homosexuality as a behavioral and psychological problem that can be "cured" through proper treatment.

This is not just an issue of ideological disagreement, but a matter of deception: the Christian Right is guilty of manipulating facts for political gain. PFAW's case is not mere conjecture, it notes, for it can be proven by a physician, an agent of science and objectivity. Not only did the Christian Right engage in deception through this manipulation, PFAW argues, but the facts they engineered about the disproportionate substance abuse and suicide among gay teens actually refer to a phenomenon that they themselves have caused ("a culture that is often unaccepting"). In this sense, the Christian Right is not only guilty of political trickery, but is culpable in harming children.

This is why the PFAW article can claim that "misrepresenting ideology as science is a favorite tactic" of the Christian Right. Having already established the Christian Right as crass, insensitive, and inappropriate (particularly in regards to Colson's comment about the Billy doll), PFAW suggests that it is unclear whether spokespersons for the Christian Right are able to accurately apprehend the truth at all.

In both excerpts of chaos rhetoric featured here, NOW and PFAW situate themselves as organizations equipped to identify propaganda so as to separate their own rhetorical moves from being similarly labeled. This special ability to sift truth from misinformation is key to preserving the nation's intrinsic sense of justice when it is under attack by conservatives. Gandy transforms anti-abortion speech into the image of a volatile, irrational domestic terrorist who threatens the nation with physical and ideological harm. Her presumed ability to identify "real oppression" (understood as Tiller's public killing and its accompanying show of intimidation) underscores her own authority. Similarly, the PFAW article claims that what the Christian Right has done amounts to little more than the manipulation and thus deactivation of "civil rights protections." These are not just religious conservatives commiserating among themselves, PFAW argues, but a group devoted to an active, politically inspired misrepresentation of reality resulting in concrete harms.

Comparing excerpts from CWA, NOW, and PFAW illuminates how groups can have much different material and legal interests that they pursue, yet still use the same rhetorical tactics to meet their common goal of public persuasion. This does not mean that all three groups use data of equal quality in their arguments, or draw equally sound conclusions, but simply that their rhetoric mirrors one another in form and symbolic usage.[15] All three question the ability of their opponent to ascertain truth and use logic on matters of sex and reproduction, throw into question their opponent's moral righteousness through claims of intentional deception, cast their opponent as a vehicle of public danger and a general threat to safety, and view them as a challenge to the workings and values of the nationalist project. Such rhetorical moves determine, as Michael Cobb puts it, "fundamental definitions of who can belong and be protected by the United States" and who will constitute "citizens that will be valued."[16] In this sense, while CWA, PFAW, and NOW all claim truth, fact, objectivity, science, safety, and health as authorities that bolster the logic contained within their chaos rhetoric, they fundamentally disagree on the criteria that constitutes a citizen worthy of protections.

Scholarship and Pathological Speech

It is apparent, then, that chaos rhetoric is not unique to the Christian Right. Yet there is an enduring sense in many circles that the rhetoric of the Christian Right is uniquely emotional, inflammatory, and manipulative. Scholars have noted how the mainstream media has often made a spectacle of the Christian Right based on this portrayal, furthering the depiction of the movement as one that controls evangelicals as if they were a monolithic puppet.[17] Similarly, it is not difficult to find other media representations of the Christian Right that capitalize heavily on war, crusade, and attack imagery to depict the group as a loathsome force hijacking America's foundations.[18] This generalized antipathy towards the tactics and politics used by conservative elites is reflected in scholar Christian Smith's remark that "American evangelicals remain one of the last social groups in the United States that people can speak disparagingly about in public and get away with it."[19]

But far fewer scholars have turned an analytical eye towards how certain members of the academy might participate in the same rhetorical moves. In fact, it is not uncommon to find scholars who produce chaos rhetoric about the Christian Right and ACPs in much the same way as do other entities, consistent with their own personal politics (which, for many scholars, includes support for liberal politics, and also frequently, liberal Protestant, thought). These political allegiances are not difficult to detect because scholars often very readily reveal them, whether in the prefaces of their books (wherein they often discuss their own religious commitments as the context for their interest in the subject), in analyses that manifestly describe the "dangers" of conservative social thought, or still in other descriptions of conservatives that demarcate their ideology as something distinct from the intellectual commitments of the academy.[20] Several of these items will be shortly discussed in further detail.

My goal in pointing out the presence of scholarly chaos rhetoric is not necessarily to delegitimize the conclusions drawn by those who use it, for again, chaos rhetoric is a persuasive tactic, not an indicator of factual inaccuracy. Rather, my intention is to show how chaos rhetoric is a truly ubiquitous persuasion technique that operates in a similar way no matter the political preferences or social locations of its producers. Adopting this approach leads to a variety of important questions: Why and how have certain scholars used chaos rhetoric to define "acceptable" religious practice? Where does CWA fit into that rubric, and why? What can one conclude about the social impact of the Christian Right and ACPs, more broadly? Are they religious zealots who have taken a nice idea too far, or are they, rather, something much more mundane?

To consider the possible answers to these questions, it is once again helpful to return to certain aspects of Judith Butler's identity formation model to discuss how the authority of words and labels is involved in the distribution of social power. In one of her most famous essays on the use of the term *queer*, Butler describes how the word was first used as a shaming interpellation against the gay community, intended to produce a pathologized subject by rendering the object of that label something abnormal—that is, a rejection of the heteronormative form. It is only because heterosexuality has been treated as normal that the term *queer* has had negative meaning, Butler notes, yet there is no universal gauge by which to essentially define why heterosexuality should be standardized. Thus, to Butler, the use of the label *queer* has functioned as a deprecatory act insomuch as it has made the user of the term the standard against which the labeled deviates. Remembering that the power behind the signifying chain depends on the concealment or altogether absence of the history and connection of certain terms and concepts, those who successfully deploy these symbols do so because they portray them as categories that have a life and reason of their own.[21]

If all groups can use chaos rhetoric to label others in ways that elicit deprecatory force, it is intriguing to consider how certain scholars who study ACPs, generally, and the Christian Right, in particular, have also worked to specifically classify, contextualize, and even pathologize such groups, thereby creating their own signifying chains. In a Butlerian move, conservative Christianity is defined through the chaos rhetoric of some scholars as an entirely distinctive—if not distinctively aberrant—phenomenon, and thus becomes an effective point of contrast against which such scholars can craft their own self-definition as individuals with a different set of political worldviews.

This chaos rhetoric occurs in a multitude of ways. For more overt examples, Linda Kintz calls conservatism's family values "chilling and alien," causing her to ask, "How can hate sound so nice?"[22] In a return to what she calls her "critical distance," she notes that even those who are mildly sympathetic to the Christian Right must understand that this sentiment still adds to the dangers that it poses.[23] Similarly, Rosemary Radford Ruether, in her work on Christianity and cultural family norms, refers to conservative family policy as "demonic distortions that impede justice and wellbeing for many."[24] And Randall Balmer, who in one work claims that conservative Christian politics have "hijacked" evangelicalism's core, elsewhere refers to "charlatan preachers" such as Pat Robertson and Jerry Falwell, who "pander to, rather than challenge, the prejudices of their flocks" as examples of "religious demagoguery."[25] In a third volume, he notes:

> Indeed, history may very well judge the ascendancy of the Religious Right in the final decades of the twentieth century as an aberration because of its distortion of the New Testament and its failure to honor the legacy of nineteenth century evangelical activists . . . the rise of the Religious Right in the late 1970s represented a response to the perceived attacks on the sanctity of the subculture. The attempt on the part of the leaders of the Religious Right to obfuscate the real origins of the movement, however, suggests a level of deception that should be disturbing to any believer. The effect of the Religious Right has been to deliver the faith into the captivity of right-wing politics.[26]

Similarly, in his own chaos rhetoric *about* chaos rhetoric, Jason Bivins remarks that taking seriously the inflammatory speech used by some evangelical leaders undermines the very fabric of democracy, for such rhetoric creates:

> . . . an American public life where responses to insecurity and crippled politics consist of a rejection of reason, an abandonment of faith in reform, and a recourse to discourses of anger and panic. When judgment and renunciation replace empathy and pluralism, democratic culture cannot survive; conversations end, and the ongoing process of democratic argumentation is snipped off.[27]

William Martin takes a more tempered and less targeted approach by avoiding the outright naming of the Christian Right in his indictment, but seeing how his comments come at the end of his book on that very group, the critique is unavoidable:

> Political zealots sometimes seem to suggest that only one political party has a legitimate claim on the American heritage. The Founding Fathers saw that attitude as dangerous. The system of checks and balances they built into the Constitution was informed not only

> by the recognition that good citizens may differ over the proper course of action, but also, at least in part, by the biblical understanding of humans as fallible and prone to wrongdoing and therefore in need of some healthy opposition from their fellows. Nobody, in their view, has a corner on Truth, Justice, and the American Way. Christians should recognize, in justified humility, that there is no single Christian position on many, perhaps most, social issues.[28]

And finally, in his study of progressive religion in America, Robert P. Jones contrasts progressives with conservative Protestants, who represent:

> the religion of the self-assured culture warriors that proffers a politicized Christianity that has drunk too deeply at the well of power and at this moment in our history has lost its way.[29]

All of the examples of chaos rhetoric just featured embrace a similar pattern: the Christian Right's activism is symbolically sealed with a threat to American cultural institutions via specific allusions to the erosion of the separation of church and state, of democracy, and in some cases, of a more righteous, original branch of Christianity that more clearly understood its proper role. In very similar fashion to how CWA deploys its own chaos rhetoric, here the nation and religion are featured together as entities that each impact the life of the other. Kintz, Bivins, and Martin capitalize on the image of America's cultural destruction, warning of the death of democracy and the compromise of the government's checks and balances, both intended to maintain justice and civil rights. While Kintz's reference is more generally targeted at the seemingly positive way in which conservatives transmit otherwise negative and exclusionary political propaganda, Bivins specifically references the "anger and panic" of conservatives, in contrast to the others capable of "empathy and pluralism" needed to make democracy work. Similarly, in his narrative, Martin employs characters frequently used by CWA (such as the Founding Fathers and the Bible) to suggest that the Christian Right's political advocacy is something outside of the intentions of both the nation and Christianity itself.

Just like CWA, several of these scholars warn that the threat to the nation is constituted precisely to the degree that "true" religion has been improperly transmitted. Ruether and Balmer both invoke this sense of a proper religious standard from which the Christian Right has fallen in

Ruether's use of the term "demonic" and Balmer's descriptions of a movement that "hijacks," "distorts," and "obfuscates" what Christianity was intended to be. Balmer's argument that the modern Christian Right has betrayed the legacy of the nineteenth-century evangelicals is, in fact, rhetorically parallel to CWA's argument that modern feminists have undermined the feminist movement of the early twentieth century.[30] Jones's remark that the Christian Right represents "politicized Christianity" that "has lost its way" also successfully deploys a chaos rhetoric that warns of America's decline at the hands of a corrupt Christianity, a defilement so far gone that Christianity has become that which it purports to oppose.

What's In a Name?

Yet these overt examples are not the only form that scholarly chaos rhetoric takes. One can find further evidence of the discursive moves Butler identifies in a more subtle and widespread brand of chaos rhetoric: in the distinctions frequently adopted by scholars that, while often treated as common sense, are propositions with a political history.

Take, for instance, the way that scholars approach liberal Protestants, the close cousins of the ACP movement. The sense that there is a major chasm between conservative and liberal Protestants is a well-established part of scholarship.[31] Conservative Protestants are often characterized by their emphasis on individual conversion, biblical literalism and inerrancy, and a strong sense of mission to transform the world for Jesus, all of which is evident in CWA's self-understanding. Yet scholars often indicate that liberal Protestants have quite a different range of concerns. Unlike their more conservative counterparts, mainline Protestants (another term for the group) are often described by their tolerance of theological differences, their commitment to diversity and ecumenical cooperation, and their sense of the need for an all-encompassing social role for religion.[32] These characteristics are enabled by a theology that, while generally Christian, is quicker to accommodate modernity by accentuating the importance of reason, which, among other things, enables a more elastic and symbolic reading of the Bible. Scholars suggest that liberal Protestants tend to see the worth and value of other religious systems and emphasize the moral teachings of Jesus over his supernatural deeds. They are also disinclined to emphasize an individual conversion experience as an explicit religious goal.[33]

Despite the fact that these two groups do, indeed, have ideological differences, interview data indicates that they are, at many points, relatively indistinguishable. For instance, studies of mainline Protestant churches have revealed that the theological diversity supposedly endemic to mainline Protestants is present only in certain congregations; many remain quite homogeneous (if not openly conservative) on a variety of issues.[34] Moreover, the political differences that are often presumed to divide the two groups are not nearly as severe as often thought. The Pew Forum on Religion and Public Life indicates that across several significant statistical measures (including voting patterns, political affiliation, positions on homosexuality and abortion, and ideal size of government), "evangelicals" and "mainline Protestants" provide opinions with significant overlap.[35] Still other scholars have published works that call into serious question the notion that most average ACPs desire national, cultural domination, confirming the sense that while their convictions may influence how they vote (as is likely true of any voter), many are, in fact, uncomfortable with the more extreme rhetoric of the Christian Right leadership.[36] And all of these measures overlook the simple fact that liberal Protestants overwhelmingly ascribe to the same basic beliefs of Christianity as their conservative relatives, espousing overtly supernatural principles for which conservatives are repeatedly critiqued as irrational and anti-intellectual. These include a fundamental belief in God, that the Bible communicates the word of God, that Jesus is God's revelation to humans, and that "Christianity is the best way to understand God."[37]

Again, this is not to deny that there are differences between the two groups. The question is whether such differences are as dramatic as the scholarly chaos rhetoric makes them appear. For instance, conservative Protestants have more often been portrayed as a group that negatively "reacts" to social change, whereas their liberal counterparts are equipped to more productively "respond" to it. This is seen in Balmer and Lauren Winner's joint assessment that conservatives were "disappointed," experienced "distress," and were "uneasy," "alarm[ed]," and "increasingly alienated" by the social changes of the nineteenth and twentieth centuries, while their more progressive cousins "rose to . . . social challenges" and "plunged into the herculean, progressive era task" of reforming society.[38] Images of psychological distress or status-deprivation have both been extremely popular means to explain why people join Christian Right movements, but neither model has been adequately substantiated as a social dynamic unique to that movement alone.[39]

Indeed, the primary critique often lodged against conservatives in scholarly chaos rhetoric has to do with the sense that they have a divisive, undemocratic nature fueled by their presumed irrationalist mindset, a worldview that does not, presumably, characterize liberal Protestants.[40] Charges of irrational thinking are based on many conservatives' firm embrace of supernatural ideas that are not reinforced through scientific thinking (i.e., miracles, a literal hell, anti-evolutionary models, etc.). Robert Wuthnow and John H. Evans describe liberal Protestantism as "a haven for American Christians who value striving for balance between faith and reason, creeds and experience, and intellect and emotion," something that presumably sets liberal Protestants apart from other Christians.[41] This aligns with Mark Noll's well-known assessment of the conservative mindset as something "scandalous" because it also, to a great degree, lacks "intellectual vitality."[42] In the same vein, James K. Wellman contrasts conservatives with liberal Protestants by calling the latter "men and women of the Enlightenment," for they "abjure most forms of what they would see as 'primitive' metaphysical and theological thinking," and yet Wellman spends considerable time discussing liberal Protestantism's unique brand of supernaturalism, which, presumably, is not part of this "primitive" genre.[43] He continues that "if liberals hate, it tends to be ideas, and not people," setting up another contrast that warns of the judgmentalism for which conservatives are stereotypically known.[44] Comparably, Robert P. Jones notes that progressive religious people embody "voices that unite rather than divide; and voices that demand attention to a broader agenda of peace, social justice, care for the environment, respect for pluralism, and the common good."[45]

In the true style of defensive argumentation previously discussed, this more subtle form of scholarly chaos rhetoric uses conservative Protestantism as a foil against which a more progressive liberal Protestantism can be construed. This leaves conservative Protestantism fused, even if subtly, with intolerance and illogic, insomuch as it is the branch of Protestantism that *cannot* be described as balancing faith and reason, embracing logic, hating ideas (but not people), and uniting together with others for the common good. The fact that the theology of liberal Protestants usually remains relatively unscathed and under-analyzed, despite the fact that it closely mirrors many aspects of conservative Protestant theology, is further evidence of the way that the defensive argumentation tactic works to highlight some aspects of social movements but avoid similar ones in others.

Yet one can find an even more indirect chaos rhetoric at work in the labeling system used by many scholars to approach conservative activism of many stripes. While conservatives have been given many labels, a representative assortment includes monikers such as "anti-intellectual"[46] or "militant anti-modernists,"[47] the "engaged orthodoxy,"[48] and even the novel term "maximalists," or those who are characterized by "the conviction that religion ought to permeate all aspects of social, indeed of human, existence."[49] While all of these terms appear at first to have some descriptive value, when considered closely, they fail to address the complexity and wide variance among the ACP and Christian Right movements. To label religious conservatives "anti-intellectual" or "anti-modern" is a questionable act on several grounds. As noted, liberal Protestants often engage many of the same supernatural ideas as ACPs, but are hardly described with such adjectives. Moreover, the scholarly standards for "rationality," "intellectualism," and "modernity" are themselves cultural products, specific historical constructs created by the Enlightenment and liberal humanist influence.

In her own work on the treatment of fundamentalist religious movements by Western scholars, Roxanne Euben shows how conservative Muslims are often dismissed by the Western academy as irrational ideologues whose beliefs are little more than psychological epiphenomena related to social and political shifts; despite this, she notes, Western scholarship has readily accepted its own scholars who have questioned these same rationalist standards.[50] Euben's larger point is to interrogate how some varieties of anti-rationalism have been accepted as important intellectual contributions while others have been dismissed as simply irrational. This is of tremendous importance to the present discussion, for even if one could demonstrate that most liberal Protestants are a dramatically different group than most conservative Protestants, this would not negate the fact that the former still overwhelmingly adopts and endorses theological perspectives that bear strong supernatural residues, at the very least embracing a belief in "God." Yet far fewer scholars spend time attempting to analyze what social circumstances might have caused liberal Protestants to profess faith in Jesus, or mining the liberal Protestant psyche for some variation that would explain their religiosity. Instead, most often such liberals are simply praised for the ways in which they create what are perceived to be productive interactions between religion and political life.

Another issue with the distinctions drawn in the construction of scholarly chaos rhetoric is that many of the terms used by scholars are so illustrative of so many social groups that they lose all descriptive power. In particular, the definitional boundaries of terms like "militant" and "orthodox" prove elusive. Could not any group that takes a strong stand on almost anything be described as such? In his own examination of the Christian Right, Kenneth Heinemann notes that while social conservatives were labeled "divisive" in the 1990s because of their strong stands on issues like abortion, their positions were no more unwavering or absolute (and thus, socially divisive) than some of the liberal advocacy groups that opposed them.[51] It seems that almost any group with a well-defined social vision that it seeks to apply cross-culturally could be similarly labeled; how does one call conservative Christians an "engaged orthodoxy," but fail to call the abortion rights activists supported by NOW any less engaged or orthodox in their positions?

Orthodoxy and militancy are, in fact, the core descriptors that often inform the popular scholarly depiction of evangelicals and the Christian Right as moral absolutists, a viewpoint that this book has sought to destabilize by showing, instead, the work of chaos rhetoric to redefine what "absolutes" a group will embrace. When considered in this light, in fact, "maximalism" is a term that could hold great weight in helping to describe the fusion of Enlightenment rationalism with liberal humanism that defines much of modern scholarship, a set of values that can operate in the same exclusionary ways used to characterize fundamentalist ideologies.[52]

While scholarly rhetoric that fuses conservative thought with danger, illogic, and threat is perhaps a more predictable form of the chaos rhetoric produced, the previous discussion pushes the boundaries of what chaos rhetoric is by describing terms that, on the surface, are less obviously critical in that they do not appear to intentionally lead the reader towards negative emotion. However, Butler's understanding of the power of pathological speech suggests that the very act of drawing distinctions and thereby establishing a "normal" state from which others deviate or differ functions in a fundamentally similar manner. Thus, the move to create distinction itself can operate as one of the underlying principles of chaos rhetoric. What this practically means is that scholarship—an activity that necessarily depends on the location, classification, and analysis of presumed difference—is a particularly fertile site for the use of such politicized strategies. Importantly, this does not render scholarship meaningless. It simply means that it is almost always political.

As previously shown, certain scholars have deployed chaos rhetoric in a multitude of ways: through speech that casts the Christian Right as dangerous and threatening; through labeling that locates characteristics in conservatives that may be otherwise ubiquitous; and through acts of attention-deflection that shift the readers' attention away from certain aspects of some religions that they wish to cast more progressively. In this sense, just as CWA uses chaos rhetoric to construct a particular rendering of its opponents so as to easily delegitimize them, some scholars have done the same by identifying and constructing the markers "progressive" and "Christian Right" in very specific ways so that these two terms cannot be synonymously rendered. This rhetorical move identifies ACPs according to their presumed theological differences, but also as psychologically (and thereby *essentially*) distinct characters, standing in contrast to a well-established scholarly norm that, like any other signifying chain, is viewed by those who identify with it as a natural or obvious description of the world.

My analysis thus far might be interpreted by some as a defense of conservative Christians, or a treatise calling for greater scholarly objectivity. It is intended to be neither one of these things. Rather, my intention is simply to show the ubiquity of chaos rhetoric, and how it successfully influences public perception by crafting persuasive linguistic realities. In a description of the politics of the academy that also readily describes the dynamics of chaos rhetoric, Russell McCutcheon notes that scholarship is often characterized by a trend towards "domesticating one form of active and public political talk and action, lending it an air of inevitability, piety, sanctity, and placing it above so-called petty, partisan politics and thus beyond any form of effective critique or commentary."[53] In this sense, removing and destabilizing the impossible image of scholars as perfectly objective, apolitical observers permits their relocation back into the cultural context in which all persons operate, resituating a more accurate understanding of scholarship as a culture-producing activity rather than a culture-describing one. Again, such an observation does not render scholarship meaningless, but simply a product of culture, just like the other phenomena that scholars purport to study. An awareness of the politics that shape the classificatory exercises essential to the scholarly enterprise thus allows scholars themselves to reflexively question the source of their own perspectives, positions, and presumptions.

Looking Elsewhere for Distinction

As a part of this questioning process, I want to consider whether there are other sources of distinction that set Christian Right groups apart on the

American political landscape. If, as the previous discussion has suggested, CWA and the Christian Right do not use unusual tactics, do not embrace significantly different theologies than other Christians, nor are they more engaged, orthodox, or otherwise involved in the political process than other advocacy groups, how, exactly, are they different?

I have already argued that the power behind CWA speech is that it can portray itself as uniquely American, and in this way, one can understand it as nothing more than another potent manifestation of American exceptionalism, to put it simply. But here exceptionalism does not merely imply national superiority, for as Richard Hughes argues, "the label 'American exceptionalism' obscures the profoundly religious origins of the chosenness vision. It is one thing to claim that America is exceptional in its own eyes. It is something else to claim that America is exceptional because God chose it and its people for a special mission in the world."[54] Thus from the beginning of the nation, America's sense of exceptionalism has depended on its ability to make religious claims—to project divine authority onto human tasks—and to use this authority to create, justify, and maintain its cultural architecture.

If faithfully reproducing moral exceptionalism has been at the heart of the American enterprise, this has involved rendering "the body . . . a hazard to the soul," as Marie Griffith puts it.[55] Insomuch as controlling sexuality—that is, creating the concept of "sexual sin"—is a convenient method of controlling the affairs of the population at large, creating and reinforcing a realm of sexual danger has been instrumental to many interpretations of the national enterprise, of a place where the rhetoric of God's covenant can be enacted in tangible ways. The continual recuperation of this theme is why, in great part, "Christian theological pronouncements have become so institutionalized in the official life of the nation that they can be taken for just good old American values."[56] There has been no time when religion has not been the foremost political element of American speech and when the nation has not promoted its own power in Christian terms.

The ability to declare ethical dominance through religion and morality speech has been, and continues to be, an essential part of the power exchange in which groups often must barter to justify their existence. So what does it mean to be a group that operates using chaos rhetoric? In the American context, it means that one's tactics are rather commonplace. What *is* distinct about the Christian Right, however, is its ability to practice this form of public persuasion armed with a pre-existing social authority that dictates its right to speak. This, in the end, is one central, unambiguous element of CWA power. As this book has shown, this power has been located in a series of marketing maneuvers that draw on the historical weight of religion and moralist rhetoric as building blocks of American culture. Whether claiming the authority of religion, the power of female speech as it regards gender and reproduction issues, the right to speak for children, or moral agency in defense of the nation, CWA has at its disposal an impressive arsenal of symbols that are powerful only to the degree that they appear to simply reflect the American mainstream. Thus through the rhetorics of both reason and religion, and the careful crafting of its opponents' identities, CWA has successfully invoked its exclusive authority to use these important emotional symbols to shape the nation in its own image.

As a religious organization—or more accurately, an organization that claims religion as its rationale—CWA has affiliated itself with the long American tradition of fusing personal morality with the health of the nation. CWA uses this identity to its benefit, drawing on it forthrightly at times and abandoning it at others. Regardless of the degree to which it chooses to overtly align itself with religion, religion's power always remains operative in the background as a major symbol that legitimizes its speech by lending it both an ultimacy and superiority that other groups cannot match.

As a women's organization, CWA has positioned itself to identify with the long history that the symbol of the moral woman has held within American culture and within Christian Right groups, in particular. Its speakers all point back to the connection between conservative religion and women's moral empowerment to claim that their speech—*female speech*—bears a particular righteousness that others cannot so easily replicate. This long history of gender dichotomization, reinforced in Christian Right rhetoric, is a necessary component of CWA power, buying it authority that other groups cannot afford. Because women still remain the primary caretakers of children in this culture, the historical power of the mother-child link is nostalgically alive and well. When, speaking as the moral female, CWA also invokes the child, CWA fuses the righteous female with national survival.

But CWA's most powerful marketing strategy lies in its rhetorical portrayal of the nation, which comes not only through overt "rights talk" but is also constituted through populist rhetoric that features itself at the helm of mainstream America. Having already drawn upon the authority of its religious ties to propel its speech into a politically persuasive realm, CWA becomes free to couch its power in images that do not intellectually or ideologically threaten the public and that also often hold great public appeal, even if the arguments that promote those symbols are sometimes extreme. In this speech that invokes liberties, "the people," common sense, and "the mainstream," CWA portrays itself as a mirror of the people rather than a machine of religion or politics. The protection and transformation of the nation through CWA's work is thus portrayed as nothing more than a democratic reflection of shared cultural sentiment.

With this said, what is perhaps not clear is whether CWA has merely reconstituted the preferences of American culture, or if it is attempting to create such a culture through its contention that its preferences are mainstream. Asking whether language creates or describes realities is, of course, a question for which no certain answer emerges, not only because of the circularity of the relationship between the two, but also because describing a reality assumes that there is a singular, self-evident, static thing to describe. Rather, if there is any reliability to Barthes's sense that persuasion depends on the melding of the known with the unknown, then there is never a moment in chaos rhetoric when cultural creation and reflection do not converge and interlock.[57]

CWA's ability to successfully equate itself with an American mainstream thus calls scholars to reconsider the common notion that the Christian Right is successful because of its embrace of unwavering moral platforms or attractive theologies. Rather, CWA is appealing because it has the symbolic tools to become almost anything that it needs to be at any given political moment. This, in the end, is one of the most formidable aspects of its chaos rhetoric. CWA's claim to be quintessentially American collapses the traditional with the modern, the conservative Christian with the progressive, and the fringe with the populist. As is the case with power, Foucault notes, those who have it can effectively manipulate what counts as the knowledge that comes from it.[58] In this sense, successfully claiming its own mainstream status, as well as setting the parameters for what constitutes the nation, guarantees the Christian Right's enduring political relevancy.

Notes

INTRODUCTION

1. Joan Wallach Scott, "The Evidence of Experience," *Critical Inquiry* 17:4(1991), 793.
2. James Morone, *Hellfire Nation: The Politics of Sin in American History* (New Haven: Yale University Press, 2003), 24.
3. Beverly LaHaye, *The Restless Woman* (Grand Rapids, MI: Zondervan, 1984), 139.
4. Ibid.
5. Beverly LaHaye, *The Spirit Controlled Woman* (Eugene, OR: Harvest House Publishers, 1976), 60.
6. Ibid.
7. Liberal feminism refers to a social movement that became both more visible and politically engaged in American culture during the 1960s and 1970s. The central idea behind its continued activism is that equal rights for women and other gender minorities (in the form of legislative action, primarily) will alleviate, if not eliminate, gender-based oppression. Most of its activism has centered on issues of reproductive rights and economic equality, although the movement has been committed to various other related issues.
8. See "New to CWA?" Concerned Women for America website, http://www.cwfa.org/content.asp?ID=18226 (posted January 1, 2010, accessed October 29, 2012).
9. See the organization's website at http://www.cwfa.org.
10. Some have called this most recent incarnation of the Christian Right the "New Christian Right," a moniker that differentiates it from a series of philosophically related movements popular in the earlier twentieth century. For the sake of simplicity, I will continue to use "Christian Right," as I see the earlier movements and the current one as manifestations of the same social sentiments.
11. CWA reports this membership number. See "New to CWA?" Concerned Women for America website, http://www.cwfa.org/content.asp?ID=18226 (posted January

1, 2010, accessed October 29, 2012). This is also corroborated by political activist Steven Gardiner, "Concerned Women for America: A Case Study," *Feminism and Women's Studies Website*, http://feminism.eserver.org/cw-of-a.txt (posted August 28, 2006, accessed December 1, 2009).

12. Clyde Wilcox and Carin Robinson, *Onward Christian Soldiers?: The Religious Right in American Politics*, 4th ed. (Boulder, CO: Westview Press, 2010), 5.
13. Susan Juster, *Disorderly Women: Sexual Politics and Evangelicalism in Revolutionary New England* (Ithaca, NY: Cornell University Press, 1996); Morone, *Hellfire Nation*, 17.
14. Janice Shaw Crouse, "Out–of–Wedlock Babies: Unintended. . . . Or Not?" *Data Digest* (Publication of the Beverly LaHaye Institute, Volume III, No. 1), http://www.cwfa.org/images/content/dd-01–07.pdf (posted January 2007, accessed May 1, 2012).
15. Ibid.
16. Ibid.
17. Judith Butler, *Bodies That Matter: On the Discursive Limits of "Sex"* (New York: Routledge, 2001), 227.
18. Jason Bivins, *Religion of Fear: The Politics of Horror in Conservative Evangelicalism* (New York: Oxford, 2008), 30.
19. Ibid.
20. Christian Smith, *American Evangelicalism: Embattled and Thriving* (Chicago: University of Chicago Press, 1998), 100–1, 118–9.
21. James Jasper, *The Art of Moral Protest: Culture, Biography, and Creativity in Social Movements* (Chicago: University of Chicago Press, 2008), 107.
22. Ibid., 106.
23. By "power dynamics," I am referring to things like the ability to exercise personal agency and access privilege, status, and resources.
24. Émile Durkheim, *The Elementary Forms of Religious Life*, trans. Karen Fields (New York: The Free Press, 1995), 220.
25. Linda Kintz, *Between Jesus and the Market: The Emotions that Matter in Right-Wing America* (Durham, NC: Duke University Press, 1997), 10.
26. This works in great part because the public is risk-averse, Jasper notes. For more of that discussion, see Jasper, *The Art of Moral Protest*, 123ff.
27. "Ladies Room." *Mad Men*, season 1, episode 2, Matthew Weiner (writer) and Alan Taylor (director). Mad Men Official Website, http://www.amctv.com/shows/mad-men/episodes/season-1/ladies-room (accessed September 4, 2012).
28. Durkheim, *The Elementary Forms of Religious Life*, 217–20, 222.
29. Julia Kristeva, *Powers of Horror: An Essay on Abjection* (New York: Columbia University Press, 1982), 4.
30. Michael Kimmel, *The Gendered Society*, 4th ed. (New York: Oxford, 2011), 74.
31. Bivins, *Religion of Fear*, 15.
32. For examples of discussions on this diversity, see Andrew Greeley and Michael Hout, *The Truth about Conservative Christians: What They Think and What They Believe*

(Chicago: University of Chicago Press, 2006); Christian Smith, *Christian America?: What Evangelicals Really Want* (Berkeley, CA: University of California Press, 2000); and John P. Bartkowski, *Remaking the Godly Marriage: Gender Negotiation in Evangelical Families* (New Brunswick, NJ: Rutgers University Press, 2001).

33. Morone, *Hellfire Nation*, 14.
34. Ibid., 14–5, 46.
35. "What ENDA Means for You and Your Family," Concerned Women for America website, http://www.cwfa.org/endapetition/endaexamples.asp (accessed September 4, 2007). All emphases in the original. Unless noted otherwise, I retain CWA's formatting in reproducing its speech throughout this book.
36. Susan Friend Harding, *The Book of Jerry Falwell: Fundamentalist Language and Politics* (Princeton: Princeton University Press, 2000), 155.
37. Janet Jakobsen, "Why Sexual Regulation? Family Values and Social Movements," in *God Forbid: Religion and Sex in American Public Life*, Kathleen Sands, ed. (New York: Oxford, 2000), 104.
38. Frances FitzGerald, "The New Evangelicals," *The New Yorker*, http://www.newyorker.com/reporting/2008/06/30/080630fa_fact_fitzgerald?currentPage = 1 (posted June 30, 2008, accessed October 5, 2009). Steve Crabtree, "Teens on Sex Education: Abstinence–Only or Safe–Sex Approach?" Gallup website, http://www.gallup.com/poll/15166/Teens-Sex-Education-AbstinenceOnly-SafeSex-Approach.aspx (posted March 8, 2005, accessed November 30, 2009); Lydia Saad, "Americans Evenly Divided on Morality of Homosexuality," Gallup website, http://www.gallup.com/poll/108115/Americans-Evenly-Divided-Morality-Homosexuality.aspx (posted June 8, 2008, accessed November 30, 2009); Lydia Saad, "More Americans "Pro–Life" Than "Pro–Choice" for First Time," Gallup website, http://www.gallup.com/poll/118399/More-Americans-Pro-Life-Than-Pro-Choice-First-Time.aspx (posted May 15, 2009, accessed November 30, 2009).
39. Kathleen Sands, "Introduction," *God Forbid: Religion and Sex in American Public Life*, Kathleen Sands, ed. (New York: Oxford, 2000), 4.
40. Nancy L. Fischer, "Purity and Pollution: Sex as a Moral Discourse," Chapter 6 in *Introducing the New Sexuality Studies*, 2nd ed., Steven Seidman, Nancy Fischer, and Chet Meeks, eds. (New York: Routledge, 2011), 41; Angus McLaren, *Twentieth-Century Sexuality: A History* (Malden, MA: Blackwell, 1999), 3.
41. McLaren, *Twentieth-Century Sexuality*, 6.
42. Fischer, "Purity and Pollution," 42.
43. Peter Berger, *The Sacred Canopy: Elements of a Sociological Theory of Religion* (New York: Anchor Books/Doubleday, 1967), 37.
44. Ibid., 39.
45. Ernest Sandeen, *The Roots of Fundamentalism: British and American Millenarianism, 1800–1930* (Chicago: University of Chicago Press, 1970), 192. Sandeen notes that there were several lists circulating at the time that defined what was "fundamentalist" about the fundamentalist movement. The particular list mentioned here became standard when it was featured in a popular tract series.

46. Scott, "The Evidence of Experience," 777.
47. Ibid.
48. Jon A. Shields, *The Democratic Virtues of the Christian Right* (Princeton: Princeton University Press, 2009), 6–15.
49. This is a definition posed by Bruce Lincoln in *Holy Terrors: Thinking about Religion after September 11th* (Chicago: University of Chicago Press, 2003), 5–7, 16.
50. Ronnee Schreiber, *Righting Feminism: Conservative Women and American Politics* (New York: Oxford, 2008), 30–1.
51. "About CWA." Concerned Women for America website, http://www.cwfa.org/about.asp (accessed June 14, 2009).
52. Gardiner, "Concerned Women for America: A Case Study," accessed December 1, 2009.
53. "CWA Spokespersons," Concerned Women for America website, http://www.cwfa.org/leadership.asp (accessed September 12, 2009).
54. Jon Meacham, "The End of Christian America," *Newsweek*, April 4, 2009, http://www.newsweek.com/id/1192583 (accessed December 4, 2009).
55. Morten T. Højsgaard and Margit Warburg, "Introduction: Waves of Research," in *Religion and Cyberspace*, Morten T. Højsgaard and Margit Warburg, eds. (London: Routledge, 2005), 5; Lorne L. Dawson and Douglas Cowan, "Introduction," in *Religion Online: Finding Faith on the Internet* (New York: Routledge, 2004), 2.
56. Jeffrey K. Hadden and Douglas Cowan, "The Promised Land or Electronic Chaos? Toward Understanding Religion on the Internet," in *Religion on the Internet: Research Prospects and Promises*, Jeffrey K. Hadden and Douglas E. Cowan, eds. (New York: Elsevier Science, Inc., 2000), 5.
57. Højsgaard and Warburg, "Introduction: Waves of Research," 8–9.
58. Christopher Helland, "Online–Religion/Religion–Online and Virtual Communitas," in *Religion on the Internet: Research Prospects and Promises*, Jeffrey K. Hadden and Douglas E. Cowan, eds. (New York: Elsevier Science, Inc., 2000), 207.
59. Birgit Meyer and Annelies Moors, "Introduction," *Religion, Media, and the Public Sphere*, Birgit Meyer and Annelies Moors, eds. (Bloomington: Indiana University Press, 2006), 4. See also Harold Mah, "Phantasies of the Public Sphere: Rethinking the Habermas of Historians," *The Journal of Modern History* 72(2000): 153–82.
60. See Sara Diamond, *Roads to Dominion: Right-Wing Movements and Political Power in the United States* (New York: The Guilford Press, 1995), 165, and Rosalind Petchesky, "Antiabortion, Antifeminism, and the Rise of the New Right," in *The New Christian Right: Political and Social Issues*, Melvin Urofsky and Martha May, eds. (New York: Garland Publishing, 1996). Rebecca Klatch argues that rather than focusing on sexuality and gender issues, the "new" aspect of the New Christian Right is the prominent participation and leadership of females. See Klatch, *Women of the New Right* (Philadelphia: Temple University Press, 1987).
61. Morone, *Hellfire Nation*, 17.

CHAPTER 1

1. Tim and Beverly LaHaye, *The Act of Marriage: The Beauty of Sexual Love* (Grand Rapids, MI: Zondervan, 1998), 257.
2. Janice Shaw Crouse, "Seven Billion People: Over-Population or Birth Dearth?" Concerned Women for America website, http://www.cwfa.org/content.asp?id = 20701 (posted October 31, 2011, accessed September 17, 2012).
3. Ibid.
4. William McLoughlin, *Revivals, Awakenings, and Reform: An Essay on Religion and Social Change in America, 1607–1977* (Chicago: University of Chicago Press, 1978), 21–3.
5. This is one of the overarching themes of DeBerg's book, *Ungodly Women: Gender and the First Wave of American Fundamentalism* (Macon, GA: Mercer University Press, 2000).
6. James Reed, *The Birth Control Movement and American Society: From Private Vice to Public Virtue* (Princeton: Princeton University Press, 1983), 23.
7. Henry Ward Beecher, "Ladies Museum," in Jeanne Boydston, "The Pastoralization of Housework," in *Women's America: Refocusing the Past*, 5th ed., Linda K. Kerber and Jane Sherron DeHart, eds. (New York: Oxford University Press, 2000), 140.
8. Rosemary Radford Ruether, *Christianity and the Making of the Modern Family* (Boston: Beacon Press, 2001), 104.
9. Ibid.
10. McLaren, *Twentieth Century Sexuality*, 44.
11. Mark Jordan, *Recruiting Young Love: How Christians Talk About Homosexuality* (Chicago: University of Chicago Press, 2011), 6–7, 15.
12. Ibid., 17–8.
13. Daniel Scott Smith, "Family Limitation, Domestic Control, and Domestic Feminism in Victorian America," in *Controlling Reproduction: An American History*, Andrea Tone, ed. (Wilmington: Scholarly Resources, Inc., 1997), 93.
14. Ibid., 106.
15. Ibid.
16. Gail Bederman, "The Women Have Had Charge of the Church Work Long Enough: The Men and Religion Forward Movement of 1911–12 and the Masculinization of Middle-Class Protestantism," in *A Mighty Baptism: Race, Gender, and the Creation of American Protestantism*, Susan Juster and Lisa MacFarlane, eds. (Ithaca: Cornell University Press, 1996), 114–15.
17. Schreiber, *Righting Feminism*, 19.
18. Ibid.
19. Ibid. This is a reference to the Men and Religion Forward movement that existed in the early twentieth century, which was extremely similar in content and tone to the later Promise Keepers movement emerging near the end of the twentieth century.

20. As quoted in Charles Lippy, "Miles to Go: Promise Keepers in Historical and Cultural Context," *Soundings* 80:2–3(Summer-Fall1997), 293.
21. This is a continuing theme found in both Margaret Lamberts Bendroth, *Fundamentalism & Gender, 1875 to the Present* (New Haven: Yale University Press), 1993 and is one of the theses of DeBerg's aforementioned *Ungodly Women.*
22. See the discussion of those "fundamentals" in the previous chapter, under "A Note About Terms."
23. Sandeen, *The Roots of Fundamentalism*, 192.
24. Margot Canaday, *The Straight State: Sexuality and Citizenship in Twentieth-Century America* (Princeton: Princeton University Press, 2009), 29, 44.
25. Ibid., 52, 252.
26. Bendroth, *Fundamentalism and Gender*, 32–4.
27. Fran Grace makes the important point that this ideal appeared in different forms across the United States. In rural areas, for instance, women played a less exclusively domestic, more economically involved role. Thus the "separate spheres" was based on a set of relatively static principles, but took a number of different shapes. See Fran Grace, *Carry A. Nation: Retelling the Life* (Bloomington: Indiana University Press, 2001), 9.
28. Peggy Pascoe, *What Comes Naturally: Miscegenation Law and the Making of Race in America* (New York: Oxford University Press, 2009), 72.
29. Angus McLaren, *A History of Conception: From Antiquity to the Present Day* (Oxford: Basil Blackwell, 1990), 193.
30. Ruether, *Christianity and the Making of the Modern Family*, 99.
31. Ellen Chesler, *Woman of Valor: Margaret Sanger and the Birth Control Movement in America* (New York: Simon and Schuster, 2007), 14.
32. Ibid.
33. Reed, *The Birth Control Movement and American Society*, xi.
34. Ibid.
35. Theodore Roosevelt, "On Race Decay and Wilfull Sterility," in *Controlling Reproduction: An American History*, ed. Andrea Tone. Wilmington, DE: Scholarly Resources, 1997, 160–1.
36. Scopes voluntarily taught the controversial subject so that the ACLU could bring the case to both public attention and the courts, and thus he was part of the resistance movement against fundamentalist thinking. See Jeffrey Moran, *The Scopes Trial: A Brief History with Documents* (New York: Bedford/Martin's Press, 2002), 26ff.
37. Ibid., 71–2.
38. Ibid, 69.
39. George Marsden, *Fundamentalism and American Culture* (New York: Oxford University Press, 2006), 149.
40. Ibid, 152.
41. McLaren, *Twentieth Century Sexuality*, 11, 15–6.
42. Ibid., 14.

43. Kelly J. Baker, *Gospel According to the Klan: The KKK's Appeal to Protestant America, 1915–1930* (Lawrence: University Press of Kansas, 2011), 12.
44. Ibid., 15, 19.
45. Morone, *Hellfire Nation*, 304ff.
46. Kathleen Blee, *Women of the Klan: Racism and Gender in the 1920s* (Berkeley: University of California Press, 2008), ch. 1, 43–4.
47. Ibid., 11.
48. Baker, *Gospel According to the Klan*, 122–3, 128–9.
49. Daniel Williams, *God's Own Party: The Making of the Christian Right* (New York: Oxford University Press, 2010), 15.
50. This process is recounted in Joel Carpenter, *Revive Us Again: The Reawakening of American Fundamentalism* (Oxford: Oxford University Press, 1997).
51. Ibid.,106.
52. Martin, *With God on Our Side*, 39; "Bios: William (Billy) F. Graham," Billy Graham Evangelistic Association website, http://www.billygraham.org/MediaRelations_Bios.asp?id=0 (accessed July 25, 2009). COPYRIGHT 2002 The Cincinnati Post. All rights reserved. Reproduced with the permission of the Dialog Corporation by Gale Group. This material is published under license from the publisher through the Gale Group, Farmington Hills, Michigan. All inquiries regarding rights should be directed to the Gale Group.
53. Carpenter, *Revive Us Again*, 113.
54. Interestingly, it should be noted that as his career went on, Graham spoke out stridently against a too-close relationship between politics and religion. This was particularly pronounced after his close friendship with Richard Nixon was jeopardized by Watergate. Graham, in turn, was pushed to rethink his personal endorsement of political platforms and figures.
55. Richard Hughes, *Myths America Lives By* (Urbana: University of Illinois Press, 2004), 172.
56. McLaren, *Twentieth Century Sexuality*, 144.
57. Jordan, *Recruiting Young Love*, 30–1.
58. Ibid., 34.
59. Steven P. Miller, *Billy Graham and the Rise of the Republican South* (Philadelphia: University of Pennsylvania Press, 2009), 166.
60. Jordan, *Recruiting Young Love*, 34.
61. Williams, *God's Own Party*, 24.
62. Lisa McGirr, *Suburban Warriors: The Origins of the New American Right* (Princeton: Princeton University Press, 2001), 69.
63. Morone, *Hellfire Nation*, 391.
64. Ibid., 387.
65. Canaday, *The Straight State*, 178.
66. Ibid., 138.
67. Martin, *With God on Our Side*, 42; Williams, *God's Own Party*, 28.

68. Martin, *With God on Our Side*, 57.
69. Diamond, *Roads to Dominion*, 74.
70. Michael Cobb, *God Hates Fags: The Rhetorics of Religious Violence* (New York: NYU Press, 2006), 127.
71. Williams, *God's Own Party*, 70.
72. Thomas Davis makes the point that this issue was divisive as early as the Truman administration and its early civil rights platforms. See Davis, *Race Relations in the United States, 1940–1960* (Santa Barbara, CA: Greenwood, 2006), 44.
73. Cobb, *God Hates Fags*, 127.
74. Ruether, *Christianity and the Making of the Modern Family*, 136. Ruether argues that despite government propaganda that portrayed women as eager to return to the home and start families, up to 75% of women declared that they wanted to continue to work in their present jobs.
75. Betty Friedan, *The Feminine Mystique* (New York: W.W. Norton, 2001; original 1963), 57.
76. Bivins, *Religion of Fear*, 10, 14.
77. Williams, *God's Own Party*, 81.
78. Ibid., 83.
79. LaHaye, *The Restless Woman*, 90.
80. Ruether, *Christianity and the Making of the Modern Family*, 160–1.
81. LaHaye, *The Spirit Controlled Woman*, 53, 59.
82. Bivins, 179–80. See also "Tim LaHaye's Biography," Tim LaHaye Ministries website, https://timlahaye.com/shopcontent.asp?type=Biography (accessed July 25, 2009).
83. Ruth Murray Brown, *For A Christian America: A History of the Religious Right* (Amherst, NY: Prometheus Books, 2002), 243. Brown's interviews with conservative Christian women show repeated employment of victimization rhetoric by her participants across the twenty-five-year survey period she examined.
84. Cobb, *God Hates Fags*, 152.
85. Natasha Zaretsky, *No Direction Home: The American Family and the Fear of National Decline, 1968–1980* (Chapel Hill: The University of North Carolina Press, 2007), 15.
86. Williams, *God's Own Party*, 113, 115.
87. Ibid., 127.
88. LaHaye, *The Restless Woman*, 95–6.
89. Williams, *God's Own Party*, 156.
90. Jordan, *Recruiting Young Love*, 136.
91. Ibid., 140.
92. Ibid., 136, 129.
93. Ibid., 166–7.
94. Brown, *For a Christian America*, 128.
95. Ibid., 29.
96. Klatch, *Women of the New Right*, 3.

97. "History," Concerned Women for America website, http://www.CWA.org/history.asp (accessed July 24, 2009).
98. Ibid.
99. Beverly LaHaye, *Who but a Woman?* (Nashville: Thomas Nelson Publishers, 1984), 25.
100. Ibid., 29.
101. *Newsweek* offered a brief reflection on the significance of that cover story thirty years later. See Jon Meacham, in "Editor's Desk" *Newsweek*, http://www.newsweek.com/id/44543 (posted November 13, 2006, accessed July 25, 2009).
102. These were the National Women's Conference (1977) and the White House Conference on Families (1980). Martin, *With God on Our Side*, 178 and Brown, *For a Christian America*, ch. 7.
103. Martin, *With God on Our Side*, 169.
104. Zaretsky, *No Direction Home*, 231–2.
105. Ibid.
106. Timothy Messer-Kruse, *Race Relations in the United States, 1980–2000* (Westport, CT: Greenwood Press, 2008), xv.
107. Jakobsen, "Why Sexual Regulation?," 105.
108. Beverly LaHaye, *Who but a Woman?* (Nashville: Thomas Nelson Publishers, 1984).
109. "History," Concerned Women for America website, http://www.cwfa.org/history.asp (accessed June 16, 2009).
110. LaHaye, *Who but a Woman?* 114–5.
111. Martin, *With God on Our Side*, 227.
112. "History," Concerned Women for America website, http://www.cwfa.org/history.asp (accessed June 16, 2009).
113. C. Everett Koop, *Koop: The Memoirs of America's Family Doctor* (New York: Random House, 1991), 250.
114. Ibid. This is the theme of Koop's chapter 9.
115. Buchanan is quoted in Lou Cannon, *President Reagan: The Role of a Lifetime* (New York: Simon and Schuster, 1991), 816.
116. Falwell is quoted in Dennis Altman, *AIDS in the Mind of America* (New York: Anchor Books, 1986), 87.
117. Koop, *Koop: The Memoirs of America's Family Doctor*, 256–8.
118. Jennifer Brier, *Infectious Ideas: U.S. Political Responses to the AIDS Crisis* (Chapel Hill: University of North Carolina Press, 2009), 80–1.
119. Ibid., ch. 3.
120. Williams, *God's Own Party*, 222.
121. Ibid.
122. Ibid, 223.
123. Ibid., 231.

124. "The Right Hand of God" *Time Magazine* (front cover), May 15, 1995, http://www.time.com/time/covers/0,16641,19950515,00.html (accessed July 29, 2009).
125. Traci West, "The Policing of Poor Black Women's Sexual Reproduction" In *God Forbid: Religion and Sex in American Public Life*, Kathleen Sands, ed. (Oxford: Oxford University Press, 2000), 136.
126. Jakobsen, "Why Sexual Regulation?," 105.
127. www.cwfa.org
128. Brown, *For a Christian America*, 174.
129. Williams, *God's Own Party*, 257.
130. "Support Our Troops Signs and Bumper Stickers Now Available," Concerned Women for America website, http://www.cwfa.org/articles/14150/FIELD/misc/index.htm (posted November 29, 2007, accessed July 25, 2009).
131. Lincoln, *Holy Terrors*, 106. The entire interview is available in this text.
132. Robert H. Knight, "The Idols of Secular Conservatism," Concerned Women for America website, http://www.cwfa.org/articles/271/CFI/cfreport/index.htm (posted October 25, 2001, accessed July 23, 2009). A similar version of this has been more recently available under the title "Defending Jerry Falwell: The Idols of Secular Conservatism" at http://www.beliefnet.com/Entertainment/2001/11/Defending-Jerry-Falwell.aspx?p=3 (accessed September 17, 2012).
133. As an example, see Wendy Wright, "Who Are These People?" Concerned Women for America website, http://www.cwfa.org/articles/7059/CWA/freedom/index.htm (posted December 29, 2004, accessed September 19, 2009).
134. "A September 11th Hijacking: How 'Gay' Activists Smeared Father Mychal Judge," Concerned Women for America website, http://www.cwfa.org/articles/682/CFI/cfreport/index.htm (posted June 28, 2002, accessed July 24, 2009); and "Q&A: Fr. Mychal Judge's Sexual Conduct Does Not Alter Moral Code," Concerned Women for America website, http://www.cwfa.org/articles/3345/CFI/cfreport/index.htm (posted February 20, 2003, accessed July 23, 2009).
135. The statistics on gay marriage were documented by the Pew Research Center and summarized by its president, Andrew Kohut. See Kohut, "The Electorate Changes, and Politics Follow," *The New York Times*, April 16, 2012, http://www.nytimes.com/roomfordebate/2012/04/16/is-support-for-gay-rights-still-controversial/the-electorate-changes-and-politics-follow?scp=4&sq=kohut%20marriage&st=cse (posted April 16, 2012, accessed September 11, 2012).
136. Janice Shaw Crouse, "Emperor Obama's Clothes are Visible and Scary," Concerned Women for America website, http://www.cwfa.org/articledisplay.asp?id=16077&department=BLI&categoryid=dotcommentary (posted November 17, 2008, accessed July 25, 2009).
137. Tony Dokoupil and Lisa Miller, "Faith Beyond His Fathers," *Newsweek*, January 17, 2009, http://www.newsweek.com/id/180107 (accessed July 25, 2009). See also Wilcox, *Onward Christian Soldiers?*, 5–6.

138. One of the most direct examples of this warning is in Janice Shaw Crouse, "Muddying the Evangelical Waters," Concerned Women for America website, http://www.beverlylahayeinstitute.org/articledisplay.asp?id=15163&department=BLI&categoryid=dotcommentary&subcategoryid=blirel (posted May 7, 2008, accessed June 17, 2009).
139. Crouse, "Emperor Obama's Clothes," (posted November 17, 2008).

CHAPTER 2

1. Daniel Maguire, "Religion and Reproductive Policy," in *God Forbid: Religion and Sex in American Public Life*, Kathleen Sands, ed. (New York: Oxford University Press, 2000), 185–6.
2. Kenneth Burke, *Language as Symbolic Action: Essays on Life, Literature, and Method* (Berkeley: University of California Press, 1968), 50.
3. Ibid., 45.
4. William Saletan, *Bearing Right: How Conservatives Won the Abortion War* (Berkeley: University of California Press, 2004), 26.
5. Michel Foucault, *Discipline and Punish: The Birth of the Prison* (New York: Vintage Books), 1995, 27.
6. Michel Foucault, *The History of Sexuality, Volume 1: An Introduction*, trans. Robert Hurley (New York: Vintage Books, 1990), 94.
7. Although this is one of the points on which Foucault is famously inconsistent, I read his discussion on the infusion of privileged discourses through the power-knowledge nexus not as the total absence of group interest in knowledge formation, but as a rejection of models of discourse whereby a privileged group knowingly deceives the less privileged. Instead, it is arguable that Foucault sees powerful groups (that is, those groups whose perceptions significantly influence the dominant discourse) as generally oblivious to the social forces that they both create and regulate . Foucault, *History of Sexuality*, Volume 1, 123–7.
8. Ibid., 86, 94–5.
9. Ibid.
10. Kristeva, *Powers of Horror*, 2–3.
11. Jasper, *The Art of Moral Protest*, 123.
12. Kristeva, *Powers of Horror*, 4.
13. See Harding, *The Book of Jerry Falwell*, ch. 1, for a discussion of how narrative shocks operate in evangelical persuasion. James Jasper also discusses a similar concept ("moral shock") in *The Art of Moral Protest*, 106–7, which is addressed in the introduction to this book.
14. Jasper, *The Art of Moral Protest*, 121.
15. Kristeva, *Powers of Horror*, 3.
16. Judith Butler, *The Psychic Life of Power: Theories in Subjection* (Stanford: Stanford University Press, 1997), 28, 147.

17. Ibid., 136–40.
18. Judith Butler, *Gender Trouble: Feminism and the Subversion of Identity* (New York: Routledge, 2006), 107ff. This chapter is Butler's commentary and engagement of Kristeva's identity formation model.
19. Bivins, *Religion of Fear*, 16–7.
20. Roland Barthes, *Mythologies*, Annette Lavers, trans. (New York: Hill and Wang, 1972), 110.
21. Ibid., 129
22. Brochures from Bryant's original campaign are available online; see http://en.wikipedia.org/wiki/File:Save_Our_Children_Brochure_inside.jpg for one example.
23. "Reactions to AAP 'Gay Parenting' Pronouncement," Concerned Women for America website, http://www.cwfa.org/articles/426/CFI/cfreport/index.htm (posted February 7, 2002, accessed September 1, 2009).
24. J. Matt Barber, "'Day of Silence' Scam Places Children at Risk," Concerned Women for America website, http://www.cwfa.org/articles/15020/CFI/education/index.htm (posted April 21, 2008, accessed September 2, 2009).
25. For a discussion on this concept's use in conservative Christian circles, see Lynne Gerber, *Seeking the Straight and Narrow* (Chicago: University of Chicago Press, 2011), 89, 96.
26. Bivins, *Religion of Fear*, 15, 27.
27. Personal email to author from alerts@cwfa.org, August 29, 2012.
28. Lincoln, *Holy Terrors*, 5–6.
29. David Van Biema, "Oral Roberts to the Rescue?" *Time* Magazine, http://www.time.com/time/nation/article/0,8599,1677098,00.html (posted October 27, 2007, accessed November 1, 2012).
30. Janet Jakobsen and Ann Pellegrini, *Love the Sin: Sexual Regulation and the Limits of Religious Tolerance* (Boston: Beacon Press, 2004), 5, 21.
31. Ibid., 41.
32. Kintz, *Between Jesus and the Market*, 6.
33. Ibid., 7.
34. Ibid., 10.
35. Kathleen Sands, "Introduction," 4.
36. Ibid.
37. Barthes, *Mythologies*, 155.
38. Robert Wuthnow, *The Restructuring of American Religion: Society and Faith Since WWII* (Princeton: Princeton University Press, 1988), 209.
39. See, for instance, charges by liberal advocacy group People for the American Way that CWA misuses data regarding the physical and psychological health of homosexuals, in "Anti–Gay Politics and the Religious Right," People For the American Way website, http://www.pfaw.org/media-center/publications/anti-gay-politics-and-the-religious-right (accessed June 21, 2010). This article is featured in Chapter 5 of this book.

40. The notes numbered 2–10 in this excerpt are original to the article and demonstrate CWA's focus on presenting its claims as ones backed by objective research. They do not correspond to footnotes or endnotes in this book.
41. Kathryn Hooks, "Results of a Thirty Year Experiment on Women," Concerned Women for America website, http://www.cwfa.org/articles/4321/BLI/dotcommentary/index.htm (posted July 23, 2003, accessed October 14, 2009).
42. Bruce Lincoln, *Authority: Construction and Corrosion* (Chicago: University of Chicago Press, 1995), 10–1.
43. Janice Shaw Crouse, "Marriage Versus the Obama/Pelosi Nanny State," Concerned Women for America website, http://www.cwfa.org/articles/18063/BLI/family/index.htm (posted November 30, 2009; accessed December 2, 2009).
44. Ibid.
45. "New to CWA?" Concerned Women for America website (posted January 1, 2010).
46. "Penny Young Nance, Chief Executive Officer and President." Concerned Women for America website, http://www.cwfa.org/content.asp?id=18286&department=CWA&categoryid=misc (posted January 14, 2010, accessed December 29, 2011).
47. Ibid.
48. "Wendy Wright, President," Concerned Women for America website, http://cwa.tcvmedia.com/about-cwa/wendy-wright (first access July 25, 2009, second access (archived at this website) January 5, 2012).
49. Ibid. According to CWA, this accolade was granted by *Washingtonian* magazine.
50. "Janice Crouse, Ph.D. Senior Fellow of the Beverly LaHaye Institute," Concerned Women for America website, http://www.cwfa.org/articledisplay.asp?id=2112&department=CWA&categoryid= (accessed August 17, 2009).
51. Ibid.
52. Fischer, "Purity and Pollution," 39.
53. Ibid.,39.
54. Foucault, *The History of Sexuality*, Volume 1, 65–8.
55. Ibid., 143–4.
56. Jakobsen, "Why Sexual Regulation?," 109.
57. Ibid.
58. John D'Emilio and Estelle B. Freedman, *Intimate Matters: A History of Sexuality in America* (Chicago: University of Chicago Press, 1998), xvii.
59. West, "The Policing of Poor Black Women's Sexual Reproduction," 135–6.
60. Ibid.
61. Jakobsen, "Why Sexual Regulation?," 114–5.
62. Foucault, *The History of Sexuality*, Volume 1, 94–5, 122–7.
63. Butler, *Bodies That Matter*, 171.
64. Harding, *The Book of Jerry Falwell*, 34.
65. Ibid., 35.
66. To CWA, the correct answers are all three false. Taken from "The Ronald Reagan Memorial Internship Program With Concerned Women for America

Application," Concerned Women for America website, http://www.cwfa.org/images/content/cwa-intern-web-app.pdf (accessed November 19, 2009).

67. "Iowa Judicial Activists Trample on Marriage and the Constitution," Concerned Women for America website, http://www.cwfa.org/articles/16772/MEDIA/family/index.htm (posted April 3, 2009, accessed September 9, 2009).
68. "Crouse Appalled at Obama's Attempts to Repeal DOMA," Concerned Women for America website, http://www.cwfa.org/articledisplay.asp?id=17562&department=MEDIA&categoryid=family (posted August 18, 2009, accessed September 9, 2009).
69. Harding, *The Book of Jerry Falwell*, 155.
70. Beverly LaHaye, *The Restless Woman*, 54.
71. Ibid., 24.
72. This is not to say, of course, that LaHaye and CWA no longer support stay-at-home motherhood; on the contrary, they are ardent advocates for it. As an example, see Pamela Pearson Wong, "Mothers Are Giving the Greatest Gift: Themselves," Concerned Women for America website, http://www.cwfa.org/familyvoice/2001–05/06–13. asp (May/June 2001 edition of *Family Voice* magazine, accessed December 7, 2009). The issue is how much ideological room is available for more kinds of "real" women other than the stay-at-home mother.
73. LaHaye, *The Restless Woman*, 101.
74. Ibid., 13.
75. In 2003, the CWA website introduced LaHaye as a woman who "raised her family before tackling the broader problems of society." Concerned Women for America website, http://gideon.cwfa.org/leadership.asp (accessed June 5, 2003).
76. "Mrs. Beverly LaHaye, Founder and Chairman, CWA," Concerned Women for America website, http://www.cwfa.org/articledisplay.asp?id=2114&department=CWA&categoryid= (posted June 5, 2007, accessed December 4, 2009).
77. This is Janice Shaw Crouse; see "Crouse Delivers Speech at Princeton: A Conservative Critique of Feminism," Concerned Women for America website, http://www.cwfa.org/articledisplay.asp?id=4693&department=BLI&categoryid=media (posted October 28, 2003, accessed August 24, 2009).
78. Cavan Sieczkowski, "Lena Dunham 'First Time' Obama Voting Ad Offends Conservatives," The Huffington Post, http://www.huffingtonpost.com/2012/10/26/lena-dunham-first-time-obama-voting-ad-_n_2023705.html (posted October 26, 2012, accessed June 13, 2013).
79. CWA Responds to Obama Campaign's "Your First Time" Ad with "Lady Smarts" Campaign," Concerned Women for America website, http://www.cwalac.org/article_1211.shtml (accessed October 30, 2012).
80. Ibid.
81. Elizabeth Hurley, "CDC Finally Acknowledges That HPV Can Cause Cervical Cancer," Concerned Women for America website, http://www.cwfa.org/

articledisplay.asp?id=7422&department=CWA&categoryid=family (posted February 10, 2005, accessed November 30, 2009).

82. Michael O. Emerson and Christian Smith, *Divided by Faith: Evangelical Religion and the Problem of Race in America* (New York: Oxford University Press, 2001), 117.
83. Charlie Savage, "A Judge's View of Judging Is on the Record," *The New York Times*, http://www.nytimes.com/2009/05/15/us/15judge.html (posted May 14, 2009, accessed December 5, 2009).
84. Steve Bruce, *The Rise and Fall of the New Christian Right: Conservative Protestant Politics in America, 1978–1988* (New York: Oxford, 1990), 23.
85. Mark Juergensmeyer argues that one of the central functions of religious speech is to lend a sense of magnitude to an issue such that individuals are compelled to act. Mark Juergensmeyer, "Is Religion the Problem?" *Hedgehog Review* 6:1 (Spring 2004), 6–7.
86. Wendy Wright, "Why More Than Ever We Must Be Involved," Concerned Women for America website, http://www.cwfa.org/brochures/morethanever.pdf (accessed December 4, 2009).
87. Although it is difficult to tell from the context that she provides, Wright references at least two arrests "for praying" in this brochure, one of them being the noteworthy Houston case where a group of anti-abortion advocates protested at abortion clinics while the Republican National Convention took place nearby. News stories about Wright indicate that she and the other protesters arrested were not jailed for the act of praying itself, but for violating court injunctions that prohibited protestors from blocking the entrance to a clinic by requiring them to remain a certain distance away from the building and its clients. See Chip Brown, "Houston Judge Orders Four Abortion Protesters Jailed," *Associated Press News Archive*, http://www.apnewsarchive.com/1992/Houston-Judge-Orders-Four-Abortion-Protesters-Jailed/id-ff910d2b074d982b026a5039ed733d4e (posted August 12, 1992, accessed June 6, 2013).
88. "Record High Teen Pregnancy and Record High Money for Comprehensive Sex Education," Concerned Women for America website, http://www.cwfa.org/articles/16641/MEDIA/family/index.htm (posted March 18, 2009, accessed September 30, 2009).
89. E-Alert Subscriber Enrollment Page, Concerned Women for America website, https://cms.mybernard.com/cwfa/subscribe.aspx (accessed June 21, 2010).
90. Personal email to author from alerts@cwalac.org, September 10, 2009.

CHAPTER 3

1. Janne Myrdal, "Feminism, Faith, and the Palin Factor," Concerned Women for America website, http://www.cwfa.org/content.asp?id=19048 (posted June 15, 2010, accessed September 29, 2012).
2. Schreiber, *Righting Feminism*, 10.

3. Klatch, *Women of the New Right*, 3; this is also the overall theme of Schreiber, *Righting Feminism*.
4. Schreiber, *Righting Feminism*, 80–1.
5. Ibid., 81. Schreiber notes that many of these women worked part-time. Even if they didn't, all understood their employment with CWA as a way to enable other women to have the option of stay-at-home motherhood that they felt liberal feminism had otherwise degraded.
6. Butler, *Bodies That Matter*, 78.
7. Ibid., 12, 146.
8. Gayatri Spivak, *Outside in the Teaching Machine* (New York: Routledge), (1993) 2009, 5–6.
9. Schreiber, *Righting Feminism*, 41–2.
10. Marsden, *Fundamentalism and American Culture*, 57.
11. Ibid., 60. While Marsden is specifically discussing the rise of pre-millennial dispensationalism, he contextualizes the Baconian emphasis on objective facts and figures as an enduring trend that has come to define the ACP movement.
12. "Abortion's Physical and Emotional Risks," Concerned Women for America website, http://www.cwfa.org/articledisplay.asp?id=3111&department=CWA&categoryid=life (posted January 18, 2003, accessed August 17, 2009).
13. "Comprehensive sexual education" is the term often used to describe sexual education programs that teach about contraceptive usage and "safe sex." These are often juxtaposed with "abstinence only education" programs that, as the name implies, teach techniques to avoid sex altogether and thus do not discuss contraception.
14. Janice Shaw Crouse, "SIECUS Slams 'Shame–Based' Abstinence," Concerned Women for America website, http://www.cwfa.org/articledisplay.asp?id=5862&department=BLI&categoryid=life (posted June 24, 2004, accessed September 2, 2009).
15. Jan LaRue, "Did You Hear About the Judges Who . . . ? Connecticut Supreme Court Rules Fetus is Part of a Woman's Body," Concerned Women for America website, http://www.cwfa.org/articledisplay.asp?id=3937&department=LEGAL&categoryid=life (posted May 12, 2003, accessed September 2, 2009).
16. Janice Shaw Crouse, "Did Progress Begin with Roe v. Wade?" Concerned Women for America website, http://www.beverlylahayeinstitute.org/zarticledisplay.asp?id=14061&department=BLI&categoryid=dotcommentary&subcategoryid=blifem (posted October 26, 2007, accessed October 26, 2009).
17. Marsden, *Fundamentalism and American Culture*, 14–5.
18. Kara Carlson and Elaine McGinnis, "Marriage Foes Outspend Marriage Defenders by 24 to 1 in Missouri," Concerned Women for America website, http://www.CWA.org/articledisplay.asp?id=6137&department=CFI&categoryid=family (posted August 11, 2004, accessed August 21, 2009).
19. Rebekah Ries, "Rights for Everyone! Except You," Concerned Women for America website, http://www.cwfa.org/articledisplay.asp?id=17449&department=CFI&categoryid=family (posted July 31, 2009, accessed September 2, 2009).

20. See the discussion of Berlant in Cobb, *God Hates Fags,* 136. Berlant's quote was originally published in Lauren Berlant, "The Subject of True Feeling: Pain, Privacy, and Politics," In *Feminist Consequences: Theory for the New Century*, eds. Elizabeth Bronfen and Misha Kavka (New York: Columbia University Press, 2001), 128–9.
21. "The Employment Non-Discrimination Act," Concerned Women for America website, http://www.CWA.org/articledisplay.asp?id=970&department=CWA&categoryid=family (posted November 18, 1997, accessed August 24, 2009).
22. Ibid.
23. Janet LaRue, "Homosexuals Hijack Civil Rights Bus." Concerned Women for America website, http://www.cwfa.org/images/content/hhcrb.pdf (accessed October 7, 2012).
24. Ibid.
25. "CWA Regrets Bias Towards Evangelicals," Concerned Women for America website, http://www.CWA.org/articledisplay.asp?id=11497&department=MEDIA&categoryid=misc (posted September 13, 2006, accessed September 2, 2009).
26. Paul A. Weyrich, "Vilified Values Voters," Concerned Women for America website, http://www.CWA.org/articledisplay.asp?id=6853&department=CWA&categoryid=misc (posted November 16, 2004, accessed August 21, 2009).
27. Wendy Wright, "Who Are These People?" Concerned Women for America website (posted December 29, 2004).
28. See the discussion in Chapter 1 on the gender norms of the early twentieth century, wherein women were granted religious power but then saw it withdrawn once they were regarded as too socially dominant.
29. "History," Concerned Women for America website, accessed November 2, 2009.
30. Jessica Anderson, "Out With the Old, in With the N.E.W.," Concerned Women for America website, http://www.cwfa.org/articles/8548/BLI/reports/index.htm (posted July 17, 2005, accessed November 3, 2009).
31. For instance, see Janice Shaw Crouse, "Feminism and the Family," Concerned Women for America website, http://www.cwfa.org/articles/5435/BLI/commentary/index.htm (posted March 31, 2004, accessed December 1, 2009), and Stephanie Porowski, "Hijacking a Noble Cause: How Feminism Has Abandoned Its Founders," Concerned Women for America website, http://www.CWA.org/images/content/early-v-mod-fem.pdf (posted September 26, 2003, accessed August 22, 2009). The latter article is discussed in this chapter.
32. Janice Shaw Crouse, "Thank You, Sarah Palin," Concerned Women for America website, http://www.cwfa.org/content.asp?id=17396 (posted July 23, 2009, accessed November 1, 2012).
33. "Crouse Delivers Speech at Princeton: A Conservative Critique of Feminism," Concerned Women for America website, accessed August 24, 2009.
34. See Chapter 1 for the discussion on how women were portrayed as moral but too emotionally fragile for public service.

35. Heide Seward, "Take Our Daughters to Work Day: Feminism Class for Young Girls?" Concerned Women for America website, http://www.cwfa.org/articles/827/BLI/dotcommentary/index.htm (posted April 26, 2002, accessed November 3, 2009).
36. Ibid.
37. Ibid.
38. Ibid.
39. Crouse, "Thank You Sarah Palin," Concerned Women for America website (posted July 23, 2009).
40. Janice Shaw Crouse, "Bless Her Heart: Poor Sarah Palin," Concerned Women for America website, http://www.cwfa.org/articledisplay.asp?id=15834&department=BLI&categoryid=dotcommentary (posted October 1, 2008, accessed September 3, 2009).
41. Emphasis added.
42. Stephanie Porowski, "Hijacking a Noble Cause: How Feminism Has Abandoned Its Founders," Concerned Women for America website (posted September 26, 2003).
43. Ibid.
44. Ibid. This formatting is different from the original, although the list format is retained.
45. Historically speaking, those who are familiar with the lives of Elizabeth Cady Stanton and Frances Willard might be surprised to find that CWA sides so strongly with them. Both women were considered radicals in their own time, often in ways that, if played out in contemporary society, would likely pit them against CWA. Here, in particular, one might consider Stanton's open defiance of organized religion on the basis of its gender discrimination, and the sense by some historians that Willard was probably a lesbian. For more on this, and for the lives of the suffragists more generally, see works such as Jean H. Baker, *Sisters: The Lives of America's Suffragists* (New York: Hill and Wang, 2005) and Ruth Bordin, *Frances Willard: A Biography* (Chapel Hill: University of North Carolina Press, 2001).
46. Myrdal, "Feminism, Faith, and the Palin Factor," Concerned Women for America website (posted June 15, 2010).
47. "Mrs. Beverly LaHaye, Founder and Chairman, CWA," Concerned Women for America website (posted June 5, 2007).
48. Brenda Zurita, "Of 'Lady Parts' and Politics," Concerned Women for America website, http://www.cwfa.org/articledisplay.asp?id=21578&department=BLI&categoryid=life&subcategoryid=blifem (accessed October 8, 2012).
49. Ibid.
50. See, for instance, the following brochure on pornography: "Pornography and Sex Trafficking: The Links" Concerned Women for America website, http://www.cwfa.org/brochures/CWA_Pornography-and-SexTrafficking.pdf (accessed November 1, 2012); also see the following description of abortion providers: Wendy Wright, "Wendy Wright: A Testimony in Kansas," Concerned Women for America

website, http://www.cwfa.org/articledisplay.asp?id=13823&department=CWA&categoryid=life (posted September 7, 2007, accessed November 1, 2012).

CHAPTER 4

1. "Glenn Interviews Jerry Falwell Jr." Glen Beck website, http://www.glennbeck.com/content/articles/article/198/42325/ (accessed October 16, 2012).
2. Falwell made this now-famous remark while being televised. Clips of that video are featured in the documentary "With God on Our Side: George W. Bush and the Rise of the Religious Right," dir. Calvin Skaggs and David Van Taylor, First Run Features, November 1, 2004.
3. Martin, *With God on Our Side*, 204.
4. "Six Core Issues," Concerned Women for America website, http://www.cwfa.org/coreissues-short.asp (accessed December 4, 2009). As this book went to press in late 2013, CWA added a seventh core issue to the list, entitled "Support for Israel."
5. Cobb, *God Hates Fags*, 125.
6. Jasper, *The Art of Moral Protest*, 120
7. My interest in this topic lies specifically with the rhetorical manufacturing of the nation as a concept in Christian Right speech. Nevertheless, there is a wealth of scholarship that has been produced about the rise of the institutional nation-state, most of which presumes that the genesis of certain technologies, intellectual movements, and shifts in physical resources led to the creation of the nation, and much of which is consistent with the sort of rhetorical moves that groups like CWA attempt. See, for instance, Benedict Anderson, *Imagined Communities* (New York: New Left Books, 1991); Ernest Gellner, "The Coming of Nationalism and Its Interpretation: The Myths of Nation and Class" in *Mapping the Nation* (New York: New Left Books, 1996); Eric J. Hobsbawm, *Nations and Nationalism since 1780* (Cambridge: Cambridge University Press, 1990); Miroslav Hroch, "From National Movement to the Fully-formed Nation: The Nation-Building Process in Europe" in *Mapping the Nation* (New York: New Left Books, 1996); and Ernest Renan, "What is a Nation?" in *Nation and Narration*, Homi Bhabha, ed. (New York: Routledge Books, 1990).
8. Butler, *Bodies That Matter*, 70–1.
9. Ibid.
10. Ibid.
11. Ibid.,108.
12. Stephanie Coontz, *The Way We Never Were: American Families and the Nostalgia Trap* (New York: Basic Books, 2000), 22.
13. Foucault, *History of Sexuality*, Volume 1, 86, 94–5.
14. Butler, *Bodies That Matter*, 108.
15. Ibid., 116.
16. Michel Foucault, "Governmentality," in *The Foucault Effect: Studies in Governmentality*, Graham Bruchell, Colin Gordon, and Peter Miller, eds. (Chicago: University of Chicago Press, 1991), 100.
17. Jakobsen, "Why Sexual Regulation?," 116.

18. Catharine Cookson, *Regulating Religion: The Courts and the Free Exercise Clause* (New York: Oxford, 2001), 131–4, 143.
19. Ibid., 9.
20. "Six Core Issues,"Concerned Women for America website (accessed December 4, 2009).
21. Ibid. The formatting here is slightly different from the CWA website, although the basic list format is preserved.
22. Kintz, *Between Jesus and the Market*, 6.
23. Ibid.
24. Ibid., 7.
25. Bullets have been added to this and the other "Six Core Issues" lists.
26. "Goals and Concerns," Concerned Women for America website, http://www.cwfa.org/goals-concerns.asp (accessed December 4, 2009).
27. Janice Shaw Crouse, "Marriage Versus the Obama/Pelosi Nanny State," Concerned Women for America website (posted November 30, 2009).
28. See, for instance, Janice Shaw Crouse, "ObamaCare: Payback Time for All the Single Ladies," Concerned Women for America website, http://www.cwfa.org/content.asp?id=18949 (published May 21, 2010, accessed November 1, 2012).
29. Brier, *Infectious Ideas*, 79, 97.
30. Robert Knight, "Gay Marriage Is Not Only Wrong; It's Socially Destructive," Concerned Women for America website, http://www.CWA.org/articledisplay.asp?id=5014&department=CFI&categoryid=family (posted June 22, 2009, accessed August 17, 2009).
31. Robert Knight, "The Undeclared War to ENDA Our Liberty," Concerned Women for America website, http://www.cwfa.org/articles/17520/CFI/family/index.htm (posted August 12, 2009, accessed November 20, 2009).
32. "Goals and Concerns," Concerned Women for America website (accessed December 4, 2009).
33. Knight, "The Undeclared War to ENDA Our Liberty," Concerned Women for America website (posted August 12, 2009).
34. "Goals and Concerns," Concerned Women for America website (accessed December 4, 2009).
35. Ibid.
36. One of the stated rationales in *Roe v. Wade* is this very fact that the status of the fetus is not something that a court can decide, for it ultimately remains a matter of personal conscience.
37. Hooks, "Results of a Thirty Year Experiment on Women" Concerned Women for America website (posted July 23, 2003, accessed July 24, 2003).
38. "Bill Summary & Status, 108th Congress (2003–2004), H.R.1997," Library of Congress website, http://thomas.loc.gov/cgi-bin/bdquery/z?d108:HR01997:@@@L&summ2=m& (accessed November 21, 2012).

39. Dean E. Murphy, "Scott Peterson Sentenced to Death for Killing Pregnant Wife," *The New York Times, http://www.nytimes.com/2005/03/17/national/17peterson.html?_r=0* (posted March 17, 2005, accessed November 1, 2012).
40. Catherine Gainous, "Fetal Homicide: Always Two Victims of Violence," Concerned Women for America website, http://www.cwfa.org/articles/17238/BLI/life/index.htm (posted June 29, 2009, accessed October 28, 2009).
41. Jessica Wadkins, Trudy Chun, and Catherina Hurlburt, "Pro-Life Action Guide: Upholding Truth, Protecting Life," Concerned Women for America website, http://www.cwfa.org/brochures/pro-life.pdf (accessed November 2, 2012).
42. Ibid.
43. While some social activists argue that pornography is morally suspect, exploits women, leads to violence against them, and has the potential to undermine marriages and families by modeling unrealistic and unhealthy sexual relationships, others have expressed legal concern over limiting pornography because to do so would violate free speech and self-expression. Arguing for the right of people to use their bodies as they please, the advocates for this latter position have also linked negative attitudes towards pornography with the demonization of sex by religious conservatives and thus the imposition of religious values on the public at large. Sexism and conservative moralities are the perspectives that create the problems, they often argue, not sex itself.
44. "Six Core Issues," Concerned Women for America website (accessed December 4, 2009).
45. Brenda Zurita, "Pornography, Ivy-League Style," Concerned Women for America website, http://www.cwfa.org/articles/15958/BLI/pornography/index.htm (posted October 23, 2008, accessed November 2, 2009).
46. Janice Shaw Crouse, "Helen Gurley Brown's Pernicious Legacy," Concerned Women for America website, http://www.cwfa.org/content.asp?id=21456 (posted August 16, 2012, accessed October 12, 2012).
47. Ibid.
48. "Indecency at the Supreme Court," Concerned Women for America website, http://www.cwfa.org/content.asp?id=20841 (posted January 1, 2012, accessed October 12, 2012).
49. Janice Shaw Crouse, "WRAP Up Porn and Throw It Out," Concerned Women for America website, http://www.cwfa.org/articles/15902/BLI/pornography/index.htm (posted October 21, 2008, accessed November 24, 2009).
50. "Six Core Issues," Concerned Women for America website (accessed December 4, 2009).
51. Kurt J. Bauman, "Home Schooling in the United States: Trends and Characteristics," U.S. Census Bureau website, http://www.census.gov/population/www/documentation/twps0053/twps0053.html (published August 2001, accessed June 21, 2010).

52. Janice Shaw Crouse, "The Crisis of the Disappearing Educated Male," Concerned Women for America website, http://www.cwfa.org/articles/17092/BLI/education/index.htm (posted June 2, 2009, accessed November 23, 2009).
53. Ibid.
54. Ibid.
55. Marilyn Frye, *The Politics of Reality: Essays in Feminist Theory* (Trumansburg, NY: Crossing Press), 1983, 1–16.
56. Ibid.
57. Jaclyn Heffernan, "News Flash: Rated X," Concerned Women for America website, http://www.cwalac.org/article_523.shtml (posted June 26, 2007, accessed November 4, 2009).
58. For examples of how CWA portrays parents and their involvement in their children's educations, see Warren Throckmorton, "Should Raunchy Be the Fourth R?," Concerned Women for America website, http://www.cwfa.org/articles/8749/CFI/education/index.htm (posted August 18, 2005, accessed June 23, 2010); and Lydia Van Matre, "Two Be or Not Two Be: Where's the Math?" Concerned Women for America website, http://www.cwfa.org/articles/17287/FIELD/education/index.htm (posted July 7, 2009, accessed June 23, 2010).
59. Van Matre, "Two Be or Not Two Be," Concerned Women for American website (posted July 7, 2009).
60. Tina Fetner, *How the Religious Right Shaped Lesbian and Gay Activism* (Minneapolis: University of Minnesota Press, 2008), 73–4.
61. Linda Harvery, "Fairy Tales Don't Come True," Concerned Women for America website, http://www.cwfa.org/articledisplay.asp?id=10633&department=CFI&categoryid=papers (posted February 13, 2006, accessed November 27, 2009).
62. Ibid.
63. Ibid.
64. "Six Core Issues," Concerned Women for America website (accessed December 4, 2009).
65. Linda Schauer, "Obama Forcing Immoral Acts by Health Care Providers," Concerned Women for America website, http://www.cwfa.org/articles/16849/FIELD/freedom/index.html (posted April 15, 2009, accessed November 24, 2009).
66. This "immoral" label is interesting because national defense and the death penalty are two platforms that contemporary social conservatives have classically supported.
67. Orin Simmerman, "The Pledge of Allegiance in Church: Mixing Church and State?" Concerned Women for America website, http://www.cwfa.org/articles/4050/BLI/commentary/index.htm (posted June 4, 2003, accessed November 29, 2009).
68. "Biased 'Hate Crimes' Bill Would Create a Caste System of Victims," Concerned Women for America website, http://www.cwfa.org/articles/16874/MEDIA/freedom/index.htm (posted April 21, 2009, accessed November 30, 2009).

69. While the laws of many countries make provisions for religious speech, some prosecutors in those countries have successfully argued for the limitation of religious speech when it is used to cause harm or to violate a group's civil rights.
For a more involved article on this topic, see Robert Knight and Lindsey Douthit, "'Hate Crime' Laws Threaten Religious Freedom," Concerned Women for America website, http://www.cwfa.org/articledisplay.asp?id=9672&department=CFI&categoryid=papers (posted December 12, 2005, accessed June 9, 2010). The text of the Canadian Hate Crimes Bill, available in both English and French, is available at http://www2. parl.gc.ca/HousePublications/Publication.aspx?pub=bill&doc=C-250&parl=37&ses=2&language=E (accessed June 2, 2010).
70. "Six Core Issues," Concerned Women for America website (accessed December 4, 2009).
71. Wendy Wright, "CEDAW Committee Rulings," Concerned Women for America website, http://www.cwfa.org/articledisplay.asp?id=1870&department=CWA&categoryid=nation (posted August 27, 2002, accessed November 30, 2009).
72. Luisa Blanchfield, "The U.N. Convention on the Elimination of All Forms of Discrimination Against Women (CEDAW): Issues in the U.S. Ratification Debate," The U.S. Department of State Foreign Press Center website,http://fpc.state.gov/documents/organization/151974.pdf (posted November 12, 2010, accessed June 7, 2013).
73. "Save Mother's Day: A Campaign to Educate America About the Dangers of CEDAW," Save Mother's Day website, http://www.savemothersday.com/ (accessed June 11, 2010).
74. Don Feder, "Democrats Are Dying to Kill Us," Concerned Women for America website, http://www.cwalac.org/article_913.shtml (posted October 29, 2009, accessed November 29, 2009).
75. David Barton, "The American Revolution: Was it an Act of Biblical Rebellion?" Concerned Women for America website, http://www.cwfa.org/articles/17271/CWA/nation/index.htm (posted July 3, 2009, accessed November 24, 2009).
76. Ibid.
77. Ibid.
78. Ibid.
79. Lincoln, *Holy Terrors*, 5–6.

CHAPTER 5

1. This chapter is a revision of an earlier article published under the following: Leslie E. Smith, "What's in a Name?: Scholarship and the Pathology of Conservative Protestantism," *Method & Theory in the Study of Religion* 20:3(2008), 191–211.
2. Jordan, *Recruiting Young Love*, 211.
3. For a representative depiction, see Clyde Wilcox, *God's Warriors: The Christian Right in Twentieth Century America* (Baltimore: Johns Hopkins University Press, 1992), xv.

Jon Shields attempts to overturn this popular rendering of conservatives in his book, *The Democratic Virtues of the Christian Right* (Princeton: Princeton University Press, 2009).

4. Wilcox, *Onward Christian Soldiers*, 14.
5. "About NOW" The National Organization for Women website, http://www.now.org/organization/info.html (accessed November 5, 2012).
6. "History," Concerned Women for America website (accessed June 16, 2009).
7. Penny Young Nance, "The Real Mean Girls," Concerned Women for America website, http://www.cwfa.org/content.asp?id=19553 (posted October 19, 2010, accessed November 5, 2012).
8. Norman Lear Official website, http://normanlear.com/backstory.html (accessed June 23, 2010).
9. For an example of CWA's rendering of PFAW, see Wendy Wright, "Iraq War Vet 'Spit On' By Democratic Senators," Concerned Women for America website, http://www.cwfa.org/articledisplay.asp?id=13550&department=CWA&categoryid=misc (posted July 31, 2007, accessed November 5, 2012). For information on Falwell's statement, see Lincoln, *Holy Terrors*, 106.
10. Laura Fitzpatrick, "Scott Roeder: The Tiller Murder Suspect," *Time* Magazine, http://www.time.com/time/nation/article/0,8599,1902189,00.html (posted June 2, 2009, accessed November 12, 2012).
11. "The State of the News Media: An Annual Report on American Journalism, 2009" The Pew Project for Excellence in Journalism, http://www.stateofthemedia.org/2009/narrative_cabletv_audience.php?cat=1 (accessed December 5, 2009).
12. Kim Gandy, "Tragedy, Hope, and the Media's Abuse of Power," The National Organization of Women website, http://www.now.org/news/note/061609.html (posted June 16, 2009, accessed November 16, 2009).
13. "Religious Right" is another commonly used name for the Christian Right, although the former term is sometimes more specifically used to describe conservative leaders of non-Christian religions who have engaged in public advocacy for conservative political platforms.
14. "Anti–Gay Politics and the Religious Right," People for the American Way website, http://site.pfaw.org/site/PageServer?pagename=report_antigay_politics (accessed November 16, 2009).
15. My thanks to Eileen Boris for pointing out how the work of people such as Dr. Heidi Hartmann of the Institute for Women's Policy Research (http://www.iwpr.org) is the product of a scientific rigor that many Christian Right groups do not embrace.
16. Cobb, *God Hates Fags*, 125.
17. Ken Waters, "The Evangelical Press," *The Oxford Handbook of Religion and the American News Media*, Diane Winston, ed. (New York: Oxford University Press, 2012), 551.
18. John Bartkowski and Ashraf Alam, "Media Portrayals of the Moral Majority," *The Oxford Handbook of Religion and the American News Media*, ed. Diane Winston (New York: Oxford University Press, 2012), 338.

19. Smith, *Christian America?*, 195.
20. For examples of this religious self-disclosure in scholars whose work will be shortly addressed, see Randall Balmer, *Mine Eyes Have Seen the Glory: A Journey into the Evangelical Subculture in America*, 4th ed. (New York, Oxford, 2006) and Mark Noll, *The Scandal of the Evangelical Mind* (Grand Rapids, MI: Eerdmans Publishing Co., 1995). This trend towards self-disclosure is actually fairly common in the study of evangelicalism.
21. Butler, *Bodies That Matter*, 227.
22. Kintz, *Between Jesus and the Market*, 271.
23. Ibid., 272.
24. Ruether, *Christianity and the Making of the Modern Family*, 229.
25. Randall Balmer, *Thy Kingdom Come: How the Religious Right Distorts the Faith and Threatens America* (New York: Basic Books, 2007) ix; Randall Balmer, *Grant Us Courage: Travels along the Mainline of American Protestantism* (New York: Oxford, 1996), 146.
26. Randall Balmer, *The Making of Evangelicalism: From Revivalism to Politics and Beyond* (Waco, TX: Baylor University Press, 2010), 75–6.
27. Bivins, *Religion of Fear*, 232.
28. Martin, *With God on Our Side*, 384.
29. Robert Jones, *Progressive and Religious: How Christian, Jewish, Muslim, and Buddhist Leaders Are Moving beyond the Culture Wars and Transforming American Public Life* (Lanham, MD: Rowman and Littlefield, 2008), 15, 19.
30. See chapter 3.
31. Although speaking specifically about conservative reform movements within liberal denominations, Cowan nevertheless describes the differences between conservative and liberal sentiments as "the precipice." See Douglas Cowan, *The Remnant Spirit: Conservative Reform in Mainline Protestantism* (Westport, CT: Praeger, 2003), 3.
32. Peter J. Thuesen, "The Logic of Mainline Churchliness: Historical Background since the Reformation," in *The Quiet Hand of God: Faith-Based Activism and the Public Role of Mainline Protestantism*, R. Wuthnow and J.H. Evans, eds. (Berkeley: University of California Press, 2002), 27.
33. Robert Wuthnow and John H. Evans, "Introduction," in *The Quiet Hand of God: Faith Based Activism and the Public Role of Mainline Protestantism*, R. Wuthnow and J.H. Evans, eds. (Berkeley: University of California Press, 2002), 9.
34. Balmer, *Grant Us Courage*, 14, 29.
35. "U.S. Religious Landscape Survey," Pew Forum on Religion and Public Life website, http://religions.pewforum.org/comparisons# (accessed December 5, 2009).
36. See Christian Smith's *Christian America?: What Evangelicals Really Want* (Berkeley: University of California Press, 2000) and Andrew Greeley and Michael Hout's *The Truth About Conservative Christians: What They Think and What They Believe* (Chicago: University of Chicago Press, 2006).

37. Wuthnow and Evans, "Introduction," 9.
38. Randall Balmer and Lauren F. Winner, *Protestantism in America* (New York: Columbia, 2002), 19, 25, 30.
39. Wilcox, *God's Warriors*, 224. See also Christian Smith, *American Evangelicalism*, ch. 3, where Smith provides a more thorough overview of the nuances of several of these (and other) approaches to explaining evangelical vigor. Addressing these representations is also the task of Jon Shields, in *The Democratic Virtues of the Christian Right* (Princeton: Princeton University Press, 2009).
40. On the issue of whether the Christian Right is compatible with democratic institutions, see Shields, *The Democratic Virtues of the Christian Right.*
41. Wuthnow and Evans, "Introduction," 15.
42. Mark Noll, *The Scandal of the Evangelical Mind* (Grand Rapids, MI: Eerdmans Publishing Co., 1995), 3.
43. James Wellman, Jr. *Evangelical vs. Liberal: The Clash of Christian Cultures in the Pacific Northwest* (New York: Oxford, 2008), 277.
44. Ibid., 273.
45. Jones, Progressive and Religious, 3.
46. Noll, *The Scandal of the Evangelical Mind,* 10.
47. Marsden, *Fundamentalism and American Culture,* 4.
48. Emerson and Smith, *Divided By Faith,* 3.
49. Lincoln, *Holy Terrors,* 5.
50. Roxanne Euben, *Enemy in the Mirror: Islamic Fundamentalism and the Limits of Modern Rationalism* (Princeton: Princeton University Press, 1999).
51. Kenneth Heineman, *God Is a Conservative: Religion, Politics, and Morality in Contemporary America* (New York: NYU Press, 1998), x–xi.
52. Janet Jakobsen and Ann Pellegrini, "World Secularisms at the Millennium: Introduction," in *Social Text* 18:3(Fall 2000), 9, 12.
53. Russell McCutcheon, *The Discipline of Religion: Structure, Meaning, Rhetoric* (New York: Routledge, 2003), 281.
54. Hughes, *Myths America Lives By,* 19.
55. R. Marie Griffith, *Born Again Bodies: Flesh and Spirit in American Christianity* (Berkeley: University of California Press, 2004), 2.
56. Jakobsen and Pellegrini, *Love the Sin,* 3.
57. Barthes, *Mythologies,* 110.
58. Foucault, *Discipline and Punish,* 27.

Bibliography

Altman, Dennis. *AIDS in the Mind of America*. New York: Anchor Books, 1986.

Anderson, Benedict. *Imagined Communities*. New York: New Left Books, 1991.

Anderson, Jessica. "Out with the Old, in with the N.E.W." Concerned Women for America website, http://www.cwfa.org/articles/8548/BLI/reports/index.htm (posted July 17, 2005, accessed November 3, 2009).

Associated Press. "Abortion Opponents Rush Wichita Clinic; 130 Arrested." *The Los Angeles Times*, http://articles.latimes.com/1991-08-21/news/mn-917_1_operation-rescue (posted August 21, 1991, accessed June 6, 2013).

Baker, Jean H. *Sisters: The Lives of America's Suffragists*. New York: Hill and Wang, 2005.

Baker, Kelly J. *Gospel According to the Klan: The KKK's Appeal to Protestant America, 1915–1930*. Lawrence: University Press of Kansas, 2011.

Balmer, Randall. *Grant Us Courage: Travels Along the Mainline of American Protestantism*. New York: Oxford, 1996.

———. *The Making of Evangelicalism: From Revivalism to Politics and Beyond*. Waco, TX: Baylor University Press, 2010.

———. *Mine Eyes Have Seen the Glory: A Journey into the Evangelical Subculture in America*, 4th ed. New York, Oxford, 2006.

———. *Thy Kingdom Come: How The Religious Right Distorts the Faith and Threatens America*. New York: Basic Books, 2007.

——— and Lauren F. Winner. *Protestantism in America*. New York: Columbia University Press, 2002.

Barber, Matt J. "CWA Responds to Wheaton College Statement." Concerned Women for America website, http://www.cwfa.org/articles/14836/CFI/education/index.htm (posted March 7, 2008, accessed December 9, 2009).

———. "'Day of Silence' Scam Places Children at Risk," Concerned Women for America website, http://www.cwfa.org/articles/15020/CFI/education/index.htm (posted April 21, 2008, accessed September 2, 2009).

Barthes, Roland. *Mythologies*. Annette Lavers, trans. New York: Hill and Wang, 1972.

Bartkowski, John P. *Remaking the Godly Marriage: Gender Negotiation in Evangelical Families*. New Brunswick, NJ: Rutgers University Press, 2001.

——— and Ashraf Alam. "Media Portrayals of the Moral Majority." In *The Oxford Handbook of Religion and the American News Media*, ed. Diane Winston. New York: Oxford University Press, 2012.

Barton, David. "The American Revolution: Was It an Act of Biblical Rebellion?" Concerned Women for America website, http://www.cwfa.org/articles/17271/CWA/nation/index.htm (posted July 3, 2009, accessed November 24, 2009).

Bauman, Kurt J. "Home Schooling in the United States: Trends and Characteristics." U.S. Census Bureau website, http://www.census.gov/population/www/documentation/twps0053/twps0053.html (published August 2001, accessed June 21, 2010).

Bederman, Gail. "The Women Have Had Charge of the Church Work Long Enough: The Men and Religion Forward Movement of 1911–12 and the Masculinization of Middle-Class Protestantism." In *A Mighty Baptism: Race, Gender, and the Creation of American Protestantism*, Susan Juster and Lisa MacFarlane, eds. Ithaca: Cornell University Press, 1996.

Bendroth, Margaret Lamberts. *Fundamentalism and Gender, 1875 to the Present*. New Haven: Yale University Press, 1993.

Berger, Peter. *The Sacred Canopy: Elements of a Sociological Theory of Religion*. New York: Anchor Books/Doubleday, 1967.

Billy Graham Evangelistic Association. "Bios: William (Billy) F. Graham." Billy Graham Evangelistic Association website, http://www.billygraham.org/MediaRelations_Bios.asp?id=0 (accessed July 25, 2009).

Bivins, Jason. *Religion of Fear: The Politics of Horror in Conservative Evangelicalism*. New York: Oxford, 2008.

Blanchfield, Luisa. "The U.N. Convention on the Elimination of All Forms of Discrimination Against Women (CEDAW): Issues in the U.S. Ratification Debate." The U.S. Department of State Foreign Press Center website, http://fpc.state.gov/documents/organization/151974.pdf (posted November 12, 2010, accessed June 7, 2013).

Blee, Kathleen. *Women of the Klan: Racism and Gender in the 1920s*. Berkeley: University of California Press, 2008.

Bordin, Ruth. *Frances Willard: A Biography*. Chapel Hill: University of North Carolina Press, 2001.

Boydston, Jeanne. "The Pastoralization of Housework." In *Women's America: Refocusing the Past*, 5th ed., Linda K. Kerber and Jane Sherron DeHart, eds. New York: Oxford University Press, 2000.

Brier, Jennifer. *Infectious Ideas: U.S. Political Responses to the AIDS Crisis*. Chapel Hill: University of North Carolina Press, 2009.

Brown, Chip. "Houston Judge Orders Four Abortion Protesters Jailed." *Associated Press News Archive*, http://www.apnewsarchive.com/1992/Houston-Judge-Orders-Four-Abortion-Protesters-Jailed/id-ff910d2b074d982b026a5039ed733d4e (posted August 12, 1992, accessed June 6, 2013).

Brown, Ruth Murray. *For a Christian America: A History of the Religious Right.* Amherst, NY: Prometheus Books, 2002.

Bruce, Steve. *The Rise and Fall of the New Christian Right: Conservative Protestant Politics in America, 1978–1988*. Oxford: Clarendon Press, 1988.

Burke, Kenneth. *Language as Symbolic Action: Essays on Life, Literature, and Method.* Berkeley: University of California Press, 1968.

Butler, Judith. *Bodies That Matter: On the Discursive Limits of "Sex."* New York: Routledge, 2011.

———. *Gender Trouble: Feminism and the Subversion of Identity*. New York: Routledge, 2006.

———. *The Psychic Life of Power: Theories in Subjection*. Stanford: Stanford University Press, 1997.

Canaday, Margot. *The Straight State: Sexuality and Citizenship in Twentieth-Century America*. Princeton: Princeton University Press, 2009.

Cannon, Lou. *President Reagan: The Role of a Lifetime*. New York: Simon and Schuster, 1991.

Carlson, Kara and Elaine McGinnis. "Marriage Foes Outspend Marriage Defenders by 24 to 1 in Missouri." Concerned Women for America website, http://www.CWA.org/articledisplay.asp?id = 6137&department = CFI&categoryid = family (posted August 11, 2004, accessed August 21, 2009).

Carpenter, Joel. *Revive Us Again: The Reawakening of American Fundamentalism.* Oxford: Oxford University Press, 1997.

Chesler, Ellen. *Woman of Valor: Margaret Sanger and the Birth Control Movement in America*. New York: Simon and Schuster, 2007.

Cobb, Michael. *God Hates Fags: The Rhetorics of Religious Violence*. New York: New York University Press, 2006.

Concerned Women for America. "Abortion's Physical and Emotional Risks." Concerned Women for America website, http://www.cwfa.org/articledisplay.asp?id = 3111&department = CWA&categoryid = life (posted January 18, 2003, accessed August 17, 2009).

———. "About CWA." Concerned Women for America website, http://www.cwfa.org/about.asp (accessed June 14, 2009).

———. "Biased 'Hate Crimes' Bill Would Create a Caste System of Victims." Concerned Women for America website, http://www.cwfa.org/articles/16874/MEDIA/freedom/index.htm (posted April 21, 2009, accessed November 30, 2009).

———. "Crouse Appalled at Obama's Attempts to Repeal DOMA." Concerned Women for America website, http://www.cwfa.org/articledisplay.asp?id = 17562&department = MEDIA&categoryid = family (posted August 18, 2009, accessed September 9, 2009).

———. "Crouse Delivers Speech at Princeton: A Conservative Critique of Feminism." Concerned Women for America website, http://www.cwfa.org/articledisplay.asp?id = 4693&department = BLI&categoryid = media (posted October 28, 2003, accessed August 24, 2009).

———. "CWA Regrets Bias Towards Evangelicals." Concerned Women for America website, http://www.CWA.org/articledisplay.asp?id=11497&department=MEDIA&categoryid=misc (posted September 13, 2006, accessed September 2, 2009).

———. "CWA Responds to Obama Campaign's 'Your First Time' Ad with 'Lady Smarts' Campaign." Concerned Women for America website, http://www.cwalac.org/article_1211.shtml (accessed October 30, 2012).

———. "CWA Spokespersons." Concerned Women for America website, http://www.cwfa.org/leadership.asp (accessed September 12, 2009).

———. E-Alert Subscriber Enrollment Page. Concerned Women for America website, https://cms.mybernard.com/cwfa/subscribe.aspx (accessed June 21, 2010).

———. "The Employment Non–Discrimination Act." Concerned Women for America website, http://www.CWA.org/articledisplay.asp?id = 970&department = CWA&categoryid = family (posted November 18, 1997, accessed August 24, 2009).

———. "Goals and Concerns." Concerned Women for America website, http://www.cwfa.org/goals-concerns.asp (accessed December 4, 2009).

———. "History." Concerned Women for America website, http://www.cwfa.org/history.asp (accessed June 16, 2009).

———. "Indecency at the Supreme Court." Concerned Women for America website, http://www.cwfa.org/content.asp?id = 20841 (posted January 1, 2012, accessed October 12, 2012).

———. "Iowa Judicial Activists Trample on Marriage and the Constitution." Concerned Women for America website, http://www.cwfa.org/articles/16772/MEDIA/family/index.htm (posted April 3, 2009, accessed September 9, 2009).

———. "Janice Crouse, Ph.D. Senior Fellow of the Beverly LaHaye Institute." Concerned Women for America website, http://gideon.cwfa.org/articledisplay.asp?id = 2112&department = CWA&categoryid = (posted May 29, 2007, accessed June 22, 2009).

———. "Mrs. Beverly LaHaye, Founder and Chairman, CWA." Concerned Women for America website, http://www.cwfa.org/articledisplay.asp?id = 2114&department = CWA&categoryid = (posted June 5, 2007, accessed December 4, 2009).

———. "New to CWA?" Concerned Women for America website, http://www.cwfa.org/articles/18226/CWA/misc/index.htm (posted January 1, 2010, accessed June 24, 2010).

———. "Q&A: Fr. Mychal Judge's Sexual Conduct Does Not Alter Moral Code." Concerned Women for America website, http://www.cwfa.org/articles/3345/CFI/cfreport/index.htm (posted February 20, 2003, accessed July 23, 2009).

———. "Penny Young Nance, Chief Executive Officer and President." Concerned Women for America website, http://www.cwfa.org/content.asp?id = 18286&department = CWA&categoryid = misc (posted January 14, 2010, accessed December 29, 2011).

———. "Pornography and Sex Trafficking: The Links." Concerned Women for America website, http://www.cwfa.org/brochures/CWA_Pornography-and-SexTrafficking.pdf (accessed November 1, 2012).

———. "Reactions to AAP 'Gay Parenting' Pronouncement." Concerned Women for America website, http://www.cwfa.org/articles/426/CFI/cfreport/index.htm (posted February 7, 2002, accessed September 1, 2009).

———. "Record High Teen Pregnancy and Record High Money for Comprehensive Sex Education." Concerned Women for America website, http://www.cwfa.org/articles/16641/MEDIA/family/index.htm (posted March 18, 2009, accessed September 30, 2009).

———. "The Ronald Reagan Memorial Internship Program with Concerned Women for America Application." Concerned Women for America website, http://www.cwfa.org/images/content/cwa-intern-web-app.pdf (accessed November 19, 2009).

———. "Save Mother's Day: A Campaign to Educate America About the Dangers of CEDAW." Save Mother's Day website, http://www.savemothersday.com/(accessed June 11, 2010).

———. "A September 11th Hijacking: How 'Gay' Activists Smeared Father Mychal Judge." Concerned Women for America website, http://www.cwfa.org/articles/682/CFI/cfreport/index.htm (posted June 28, 2002, accessed July 24, 2009).

———. "Six Core Issues." Concerned Women for America website, http://www.cwfa.org/coreissues-short.asp (accessed December 4, 2009).

———. "Support Our Troops Signs and Bumper Stickers Now Available." Concerned Women for America website, http://www.cwfa.org/articles/14150/FIELD/misc/index.htm (posted November 29, 2007, accessed July 25, 2009).

———. "Wendy Wright, President." Concerned Women for America website, http://gideon.cwfa.org/articledisplay.asp?id = 2107&department = CWA&categoryid =. Archived at http://cwa.tcvmedia.com/about-cwa/wendy-wright (posted February 2, 2002, accessed July 25, 2009).

———. "What ENDA Means for You and Your Family." Concerned Women for America website, http://www.cwfa.org/endapetition/endaexamples.asp (accessed September 4, 2007).

Cookson, Catharine. *Regulating Religion: The Courts and the Free Exercise Clause*. New York: Oxford, 2001.

Coontz, Stephanie. *The Way We Never Were: American Families and the Nostalgia Trap*. New York: Basic Books, 2000.

Cowan, Douglas. *The Remnant Spirit: Conservative Reform in Mainline Protestantism*. Westport, CT: Praeger, 2003.

Crabtree, Steve. "Teens on Sex Education: Abstinence–Only or Safe–Sex Approach?" Gallup website, http://www.gallup.com/poll/15166/Teens-Sex-Education-AbstinenceOnly-SafeSex-Approach.aspx (posted March 8, 2005, accessed November 30, 2009).

Crouse, Janice Shaw. "Bless Her Heart: Poor Sarah Palin." Concerned Women for America website, http://www.cwfa.org/articledisplay.asp?id = 15834&department = BLI&categoryid = dotcommentary (posted October 1, 2008, accessed September 3, 2009).

———. "The Crisis of the Disappearing Educated Male." Concerned Women for America website, http://www.cwfa.org/articles/17092/BLI/education/index.htm (posted June 2, 2009, accessed November 23, 2009).

———. "Did Progress Begin with Roe v. Wade?" Concerned Women for America website, http://www.beverlylahayeinstitute.org/articledisplay.asp?id = 14061&department = BLI&categoryid = dotcommentary&subcategoryid = blifem (posted October 26, 2007, accessed October 26, 2009).

———. "Emperor Obama's Clothes Are Visible and Scary." Concerned Women for America website, http://www.cwfa.org/articledisplay.asp?id = 16077&department = BLI&categoryid = dotcommentary (posted November 17, 2008, accessed July 25, 2009).

———. "Feminism and the Family." Concerned Women for America website, http://www.cwfa.org/articles/5435/BLI/commentary/index.htm (posted March 3, 2004, accessed December 1, 2009).

———. "Helen Gurley Brown's Pernicious Legacy." Concerned Women for America website, http://www.cwfa.org/content.asp?id = 21456 (posted August 16, 2012, accessed October 12, 2012).

———. "Marriage Versus the Obama/Pelosi Nanny State." Concerned Women for America website, http://www.cwfa.org/articles/18063/BLI/family/index.htm (posted November 30, 2009, accessed December 2, 2009).

———. "Muddying the Evangelical Waters." Concerned Women for America website, http://www.beverlylahayeinstitute.org/articledisplay.asp?id = 15163&department = BLI&categoryid = dotcommentary&subcategoryid = blirel (posted May 7, 2008, accessed June 17, 2009).

———. "ObamaCare: Payback Time for All the Single Ladies." Concerned Women for America website, http://www.cwfa.org/content.asp?id = 18949 (published May 21, 2010, accessed November 1, 2012).

———. "Out-of-Wedlock Babies: Unintended. . . . Or Not?" *Data Digest* (Publication of the Beverly LaHaye Institute, Volume III, No. 1), http://www.cwfa.org/images/content/dd-01-07.pdf (posted January 2007, accessed May 1, 2012).

———. "Seven Billion People: Over-Population or Birth Dearth?" Concerned Women for America website, http://www.cwfa.org/content.asp?id=20701 (posted October 31, 2011, accessed September 17, 2012).

———. "SIECUS Slams 'Shame-Based' Abstinence." Concerned Women for America website, http://www.cwfa.org/articledisplay.asp?id = 5862&department=BLI&categoryid=life (posted June 24, 2004, accessed September 2, 2009).

———. "Thank You, Sarah Palin." Concerned Women for America website, http://www.cwfa.org/content.asp?id = 17396 (posted July 23, 2009, accessed November 1, 2012).

———. "They Put My Daughter in a Homosexual Studies Class!" Personal Email from Concerned Women for America, alerts@cwfa.org. August 29, 2012.

———. "WRAP Up Porn and Throw It Out." Concerned Women for America website, http://www.cwfa.org/articles/15902/BLI/pornography/index.htm (posted October 21, 2008, accessed November 24, 2009).

Davis, Thomas. *Race Relations in the United States, 1940–1960*. Santa Barbara, CA: Greenwood Press, 2006.

Dawson, Lorne L. and Douglas E. Cowan. *Religion Online: Finding Faith on the Internet*. New York: Routledge, 2004.

DeBerg, Betty. *Ungodly Women: Gender and the First Wave of American Fundamentalism*. Minneapolis: Fortress Press, 1990.

D'Emilio, John and Estelle B. Freedman. *Intimate Matters: A History of Sexuality in America*. Chicago: University of Chicago Press, 1998.

Diamond, Sara. *Roads to Dominion: Right-Wing Movements and Political Power in the United States*. New York: The Guilford Press, 1995.

Dokoupil, Tony and Lisa Miller. "Faith Beyond His Fathers." *Newsweek*, January 17, 2009, http://www.newsweek.com/id/180107 (accessed July 25, 2009).

Durkheim, Emile. *The Elementary Forms of Religious Life*, trans. Karen Fields. New York: The Free Press, 1995.

Emerson, Michael O. and Christian Smith. *Divided By Faith: Evangelical Religion and the Problem of Race in America*. New York: Oxford University Press, 2000.

Euben, Roxanne. *Enemy in the Mirror: Islamic Fundamentalism and the Limits of Modern Rationalism*. Princeton: Princeton University Press, 1999.

Feder, Don. "Democrats are Dying to Kill Us." Concerned Women for America website, http://www.cwalac.org/article_913.shtml (posted October 29, 2009, accessed November 29, 2009).

Fetner, Tina. *How the Religious Right Shaped Lesbian and Gay Activism*. Minneapolis: University of Minnesota Press, 2008.

Fischer, Nancy L. "Purity and Pollution: Sex as a Moral Discourse." Chapter 6 in *Introducing the New Sexuality Studies*, 2nd ed., eds. Steven Seidman, Nancy Fischer, and Chet Meeks. New York: Routledge, 2011.

FitzGerald, Frances. "The New Evangelicals." *The New Yorker*, http://www.newyorker.com/reporting/2008/06/30/080630fa_fact_fitzgerald?currentPage = 1 (posted June 30, 2008, accessed October 5, 2009).

Fitzpatrick, Laura. "Scott Roeder: The Tiller Murder Suspect." *Time*, http://www.time.com/time/nation/article/0,8599,1902189,00.html (posted June 2, 2009, accessed November 12, 2012).

Foucault, Michel. *Discipline and Punish: The Birth of the Prison*. New York: Vintage Books, 1995.

———. "Governmentality." In *The Foucault Effect: Studies in Governmentality*, eds. Graham Bruchell, Colin Gordon, and Peter Miller. Chicago: University of Chicago Press, 1991.

———. *The History of Sexuality, Volume I*. New York: Vintage Books, 1990.

Friedan, Betty. *The Feminine Mystique*. New York: W.W. Norton, 2001 (original 1963).

Frye, Marilyn. *The Politics of Reality: Essays in Feminist Theory*. Trumansburg, NY: Crossing Press, 1983.

Gainous, Catherine. "Fetal Homicide: Always Two Victims of Violence." Concerned Women for America website, http://www.cwfa.org/articles/17238/BLI/life/index.htm (posted June 29, 2009, accessed October 28, 2009).

Gandy, Kim. "Tragedy, Hope, and the Media's Abuse of Power." The National Organization of Women website, http://www.now.org/news/note/061609.html (posted June 16, 2009, accessed November 16, 2009).

Gardiner, Steven. "Concerned Women for America: A Case Study." Feminism and Women's Studies website, http://feminism.eserver.org/cw-of-a.txt (posted August 28, 2006, accessed December 1, 2009).

Gellner, Ernest. "The Coming of Nationalism and Its Interpretation: The Myths of Nation and Class." *Mapping the Nation*, ed Gopal Balakrishnan. New York: New Left Books, 1996.

Gerber, Lynne. *Seeking the Straight and Narrow*. Chicago: University of Chicago Press, 2011.

The Glenn Beck Show. "Glenn Interviews Jerry Falwell Jr." Glen Beck Show Official website, http://www.glennbeck.com/content/articles/article/198/42325/ (accessed October 16, 2012).

Grace, Fran. *Carry A. Nation: Retelling the Life*. Bloomington: Indiana University Press, 2001.

Greeley, Andrew and Michael Hout. *The Truth About Conservative Christians: What They Think and What They Believe*. Chicago: University of Chicago Press, 2006.

Griffith, R. Marie. *Born Again Bodies: Flesh and Spirit in American Christianity*. Berkeley: University of California Press, 2004.

Hadden, Jeffrey K. and Douglas E. Cowan. "The Promised Land or Electronic Chaos? Toward Understanding Religion on the Internet." In *Religion on the Internet: Research Prospects and Promises*, Jeffrey K. Hadden and Douglas E. Cowan, eds. New York: Elsevier Science, Inc., 2000.

Harding, Susan. *The Book of Jerry Falwell: Fundamentalist Language and Politics*. Princeton: Princeton University Press, 2000.

Harvery, Linda. "Fairy Tales Don't Come True." Concerned Women for America website, http://www.cwfa.org/articledisplay.asp?id=10633&department=CFI&categoryid = papers (posted February 13, 2006, accessed November 27, 2009).

Heffernan, Jaclyn. "News Flash: Rated X." Concerned Women for America website, http://www.cwalac.org/article_523.shtml (posted June 26, 2007, accessed November 4, 2009).

Heineman, Kenneth. *God Is a Conservative: Religion, Politics, and Morality in Contemporary America*. New York: NYU Press, 1998.

Helland, Christopher. "Online-Religion/Religion-Online and Virtual Communitas." In *Religion on the Internet: Research Prospects and Promises*, Jeffrey K. Hadden and Douglas E. Cowan, eds. New York: Elsevier Science, Inc., 2000.

Hobsbawm, Eric J. *Nations and Nationalism Since 1780*. Cambridge: Cambridge University Press, 1990.

Højsgaard, Morten T. and Margit Warburg. "Introduction: Waves of Research." In *Religion and Cyberspace*, Morten T. Højsgaard and Margit Warburg, eds. London: Routledge, 2005.

Hooks, Katherine. "Results of a Thirty Year Experiment on Women." Concerned Women for America website, http://www.cwfa.org/articles/4321/BLI/dotcommentary/index.htm (posted July 23, 2003, accessed October 14, 2009).

Hroch, Miroslav. "From National Movement to the Fully–formed Nation: The Nation–Building Process in Europe." *Mapping the Nation*, ed. Gopal Balakrishnan. New York: New Left Books, 1996.

Hughes, Richard. *Myths America Lives By*. Urbana: University of Illinois Press, 2004.

Hurley, Elizabeth. "CDC Finally Acknowledges that HPV Can Cause Cervical Cancer." Concerned Women for America website, http://www.cwfa.org/articledisplay.asp?id = 7422&department = CWA&categoryid = family (posted February 10, 2005, accessed November 30, 2009).

Jakobsen, Janet. "Why Sexual Regulation? Family Values and Social Movements." In *God Forbid: Religion and Sex in American Public Life*, Kathleen Sands, ed. New York: Oxford, 2000.

——— and Ann Pellegrini. *Love the Sin: Sexual Regulation and the Limits of Religious Tolerance*. Boston: Beacon Press, 2004.

——— and Ann Pellegrini. "World Secularisms at the Millennium: Introduction." *Social Text* 18:3 (2000), 1–27.

Jasper, James. *The Art of Moral Protest: Culture, Biography, and Creativity in Social Movements*. Chicago: University of Chicago Press, 2008.

Jones, Robert P. *Progressive and Religious: How Christian, Jewish, Muslim, and Buddhist Leaders Are Moving Beyond the Culture Wars and Transforming American Public Life*. Lanham, MD: Rowman and Littlefield, 2008.

Jordan, Mark. *Recruiting Young Love: How Christians Talk About Homosexuality*. Chicago: University of Chicago Press, 2011.

Juergensmeyer, Mark. "Is Religion the Problem?" *Hedgehog Review* 6:1 (Spring 2004).

Juster, Susan. *Disorderly Women: Sexual Politics and Evangelicalism in Revolutionary New England*. Ithaca, NY: Cornell University Press, 1996.

Kimmel, Michael. *The Gendered Society*, 4th ed. New York: Oxford, 2011.

Kintz, Linda. *Between Jesus and the Market: The Emotions That Matter in Right Wing America*. Durham: Duke University Press, 1997.

Klatch, Rebecca. *Women of the New Right*. Philadelphia: Temple University Press, 1987.

Knight, Robert. "Gay Marriage is Not Only Wrong; It's Socially Destructive." Concerned Women for America website, http://www.CWA.org/articledisplay.asp?id = 5014&department = CFI&categoryid = family (posted June 22, 2009, accessed August 17, 2009).

———. "The Idols of Secular Conservatism." Concerned Women for America website, http://www.cwfa.org/articles/271/CFI/cfreport/index.htm. Archived at http://www.beliefnet.com/Entertainment/2001/11/Defending-Jerry-Falwell.aspx?p = 3 (posted October 25, 2001, accessed July 23, 2009).

———. "The Undeclared War to ENDA Our Liberty." Concerned Women for America website, http://www.cwfa.org/articles/17520/CFI/family/index.htm (posted August 12, 2009, accessed November 20, 2009).

——— and Lindsey Douthit. "Hate Crime Laws Threaten Religious Freedom." Concerned Women for America website, http://www.cwfa.org/articledisplay.asp?id = 9672&department = CFI&categoryid = papers (posted December 12, 2005, accessed June 9, 2010).

Kohut, Andrew. "The Electorate Changes, and Politics Follow." *The New York Times*, http://www.nytimes.com/roomfordebate/2012/04/16/is-support-for-gay-rights-still-controversial/the-electorate-changes-and-politics-follow?scp=4&sq=kohut%20marriage&st = cse (posted April 16, 2012, accessed September 11, 2012).

Koop, C. Everett. *Koop: The Memoirs of America's Family Doctor*. New York: Random House, 1991.

Kristeva, Julia. *Powers of Horror: An Essay on Abjection*. New York: Columbia University Press, 1982.

LaHaye, Beverly. *The Restless Woman*. Grand Rapids: Zondervan Publishing House, 1984.

———. *The Spirit Controlled Woman*. Eugene, OR: Harvest House Publishers, 1976.

———. *Who But A Woman?* Nashville: Thomas Nelson Publishers, 1984.

LaHaye, Tim and Beverly. *The Act of Marriage: The Beauty of Sexual Love*. Grand Rapids, MI: Zondervan, 1998.

LaRue, Jan. "Did You Hear About the Judges Who . . . ? Connecticut Supreme Court Rules Fetus is Part of a Woman's Body." Concerned Women for America website, http://www.cwfa.org/articledisplay.asp?id=3937&department=LEGAL&categoryid = life (posted May 12, 2003, accessed September 2, 2009).

———. "Homosexuals Hijack Civil Rights Bus." Concerned Women for America website, http://www.cwfa.org/images/content/hhcrb.pdf (accessed October 7, 2012).

Library of Congress. "Bill Summary & Status, 108th Congress (2003–2004), H.R.1997." Library of Congress website, http://thomas.loc.gov/cgi-bin/bdquery/z?d108:HR01997:@@@L&summ2 = m& (accessed November 21, 2012).

Lincoln, Bruce. *Authority: Construction and Corrosion*. Chicago: University of Chicago Press, 1995.

———. *Holy Terrors: Thinking About Religion After September 11*. Chicago: University of Chicago Press, 2003.

Lippy, Charles. "Miles to Go: Promise Keepers in Historical and Cultural Context." *Soundings* 80(Summer/Fall 1997): 2–3.

Maguire, Daniel. "Religion and Reproductive Policy." In *God Forbid: Religion and Sex in American Public Life*, Kathleen Sands, ed. New York: Oxford University Press, 2000.

Mah, Harold. "Phantasies of the Public Sphere: Rethinking the Habermas of Historians." *The Journal of Modern History* 72 (March 2000):1.

Marsden, George. *Fundamentalism and American Culture*. New York: Oxford University Press, 2006.

Martin, William. *With God on Our Side: The Rise of the Religious Right in America*. New York: Broadway Books, 1996.

McCutcheon, Russell. *The Discipline of Religion: Structure, Meaning, Rhetoric*. New York: Routledge, 2003.

McGirr, Lisa. *Suburban Warriors: The Origins of the New American Right*. Princeton: Princeton University Press, 2001.

McLaren, Angus. *A History of Conception: From Antiquity to the Present Day*. Oxford: Basil Blackwell, 1990.

———. *Twentieth-Century Sexuality: A History*. Malden, MA: Blackwell, 1999.

McLoughlin, William. *Revivals, Awakenings, and Reform: An Essay on Religion and Social Change in America, 1607–1977*. Chicago: University of Chicago Press, 1978.

Meacham, John. "Editor's Desk." *Newsweek*, http://www.newsweek.com/id/44543 (posted November 13, 2006, accessed July 25, 2009).

———. "The End of Christian America." *Newsweek*, http://www.newsweek.com/id/192583 (posted April 4, 2009, accessed December 4, 2009).

Messer-Kruse, Timothy. *Race Relations in the United States, 1980–2000*. Westport, CT: Greenwood Press, 2008.

Meyer, Birgit and Annelies Moors. "Introduction." In *Religion, Media, and the Public Sphere*, Birgit Meyer and Annelies Moors, eds. Bloomington: Indiana University Press, 2006.

Miller, Steven P. *Billy Graham and the Rise of the Republican South*. Philadelphia: University of Pennsylvania Press, 2009.

Moran, Jeffrey. *The Scopes Trial: A Brief History with Documents*. New York: Bedford/St. Martin's Press, 2002.

Morone, James. *Hellfire Nation: The Politics of Sin in American History*. New Haven: Yale University Press, 2003.

Murphy, Dean E. "Scott Peterson Sentenced to Death for Killing Pregnant Wife." *The New York Times*, March 17, 2005, http://www.nytimes.com/2005/03/17/national/17peterson.html?_r = 0(posted March 17, 2005, accessed November 1, 2012).

Myrdal, Janne. "Feminism, Faith, and the Palin Factor." Concerned Women for America website, http://www.cwfa.org/content.asp?id = 19048 (posted June 15, 2010, accessed September 29, 2012).

Nance, Penny Young. "The Real Mean Girls." Concerned Women for America website, http://www.cwfa.org/content.asp?id = 19553 (posted October 19, 2010, accessed November 5, 2012).

The National Organization of Women. "About NOW." The National Organization of Women website, http://www.now.org/organization/info.html (accessed November 5, 2012).

Noll, Mark. *The Scandal of the Evangelical Mind.* Grand Rapids, MI: Eerdmans Publishing Co., 1995.

Norman Lear Official Website, http://normanlear.com/backstory.html (accessed June 23, 2010).

Pascoe, Peggy. *What Comes Naturally: Miscegenation Law and the Making of Race in America.* New York: Oxford University Press, 2009.

People For the American Way. "Anti-Gay Politics and the Religious Right." People For the American Way website, http://www.pfaw.org/media-center/publications/anti-gay-politics-and-the-religious-right (accessed June 21, 2010).

Petchesky, Rosalind. "Antiabortion, Antifeminism, and the Rise of the New Right." In *The New Christian Right: Political and Social Issues,* Melvin Urofsky and Martha May, eds. New York: Garland Publishing, 1996.

The Pew Forum on Religion and Public Life. "U.S. Religious Landscape Survey." The Pew Forum on Religion and Public Life website, http://religions.pewforum.org/comparisons# (accessed December 5, 2009).

The Pew Project For Excellence in Journalism. "The State of the News Media: An Annual Report on American Journalism, 2009." The Pew Project for Excellence in Journalism Website, http://www.stateofthemediaorg/2009/narrative_cabletv_audience.php?cat-1 (accessed December 5, 2009).

Porowski, Stephanie. "Hijacking a Noble Cause: How Feminism Has Abandoned Its Founders." Concerned Women for America website, http://www.CWA.org/images/content/early-v-mod-fem.pdf (posted September 26, 2003, accessed August 22, 2009).

Reed, James. *The Birth Control Movement and American Society: From Private Vice to Public Virtue.* Princeton: Princeton University Press, 1983.

Renan, Ernest. "What Is a Nation?" *Nation and Narration,* ed. Homi K. Bhabha. New York: Routledge Books, 1990.

Ries, Rebekah. "Rights for Everyone! Except You." Concerned Women for America website, http://www.cwfa.org/articledisplay.asp?id = 17449&department = CFI&categoryid = family (posted July 31, 2009, accessed September 2, 2009).

Roosevelt, Theodore. "On Race Decay and Wilfull Sterility." In *Controlling Reproduction: An American History,* ed. Andrea Tone. Wilmington, DE: Scholarly Resources, 1997.

Ruether, Rosemary Radford. *Christianity and the Making of the Modern Family.* Boston: Beacon Press, 2001.

Saad, Lydia. "Americans Evenly Divided on Morality of Homosexuality." Gallup website, http://www.gallup.com/poll/108115/Americans-Evenly-Divided-Morality-Homosexuality.aspx (posted June 8, 2008, accessed November 30, 2009).

———. "More Americans 'Pro–Life' Than 'Pro–Choice' for First Time." Gallup website, http://www.gallup.com/poll/118399/More-Americans-Pro-Life-Than-Pro-Choice-First-Time.aspx (posted May 15, 2009, accessed November 30, 2009).

Saletan, William. *Bearing Right: How Conservatives Won the Abortion War.* Berkeley: University of California Press, 2004.

Sandeen, Ernest. *The Roots of Fundamentalism: British and American Millenarianism, 1800–1930.* Chicago: University of Chicago Press, 1970.

Sands, Kathleen. "Introduction." In *God Forbid: Religion and Sex in American Public Life,* Kathleen Sands, ed. New York: Oxford, 2000.

Savage, Charlie. "A Judge's View of Judging Is on the Record." *The New York Times* website, http://www.nytimes.com/2009/05/15/us/15judge.html (posted May 14, 2009, accessed December 5, 2009).

Schauer, Linda. "Obama Forcing Immoral Acts by Health Care Providers." Concerned Women for America website, http://www.cwfa.org/articles/16849/FIELD/freedom/index.html (posted April 15, 2009, accessed November 24, 2009).

Schreiber, Ronnee. *Righting Feminism: Conservative Women and American Politics.* New York: Oxford, 2008.

Scott, Joan Wallach. "The Evidence of Experience." *Critical Inquiry* 17:4(1991), 773–797.

Seward, Heide. "Take Our Daughters to Work Day: Feminism Class for Young Girls?" Concerned Women for America website, http://www.cwfa.org/articles/827/BLI/dotcommentary/index.htm (posted April 26, 2002, accessed November 3, 2009).

Shields, Jon A. *The Democratic Virtues of the Christian Right.* Princeton: Princeton University Press, 2009.

Sieczkowski, Cavan. "Lena Dunham 'First Time' Obama Voting Ad Offends Conservatives." The Huffington Post, http://www.huffingtonpost.com/2012/10/26/lena-dunham-first-time-obama-voting-ad-_n_2023705.html (posted October 26, 2012, accessed June 13, 2013).

Simmerman, Orin. "The Pledge of Allegiance in Church: Mixing Church and State?" Concerned Women for America website, http://www.cwfa.org/articles/4050/BLI/commentary/index.htm (posted June 4, 2003, accessed October 5, 2009).

Skaggs, Calvin and David Van Taylor. "With God On Our Side: George W. Bush and the Rise of the Religious Right." Video. Dir. Calvin Skaggs and David Van Taylor. First Run Features, November 1, 2004.

Smith, Christian. *American Evangelicalism: Embattled and Thriving.* Chicago: University of Chicago Press, 1998.

———. *Christian America?: What Evangelicals Really Want*. Berkeley: University of California Press, 2000.

Smith, Daniel Scott. "Family Limitation, Domestic Control, and Domestic Feminism in Victorian America." In *Controlling Reproduction: An American History*, Andrea Tone, ed. Wilmington: Scholarly Resources, Inc., 1997.

Spivak, Gayatri. *Outside in the Teaching Machine*. New York: Routledge, 2009 (original publication 1993).

Throckmorton, Warren. "Should Raunchy Be the Fourth R?" Concerned Women for America website, http://www.cwfa.org/articles/8749/CFI/education/index.htm (posted August 18, 2005, accessed June 23, 2010).

Thuesen, Peter J. "The Logic of Mainline Churchliness: Historical Background Since the Reformation." In *The Quiet Hand of God: Faith-Based Activism and the Public Role of Mainline Protestantism*, R. Wuthnow and J.H. Evans, eds. Berkeley: University of California Press, 2002.

Tim LaHaye Ministries. "Tim LaHaye's Biography." Tim LaHaye Ministries website,https://timlahaye.com/shopcontent.asp?type = Biography (accessed July 25, 2009).

Time Magazine. "The Right Hand of God." *Time* (Front Cover), May 15, 1995, http://www.time.com/time/covers/0,16641,19950515,00.html (accessed July 29, 2009).

Van Biema, David. "Oral Roberts to the Rescue?" *Time*, October 27, 2007, http://www.time.com/time/nation/article/0,8599,1677098,00.html (posted October 27, 2007, accessed November 1, 2012).

Van Matre, Lydia. "Two Be or Not Two Be: Where's the Math?" Concerned Women for America website, http://www.cwfa.org/articles/17287/FIELD/education/index.htm (posted July 7, 2009, accessed June 23, 2010).

Wacker, Grant. *Heaven Below: Early Pentecostals and American Culture*. Cambridge: Harvard University Press, 2003.

Wadkins, Jessica, Trudy Chun, and Catherina Hurlburt. "Pro-Life Action Guide: Upholding Truth, Protecting Life." Concerned Women for America website, http://www.cwfa.org/brochures/pro-life.pdf(accessed November 2, 2012).

Waters, Ken. "The Evangelical Press." *The Oxford Handbook of Religion and the American News Media*, ed. Diane Winston. New York: Oxford University Press, 2012.

Weiner, Matthew. "Ladies Room." *Mad Men*, season 1, episode 2. Matthew Weiner (writer) and Alan Taylor (director). Mad Men Official website, http://www.amctv.com/shows/mad-men/episodes/season-1/ladies-room (accessed September 4, 2012).

Wellman, James Jr. *Evangelical vs. Liberal: The Clash of Christian Cultures in the Pacific Northwest*. New York: Oxford University Press, 2008.

West, Traci C. "The Policing of Poor Black Women's Sexual Reproduction." In *God Forbid: Religion and Sex in American Public Life*, Kathleen Sands, ed. Oxford: Oxford University Press, 2000.

Weyrich, Paul A. "Vilified Values Voters." Concerned Women for America website, http://www.CWA.org/articledisplay.asp?id=6853&department=CWA&categoryid = misc (posted November 16, 2004, accessed August 21, 2009).

Wilcox, Clyde. *God's Warriors: The Christian Right in Twentieth Century America*. Baltimore: Johns Hopkins University Press, 1992.

Wilcox, Clyde and Carin Robinson. *Onward Christian Soldiers?: The Religious Right in American Politics*, 4th ed. Boulder, CO: Westview Press, 2010.

Williams, Daniel. *God's Own Party: The Making of the Christian Right*. New York: Oxford University Press, 2010.

Wong, Pamela Pearson. "Mothers Are Giving the Greatest Gift: Themselves." *Family Voice* Magazine, Concerned Women for America website, http://www.cwfa.org/familyvoice/2001–5/06–13.asp (posted May/June 2001, accessed December 7, 2009).

Wright, Wendy. "CEDAW Committee Rulings." Concerned Women for America website, http://www.cwfa.org/articledisplay.asp?id=1870&department=CWA&categoryid = nation (posted August 27, 2002, accessed November 30, 2009).

———. "Iraq War Vet 'Spit On' By Democratic Senators." Concerned Women for America website, http://www.cwfa.org/articledisplay.asp?id = 13550&department = CWA&categoryid = misc (posted July 31, 2007, accessed November 5, 2012).

———. "Wendy Wright: A Testimony in Kansas." Concerned Women for America website, http://www.cwfa.org/articledisplay.asp?id = 13823&department = CWA&categoryid = life (posted September 7, 2007, accessed November 1, 2012).

———. "Who Are These People?" Concerned Women for America website, http://www.cwfa.org/articles/7059/CWA/freedom/index.htm (posted December 29, 2004, accessed September 19, 2009).

———. "Why More Than Ever We Must Be Involved." Concerned Women for America website, http://www.cwfa.org/brochures/morethanever.pdf (accessed December 4, 2009).

Wuthnow, Robert. *The Restructuring of American Religion: Society and Faith Since WWII*. Princeton: Princeton University Press, 1988.

———and John H. Evans. "Introduction." In *The Quiet Hand of God: Faith Based Activism and the Public Role of Mainline Protestantism*, R. Wuthnow and J.H. Evans, eds. Berkeley: University of California Press, 2002.

Zaretsky, Natasha. *No Direction Home: The American Family and the Fear of National Decline, 1968–1980*. Chapel Hill: The University of North Carolina Press, 2007.

Zurita, Brenda. "Of 'Lady Parts' and Politics." Concerned Women for America website, http://www.cwfa.org/articledisplay.asp?id=21578&department=BLI&category id = life&subcategoryid = blifem (accessed October 8, 2012).

———. "Pornography, Ivy–League Style." Concerned Women for America website, http://www.cwfa.org/articles/15958/BLI/pornography/index.htm (posted October 23, 2008, accessed November 2, 2009).

Index

NOTE: The letter 'n' following locators refers to notes